EAST ASIAN MEDICINE IN URBAN JAPAN

Comparative Studies of Health Systems

and Medical Care

Number 4

Comparative Studies of Health Systems and Medical Care

General Editor
CHARLES LESLIE

Varieties of Medical Experience

EAST ASIAN MEDICINE IN URBAN JAPAN

Margaret M. Lock

University of California Press
Berkeley · Los Angeles · London

For Richard and his understanding

This book is a print-on-demand volume. It is manufactured using toner in place of ink.
Type and images may be less sharp than the same material seen in traditionally
printed University of California Press editions.

University of California Press
Berkeley and Los Angeles, California

University of California Press, Ltd.
London, England

© 1980 by
The Regents of the University of California

First Paperback Printing 1984
ISBN 0-520-05231-5
Library of Congress Catalog Card Number: 78-55187
Printed in the United States of America

The paper used in this publication meets the
minimum requirements of ANSI/NISO Z39.48-1992
(R 1997) (Permanence of Paper).

PREFACE to the Paperback edition

It is now more than ten years since New York Times reporter James Reston had his appendix removed in China with acupuncture anesthesia. The timing of this incident contributed to a flurry of interest in traditional Asian medicine which spread rapidly through North America. Among the many therapeutic techniques of Asian medicine, massage received the widest acceptance, but the fad soon peaked, leaving behind it some institutionalized changes such as the right for licensed practitioners in some States to practice acupuncture on patients who had been referred to them by a physician.

Although interest in these therapeutic techniques was not generally sustained, nevertheless, their application did contribute, along with many other factors, to the rise of the holistic health movement in North America. It became fashionable to refer to traditional Asian medicine as exemplary of a humanistic integrated approach to health and illness, particularly since it was grounded in a tradition in which mind and body had not been rent asunder.

My purpose ten years ago, while researching traditional medicine in Japan, was to examine its historical roots and the current social and cultural context of its practice. My findings, not surprising in retrospect, were firstly that there are numerous approaches to the practice of traditional medicine which reflect not only the pluralistic philosophical heritage of Japan but also its embrace of modern scientific thinking and techniques, as well as the institutional forms of organization in which they exist. Secondly, it became clear early on in the research that the practice of this type of medicine, despite its Asian heritage, did not usually operate within an integrated approach to health and illness or to mind and body. In fact, in the majority of clinics, practitioners appeared to be engaged in an attempt to remove physical symptoms in a fashion reminiscent of that of most biomedical physicians, although their tools were those of traditional medicine.

It was only through an extensive investigation outside the clinical setting that I was able to understand that what at first sight often appeared to be a rather non-communicative encounter between patient and practitioner could indeed potentially serve to focus and stimulate social and psychological change, although this was by no means always realized. Indeed, consideration of the social dimensions of illness is something which people are usually reluctant to examine for reasons which are explored in the text. East Asian medicine as it is practiced in Japan today is therefore not an example of the holistic approach which many Westerners believe it to be.

Nevertheless, traditional medicine over the past twenty years has enjoyed a great revival in Japan, an occurrence which has run parallel to the rise of the holistic health movement in North America. It evolved for some of the same reasons and shares many of its objectives, including an emphasis on self-responsibility for health and illness.

The material for this book was collected at the time when the Japanese mass media had just coined the phrase "*kanpo* boom" (see pages 15, 152) to describe the renewed interest in traditional medicine. One of the concerns of many practitioners of East Asian medicine at that time was how to provide a comprehensive service to their increased clientele within certain given constraints. The full range of East Asian medicine has always been a service limited to the elite of Japanese society and has probably never been available in more than a fragmentary form for the ordinary citizen. A complete work up and treatment is highly individualized and takes at least 30 to 40 minutes, and the raw materials for a prescription of herbal medication, most of which have to be imported, are costly. Japan has a socialized health care system but until recently, with certain exceptions (see page 168), patients could not be reimbursed if they received care from a traditional practitioner. With the obvious increased demand for herbal medication in Japan, the Chinese, who provide most of the raw materials, and who could not grow plants in sufficient quantity to meet the increased orders both from within their own country and Japan, raised considerably the cost of most of the plant material grown for export. The practitioners in Japan who were trying to apply traditional medicine in a comprehensive form had to face the dilemma of how to provide time consuming, individualized care, involving therapeutic techniques which were rapidly becoming more costly, to a burgeoning number of eager clients.

The pharmaceutical industry in Japan was quick to notice this dilemma and several companies radically increased their sponsorship of research into the physiological effects and the mass production of herbal medication. The culmination of this interest occured in 1975 when representatives of the largest drug company involved in the production of herbal medication approached the head of the Japanese medical association and, within a very short time, meetings were held between representatives of the Ministry of Health and Welfare, the drug company, and the Japanese medical association to discuss the possibility of including the prescription of herbal medication in the health insurance system. A senior *Kanpō-i* (a biomedically trained physician who specialized in the use of herbal medication) was present at these meetings and was opposed to this suggestion, although he wanted it to be included slowly in the future and after careful experimentation and re-education of physicians and other involved personnel.

The *kanpō-i* was over-ruled, the law was changed, and mass production and promotion of herbal medication commenced in 1976. This led to an escalation in the revival of traditional medicine since ordinary physicians could now freely prescribe and be reimbursed from insurance companies on behalf of the government for the use of more than 100 herbal prescriptions.

A recent survey reported by Nikkei Medical (1981) indicates that 37% of all Japanese physicians now prescribe herbal medication with some frequency; of these physicians, 36% reported that they use it very frequently, 46% reported that they use it regulary, while 18% said that they occasionally use it. On close examination what was known as a "boom" in traditional medicine has become largely a boom in the use of traditional medication, the preparation and prescription of which has been absorbed into the commercial and biomedical sectors of society, ostensibly to make it readily available to all patients. The philosophy and theories underlying the traditional system, including techniques of preventive medicine and diagnosis are generally ignored or despised. Consequently, traditional methods for the selection, mixing and prescription of herbal medication (see pages 40-44) are also ignored and herbs are prescribed, contrary to traditional practice, as though they are synthetic drugs to be applied against named diseases or highly specific symptoms.

In the last six years there have been huge promotional campaigns by many drug companies to encourage the medical profession to use their new products. Physicians are not required to undergo any special training in the use of traditional medicine but are given some written advice distributed by the drug companies on suggested application of medications and their possible contraindications. Newspapers, magazines and journals are now beginning to report side effects, some serious, for the first time in connection with the use of herbal medication (Mainichi shinbun, Dec. 1981; Nikkei Medical: 1981). An advisory bulletin put out by the Japanese association of pharmacists reports that in recent years there were more complaints about side-effects from herbal medication than any other type of drug, and a questionnaire to physicians revealed that most doctors use it on an ad hoc basis in combination with synthetic medication (Modern Medicine: 1982). Experimental evidence indicates that the quality control on these medications is not adequate—something which is not highly significant when using mixtures of crude drugs in small quantities as is done by traditional practitioners. When the medication is refined and concentrated in a laboratory the effect is different, its physiological actions, both those that are desired, and unwanted side-reactions, become much more potent. Moreover, the clinical effects of mixing herbal extracts with synthetic drugs is a topic on which there is virtually no research.

East Asian medicine survived the blow it received at the 1876 Meiji Restoration when it was legislated as inadequate in comparison to European style medicine; it may not survive the onslaught it is at present experiencing from politicians, physicians, industry, and the general public. Each of these groups is now eager to embrace traditional medicine to some extent, to use it, hopes to benefit from it, but rarely to learn from, adjust to, or accept it on its own terms. They believe that East Asian medicine must be made scientific, neatly packaged and advertized—the price of success in today's world. Experienced traditional practitioners can now take part in the socialized health care system, but they must conform to the restraints imposed by that system, the most disquieting of which is that one is reimbursed according to what procedures are performed, and that even a meagre existence cannot be eked out through the practice of a preventive and an educational approach to health care (see pages 17 and 233-235). Practitioners have the choice of sacrificing their philosophical and theoretical principles in order to make a living, or of practicing an elitist type of medicine available only to the relatively wealthy. Meanwhile, they watch their 1200-year-old tradition being contorted and led into ill repute, paradoxically largely as the result of its own recent popularity. A few biomedical physicians are undertaking special training offered by kanpō-i but most see no reason for further education.

Some malpractice and iatrogenesis is inevitable in connection with all medical systems, and East Asian medicine undoubtedly has been, and continues to be no exception, but its popularity in modern Japan has exacerbated this situation excessively. I believe that one of the gravest problems is the assumption on the parts of the vast majority of the people involved, whether government officials, biomedical physicians, salesmen, chemists, or the general public, that traditional medicine can be made more effective by subjecting it completely to the principles of "science" as we apply them today. The theory and practice of traditional Asian medicine deserves a much closer analysis in its own terms before it is relegated to the equivalent antiquated status granted to phlogiston theory. Meanwhile there are indications that much of the iatrogenesis which has arisen in connection with herbal medication can be attributed to its application in what is considered to be a scientific fashion (Lock: 1984). Of course we need more research into the physiological actions of herbal medication and acupuncture, something which is being seriously undertaken in most of the major teaching hospitals and some research institutes in Japan. It is a most impressive sight, for example, to see row upon row of tiny ginseng plants lined up in conical flasks containing nourishing solutions, growing apace from a tissue culture of a single cell into their characteristic form. But we are a long way from being able to analyse chemically the action on the human body of ten or more crude drugs containing possibly hundreds of active ingredients. Since we cannot apply science reasonably accurately then it seems more appropriate to draw upon the accumulated empirical wisdom of over one thousand years. The kanpō-i who apply this knowledge use both their scientific training and an empirically derived approach in their clinics; there is unanimous agreement among them that at the present time an empirical approach is superior to a scientific approach for the prescription of herbal medication. When such an approach is used prescriptions must be prepared especially for each patient and hence pre-prepared standard medication is regarded as inadequate.

Diagnosis is another area where the traditional approach deserves careful consideration. Many modern diagnostic techniques are highly refined and readily reproduceable, but slowly we are learning that reliance upon average values as standards for normality has its dangers, and that single measurements of, for example, blood pressure or blood sugar levels are relatively meaningless (Mishler et al.: 1981). It has also been shown that the increasing dependence on laboratory tests and machines which aid in diagnosis has raised the cost, the hazards, and the sense of patient alienation associated with biomedicine (Reiser: 1978). Contemporary practitioners of East Asian medicine do not rely wholly on traditional methods these days; they value a scientific approach to diagnosis but they also retain the time honored techniques of observation, questioning, listening, and palpation, and they relate their findings to such variables as the diurnal and annual cycles of nature.

The changes over the past ten years do not seem very encouraging to me. One of the conclusions drawn from my original research was that if acupuncture, or any other therapeutic technique, is torn from its cultural context and put to use as part of biomedical practice, then it becomes transformed into a different technique, since the context, meanings, and objectives associated with its practice are now different. I had the use of acupuncture in North America in mind when I reached this conclusion, but it seems to be equally true for the contemporary Japanese situation. East Asian medicine has not been made available to all by incorporating parts of it into the socialized health care system. On the contrary, herbal medication has simply become a new class of drug. Furthermore, experienced traditional practitioners who remain in private practice are losing patients who believe that they can now receive quality traditional-style care in an ordinary hospital. Some patients, no doubt, will soon realize that this is not so, but meantime the reputation of traditional medicine is muddied, perhaps beyond repair. This situation cannot be remedied until the organization of biomedical practice, the health insurance reimbursement system for physicians, and the virtually unquestioned reliance on as scientific an approach as possible are modified. A few isolated experiments by imaginative and concerned kanpō-i and other physicians are the only bright spots on the horizon at present.

In conclusion I would like to stress that both biomedicine and East Asian medicine focus upon biological interventions (although those of East Asian medicine are less invasive) as central to the healing process. Hence both systems tend to avoid dealing with the social aspects of illness, although for different reasons (see page 137). In modern Japan, however, patients, like those in the industrial West, are suffering from problems in which social and environmental aspects are crucial, such as diseases caused or exacerbated by pollution, poor nutritional habits, being moved by one's employer, lack of security for the elderly, and so on. Both biomedicine and East Asian medicine, since they focus primarily on curative measures, tend to deflect attention away from the urgent social problems which affect health and illness in modern Japan.

In North America the holistic health movement emerged partly as a response to the barrage of criticism directed at biomedicine. Guttmacher, after indicating some of the advantages in the style of thinking which is representative of this movement, adds that by viewing health as an end in itself, and by emphasizing individual responsibility for health and illness, the movement has in fact exacerbated the "medicalization" of many areas of life and reinforced a basic biomedical premise: that disorders should be dealt with largely at the personal level (Guttmacher: 1979:16). She adds that this attitude receives government support since it is equated with cost containment.

In Japan, although something as clearly defined as a holistic health movement cannot be detected, there is, nevertheless, an even stronger tendency than in North America to reify health, to consider it a personal or family problem, and to rush to the doctor for medication and psychological support. The roots of this behavior can be found in traditional East Asian medicine, in indigenous psychotherapeutic systems (Reynolds: 1976), and their associated philosophical systems. No medical system can be expected to fully answer the patient's question "why me?" But while the social dimensions of an illness are ignored or reinterpreted as due to lack of personal care, the burden of responsibility for an illness becomes that of the patient, many of whom are victims of a social situation completely beyond their control.

Margaret Lock
Kyoto, January 1984

REFERENCES

Guttmacher, Sally, 1979, "Whole in Body, Mind and Spirit: Holistic Health and the Limits of Medicine." *Hastings Center Report*. April pp. 15–21.

Lock, Margaret, 1984, "Licorice in Leviathan: The Medicalization of Care for the Japanese Elderly." *Culture, Medicine and Psychiatry*. In press.

Mainichi Shinbum, 1981, "Excessive use of *kanpō* medicine is ill advised." December 19th.

Mishler, Elliot G., Lorna R. AmaraSingham, Stuart T. Hauser, Ramsay Liem, Samuel D. Osherson, Nancy E. Waxler, 1981, *Social Contexts of Health, Illness and Patient Care*. New York: Cambridge University Press.

Modern Medicine, 1982, "*Kanpō-yaku*: an essay on side reactions". No. 1 pp. 80-81.

Nikkei Medical, 1981, "A survey of the Use of *kanpōyaku* by Practicing Physicians" No. 10, pp. 28-31.

Reiser, Stanley J., 1978, *Medicine and the Reign of Technology*. Cambridge: Cambridge University Press.

Reynolds, David K., 1976, *Morita Psychotherapy*. Berkeley: University of California Press.

CONTENTS

Contents

ILLUSTRATIONS

TABLES

xvi

PREFACE

This study is based on fieldwork carried out in Japan in 1973 and 1974. The purpose was to present a facet of Japanese culture which had not been examined to any great extent before, and with this in mind I wrote to Professor William Caudill, shortly before his death, expressing my interest in the topic of East Asian medicine. It was his introduction to Dr. Yasuo Ōtsuka, a practicing East Asian physician, which provided the impetus to develop and focus the project. Dr. Ōtsuka not only facilitated a smooth entry for me into the East Asian medical world, but was the first of many Japanese informants to undo gently my preconceptions and set me on a firmer course.

Fieldwork was conducted over a period of sixteen months. As formal introductions are usually necessary to establish good rapport in Japan, a considerable amount of time had to be spent in building up the necessary contacts. Once entry to each clinic was established, I received nothing but friendly cooperation, with only one exception. The confidence with which each doctor welcomed me and explained his practice was a clear indication of their faith in the importance of their own work. The clinics were selected so that as many as possible of the various approaches to East Asian medicine could be studied. All interviews were conducted personally in Japanese and tape recorded.

The medical practitioners were interviewed initially in private with loosely structured questionnaires; later, I was frequently welcomed into their family circles and spent many hours sharing their lives both formally and informally. Patients were interviewed initially for about thirty minutes. My plan was to follow up a small sample of the patients by interviewing them at six-month intervals, but there is no appointment system in the clinics, and the task of sitting and waiting to catch particular patients on the off chance that they would appear became impossible. Nevertheless, I did see some patients quite regularly and could watch their progress.

I was allowed to observe doctor and patient interaction freely during the examination and treatment sessions, and I actually underwent all forms of therapy myself in almost all of the clinics discussed. My husband and my two children, aged four and one-and-a-half on our arrival in Kyoto, received all their medical care, for the duration of our stay, in East Asian medical clinics.

For comparative purposes, nine Kyoto doctors practicing cosmopolitan medicine were interviewed regarding their own medical practice and attitudes toward East Asian medicine. These doctors were selected because they were in private practice and were independent owners of medical clinics and so that I might cover a variety of specialties.

In order to establish general attitudes toward health beliefs and practices, rather than simply record those of people who were actually sick, I selected fifty Kyoto families for interviews. Half the sample was composed of families from a middle- to upper-middle-class residential area, and the other twenty-five families were selected from a lower-middle-class area of shopkeepers and small entrepreneurial families. Interviews of the families were conducted in their homes by Japanese research assistants and lasted about an hour for each family.

Observations of mother-and-child and teacher-and-child behavior regarding health were carried out personally in ten families and two schools at intervals over a nine-month period.

I visited eight herbal pharmacies, and after interviewing the pharmacists I spent half a day in three of them observing interaction between customers and pharmacist. I also visited a few clinics in Osaka and Tokyo and spent one day in each of three schools that teach East Asian medicine in Kyoto and Osaka. During the final six months of the fieldwork, I attended a private seminar in classical East Asian medicine conducted by a practicing doctor.

Finally, I attended festivals and ceremonies at temples and shrines related to health care, visited two of the new religions that make use of traditional medicine, and spent some of my "free time" in public baths and at hot-spring resorts.

My ultimate aim was to observe, experience, and discuss as <u>full a range of</u> East Asian medicine as was possible within the given limitations of time and financial resources.

I am indebted to all the doctors, patients, pharmacists, and residents of Kyoto who cooperated and contributed so willingly with my intrusion into their lives and with my endless questions. In particular, my thanks go to Drs. Hiroshi Sakaguchi, Keigo Nakata, and Masakasu Yamazaki, who not only welcomed me in their midst, but provided excellent medical care for my family. Among the other practitioners to whom I am indebted, Drs. Yasuji Nagao, Kazuo Komai, Kunzo Nagayama, Otoharu Takagi, Eizō Asayama, and Yoshitaka Tsunokawa must be credited with special thanks. The patients remain anonymous, but they have contributed to this study as much as have the members of the medical profession. It was they who taught me, in a way I could never have understood so readily in the Western Hemisphere, about the social nature of illness.

Professor Mamoru Tabata of the pharmacognosy department of Kyoto University has been of unfailing support both in the field and afterward. His criticisms and suggestions are gratefully acknowledged. Professor Mitsukuni Yoshida, of the Center for Research into the Human and Cultural Sciences in Kyoto, was kind enough to help me with some of the historical material, and Professors Takeo Doi (Tokyo University) and Toshinao Yoneyama (Kyoto University) provided helpful criticism and advice regarding research techniques and analysis of data.

Informal discussions and assistance with transcription of data furnished by my Japanese friends have been invaluable. To Yasuhito Kinoshita, for his encouragement at our meetings in the Almond Coffee Shop, Akasakamitsuke, where I really started to speak Japanese, and for his help throughout all the fieldwork and after, to Machiko Hayase, the best of research assistants and baby-sitters, to Yasuko Yabe and to Fumiko Bielefeldt, go my special thanks.

Professors George DeVos, Elizabeth Colson, and Robert Bellah of the University of California at Berkeley have helped me formulate my ideas over the years; their encouragement, advice, and guidance are warmly acknowledged. More recently, Donald Bates and Joseph Lella of the Department of the History of Medicine at McGill University have provided useful and stimulating discussions, which have served to temper my ideas in fruitful ways. I should also like to thank Gladys Castor for her careful editing of the manuscript.

The Social Science Research Council furnished the grant for the field-work in Japan and for some of the time spent in writing up the data.

Finally, my warmest thanks go to my husband, Richard, for his unfailing support, and to my children, Adam and Gudrun, each of whom experienced a different Japan and taught me so much more than I could have understood on my own.

All of the photographs in this volume were taken by Richard and Margaret Lock, with the exception of those which were taken from books.

Photographs 4 and 5 are taken from the *Fukushō-Kiran-Yoku* and are reproduced with the kind permission of Dr. Hiroshi Sakaguchi. Photographs 2, 3, and 12 are reproduced from the volume *Edo Shokunin Zukushi Shū*, with the kind permission of the author, Kazuo Hanazaki, and the publishers, Watanabe Shoten of Tokyo. The book was published in 1973, and the pictures are reproductions from the original volumes in which they appeared: *Shokunin Zukushi Hokku Awase* and *Edo Shokunin Uta Awase*. Photograph 1 is reproduced from the collection of the Yamato Bunkakan, Nara, with the permission of the curator.

1

Introduction: The Pendulum
Swings to Holism

There are and can be only two ways of searching into and
discovering the truth. The one flies from the senses and particulars
to the most general axioms . . . this way is now in fashion. The
other derives axioms from the senses and particulars, rising by a
gradual and unbroken ascent, so that it arrives at the most
general axioms last of all. This is the true way, but as yet untried.

Francis Bacon,
Novum Organum, 1620

The nature of most human problems is such that universally valid
answers do not exist, because there is more than one aspect to each
of these problems.

Victor Weisskopf,
*Physics in the Twentieth
Century,* 1972

Concepts of health and illness are based on, among other things, value
systems and both individual and collective experiences; they are therefore
culture-bound and subject to changes according to their historical and social
context. As explanations for health and illness change with the mores of the
times, actual medical theory and practice change, and these in turn have an
effect on the epidemiology of disease.

In the industrial world, with its enormous problems of pollution, over-
population, and chronic disease, concepts of health and illness are currently

being reevaluated; at the same time the theoretical assumptions and practices of cosmopolitan medicine have been subjected to much criticism and close examination.[1] (See Carlson 1975; Fuchs 1974; Illich 1976; McKeown 1976; Navarro 1976; Rhodes 1976.) It is in this context that an interest in medical systems of other periods of history and other cultures has recently emerged.

This criticism is also manifest in Japan, the country with the third largest gross national product in the world. The Japanese, like people in the West, have alternative medical systems that they can turn to when they are dissatisfied, and the traditional East Asian medical system,[2] established in Japan in the sixth century, is presently undergoing a revival. This medical system, which has caught the attention of Western observers from many walks of life, is the subject for analysis in this book.

Earlier studies of both cosmopolitan and other medical systems have usually concentrated on only one principal system of medical thought for any given culture at any given time. Where a medical system was in contact with cosmopolitan medicine it was generally assumed that, given enough exposure, cosmopolitan medicine would eclipse traditional medicine. More recent studies emphasize pluralism as the norm; in complex cultures where several medical systems are readily available it has been established that, although adaptation may take place as the result of culture contact, pluralism rather than assimilation is usual (Leslie 1975; Kunstadter 1975; Topley 1975). Moreover, when any one medical system is analyzed in detail, several persistent modes of thought, often radically different, can be detected, although certain modes attain dominance as a particular world view holds sway at any given historical time (Engel 1977; Ōtsuka 1976; Smith 1973; Virchow 1958). Recent studies of the decision-making process in general and the selection of medical care in particular stress the ability of an individual to sustain potentially conflicting points of view, any one of which may be drawn upon depending on the situation (Janzen 1978; Kleinman 1979).

1 The medical system usually referred to as "Western," "scientific," or "modern" will hereafter be referred to as "cosmopolitan" in accord with the argument put forward by Dunn (1976, p. 135) for use of this term.

2 The term "East Asian medical system" is used to refer to the medical beliefs that were dominant until the nineteenth century among the literate populations of China, Korea, and Japan and which are usually referred to in the literature as classical Chinese medicine or oriental medicine.

Our present willingness to analyze and understand medical systems as pluralistic institutions, and our interest in the complexity and in the wide variations of normal human behavior, are in themselves a reflection of changing values in contemporary times.

A glance at the history of Western medicine reveals perennial sources of tension in medical thinking and the swing back and forth from one mode of thought to another. This tension is apparent in the Hippocratic corpus, becomes polarized in the rationalist and empirical schools of Greece and Rome, and continues until the present day. Theories of disease causation furnish a recurrent issue for debate. Dubos (1965, p. 319) describes the two dominant modes of thought as the "ontological" versus the "physiological" viewpoint. According to the "ontological" doctrine, disease is regarded as a specific entity, "a thing in itself, essentially unrelated to the patient's personality, his bodily constitution, or his mode of life" (p. 320), while in the "physiological" model disease is seen simply as an abnormal state that is due to imbalance experienced by the individual organism at a given time. These types of explanations are used in many medical systems, but either one may receive greater emphasis, depending on the prevailing ideas of the time and the specific medical problem under consideration.

Since the seventeenth century in Europe, and the emergence of the mechanistic and reductionistic approach to biology and medicine under the influence of Newton and Descartes, the ontological theory has held considerable but not exclusive sway. Toward the end of the nineteenth century when the doctrine of "specific etiology of disease" (Dubos 1959, p. 101) came to the fore, ontological theory seemed destined to be the final answer to disease causation. The discoveries of Pasteur and Koch in the realms of bacteriology are of the greatest relevance during this period, and they led to the notion that all infectious disease could be controlled by means of specific drugs and vaccines. This belief was reinforced with the discovery of the sulfa drugs in the 1930s and antibiotics in the 1940s. It continues to dominate our approach to clinical research today when, for example, we look for the cause and cure of cancer.

Despite the tremendous success of the ontological, biomedical approach, the physiological model with its emphasis on psychosomatic theories and the relationship of the individual to the environmental milieu has always had a following, spearheaded until recently by epidemiologists and public health

3

workers and to a lesser extent by psychiatrists and psychologists. Over the past twenty years as an overwhelming adherence to the biomedical model has come into question, a reawakening interest in the physiological or "holistic" approach has gradually gained momentum. This is due not only to criticism of the biomedical approach but also to a change in values and attitudes toward knowledge in general.

There are complex reasons for a reexamination of the biomedical model related both directly and indirectly to the medical world itself. Intolerable costs (either to individuals or to governments), inaccessibility of medical care because of poor distribution by locality and specialty, and dissatisfaction with the "quality" of the medical encounter when it takes place, are cited by Eisenberg (1977, p. 235) as important factors. These problems are thought to arise largely because of the historical bias of cosmopolitan medicine in which an "engineering" approach was established in order to put medicine on a scientific footing. McKeown (1971) expresses it as follows:

> The approach to biology and medicine established during the seventeenth century was an engineering one based on a physical model. Nature was conceived in mechanistic terms, which lead in biology to the idea that a living organism could be regarded as a machine which might be taken apart and reassembled if its structure and function were fully understood. In medicine, the same concept leads further to the belief that an understanding of disease processes and of the body's response to them would make it possible to intervene therapeutically, mainly by physical (surgical), chemical, or electrical methods. (P. 36)

Von Mering and Earley (1965) state that the legacy of this attitude can be observed in modern medical practice:

> It has . . . been our observation that the clinic physician and the general practitioner share a kind of "molecular man" orientation which seems to predispose them to be more concerned with the specifics of the presenting complaint and to look eagerly for major disease in every bed or consulting room. (P. 198)

They believe that the "growth of medicine as a science of tests and measurements rather than an art involving the five senses" is largely to blame, along with the impersonal use of large hospitals as the usual site for diagnosis and treatment.

Specialization and the attempt to attain objectivity necessitated by a scientific approach are seen as major problems in the actual delivery of health care, leading to a lack of concern with the outcome of therapy, little interest in the experience of illness, and a tendency to equate the removal of symptoms with a complete and successful cure. Dedication to progress in medical technology, described by Carlson (1975, p. 12), is cited as the principal cause of iatrogenesis (damage caused by the medical profession itself). Iatrogenesis occurs in all medical traditions, but because cosmopolitan medicine is theoretically based on scientific tenets, it is particularly hard for doctors in this system to admit to fallibility and for patients to accept that doctors *are* fallible.

Not only the theoretical approach but the professionalization of medicine has also come under censure. In the words of Freidson (1970, p. 5), "Medicine's position today is akin to that of state religions yesterday—it has an officially approved monopoly of the right to define health and illness and to treat illness." In *Medical Nemesis* (1976, p. 40), although Illich's argument is often overstated, he makes the important point that in industrial societies where medicine is highly professionalized the public is stripped of its ability to care for itself; this he terms social iatrogenesis. He cites, among other things, the management of old age, childbirth, and death as areas where the medical profession has defined its right to be in control. The interrelationship of medicine with politics (Navarro 1976) and with the drug industry (Silverman and Lee 1974) provide further areas for critical analysis.

Recent developments in the field of epidemiology furnish data which, while not being critical of the biomedical model, indicate that its success may not be as dramatic as was formerly believed. Rosen (1958, pp. 225 ff.), Dubos (1961, p. 131), and McKeown (1965, pp. 21–58) put forward the argument that the general improvement in health and the decrease in mortality rates in the Western world largely took place *before* the advent of modern drugs and technology. These changes toward the end of the nineteenth century are attributed to better nutrition and to the introduction of certain standards of public hygiene instigated by medical reformers who were, in

5

fact, sometimes opposed to the germ theory of disease. McKeown (1971, p. 36) also stresses the importance of the introduction of birth control and believes that this is the most significant variable to consider in accounting for improved health conditions. According to McKeown, the contribution of clinical medicine to general health standards was not significant until the second quarter of the twentieth century, and by that time most of the total decline in mortality had already been achieved. The conclusions that are drawn from these articles are that social and cultural factors and man's relationship to his environment are of crucial importance in the occurrence and control of disease.

Change in epidemiology of disease from largely acute to chronic problems was thought to be due, on the one hand, to longer life expectancy and, on the other, to the conquest of acute problems, but epidemiologists see the issue as more complex than this. John Powles, in an article (1973) in which he makes use of the literature on epidemiology in hunter-gatherer, agricultural, and industrial societies, demonstrates that the rise in chronic and degenerative diseases in the modern industrial world is not just simply due to increased life expectancy, but is due rather to maladaptation to the environment that we have created for ourselves. He states:

> Industrial populations owe their current health standards to a pattern of ecological relationships which serves to reduce their vulnerability to death from infection and to a lesser extent to the capabilities of clinical medicine. Unfortunately this new way of life, because it is so far removed from that to which man is adapted by evolution, has produced its own disease burden. These diseases of maladaptation are, in many cases, increasing. (P. 12)

Other data, though still controversial, focus on the interrelationship of personality type with the incidence of many kinds of disease, including coronary heart disease, cancer, arthritis, migraine, low back pain, and asthma among others. (See LeShan 1959, 1966; Scotch and Geiger 1962; Simonton and Simonton 1975; Thomas and Duszynski 1974.)

In the light of these recent developments new trends in health policy planning are beginning to appear (Lalonde 1975). The fact that chronic diseases, for whatever reason, are the major medical problems in industrial societies has probably spurred on this development: first, treatment of chronic disease causes the largest drain on budgets for health; second, the incidence of chronic disease brings into sharp focus the problem of why only certain members of the population show a high morbidity; and last, the question of quality in health care becomes central. Powles (1973) describes the situation thus:

> With a rising proportion of illness evidently man-made and increasing restrictions on the further increase of resource consumption for medical care, medicine seems bound to move in an "ecological" direction. . . . With less confidence in his ability to master nature man will have to learn to live more openly with his vulnerability to forces he cannot control and with the frailty of the individual human existence. Man's domination of nature has been the central impetus of modern industrial culture. Further pursuit of this within the already industrialized countries is likely to be self-defeating and could well be disastrous. (P. 25)

This need to move in an "ecological" direction was expressed in 1975 as part of official health policy planning by the Deputy Director-General of the World Health Organization, Dr. Lambo, who made the following observation:

> The health status of an individual becomes meaningful only in terms of his human environment, i.e., his social and cultural milieu. The lessons of the last few decades have shown that social and economic changes have at least as much influence on health as medical interventions. . . . We must be sensitive to the issues involved in these changes and relate them to the rhythms and needs of individuals. (P. 7)

This statement and that of John Powles hint at some of the changes in values and attitudes toward knowledge which stem not simply from medicine but from changes in our approach to science itself. Heisenberg's Uncertainty Principle is the first expression in mathematical form of the problems which the pure scientists are facing. He demonstrates conclusively that the concept of a distinct physical entity, such as a particle, is an idealization that has no fundamental significance. It can only be defined in terms of its *connections* with the whole, and these connections are of a statistical nature, that is, probabilities rather than certainties. Heisenberg (1958) therefore concludes:

> [In modern physics], one has now divided the world not into different groups of objects but into different groups of connections. . . . What can be distinguished is the kind of connection which is primarily important in a certain phenomenon. . . . The world thus appears as a complicated tissue of events, in which connections of different kinds alternate or overlap or combine and thereby determine the texture of the whole. (P. 107)

Once Heisenberg's ideas were put into mathematical formulation, the way was open for some scientists to join forces with philosophers and other thinkers in seeking alternatives to explanations and answers for everything in finite scientific terms. The natural world is at present best explained with a model similar to that which Durkheim postulated sixty years ago for the social world: that the whole is greater than the sum of the parts and has a "reality" of its own, which cannot be totally explained by an examination of the parts. Man and the universe are not simply a jigsaw puzzle that will be made entirely comprehensible when the last piece is slotted into place.

The new trend in the sciences is therefore to appreciate the interrelationship of parts—ecological, holistic models are fashionable. The biologist Theobald (1972) states:

> All other species work within the existing habitat. Their success or failure depends upon their ability to adapt to the conditions in which they find themselves. Their survival depends upon a complex, interrelated ecosystem of which they form a small part and over which they have very limited control. . . . Man alone has tried to deny his relationship to the total ecosystem of which he forms a part by continuously cutting off feedback which he finds undesirable. He has developed the habit of seeing his habitat as totally flexible according to his own wishes and desires. (P. 1)

Fred Hoyle (1955), the astronomer, pushes the argument to its limits:

> Present-day developments in cosmology are coming to
> suggest rather insistently that everyday conditions could not
> persist but for the distant parts of the Universe, that all our
> ideas of space and geometry would become entirely invalid if
> the distant parts of the Universe were taken away. Our
> everyday experience even down to the smallest details seems
> to be so closely integrated to the grand-scale features of the
> Universe that it is well-nigh impossible to contemplate the
> two being separated. (P. 304)

When a holistic approach is applied to medicine new questions and attitudes emerge. Cosmopolitan medicine, with its technological bias, stresses the removal of specific symptoms by therapeutic intervention. But when a man is considered in relation to his environment, then the emphasis becomes one of maintaining health and balance rather than restoring lost health. Naming a specific cause for a disease is not considered sufficient. A search is made for a pattern of events that could have allowed the patient to become vulnerable to specific causes of disease. Social, psychological, environmental, and genetic factors should all be considered, not only to solve the present medical problem, but to aid in prevention of future problems. Emphasis is on adjustment rather than cure.

The range of cosmopolitan medicine is once again expanding to include a variety of factors beyond the biomedical model and is now similar to medical systems in nontechnological societies (Frank 1964, p. vii), to Western medicine until the early twentieth century, and also to that laid out in the classics of Ayurvedic, Yūnānī, and East Asian medical traditions.

Dubos (1968) puts the holistic approach into contemporary language:

> The activities of various hormones influence all of the human
> organism's responses to noxious agencies. The secretion of
> these hormones is in turn affected by psychological factors
> and by the symbolic interpretation the mind attaches to
> environmental agents and stimuli. This individual
> interpretation is so profoundly conditioned by the experiences
> of the past and by the anticipations of the future that the

9

> physiochemical characteristics of noxious agents rarely
> determine the character of the pathological processes they set
> in motion. (P. 75)

The biomedical model, however, remains the most persuasive viewpoint for its many adherents; the classical debate is still very much alive, as Lewis Thomas demonstrates:

> Since we have got rid of a few very important diseases, I
> think there is good reason to believe that we can keep at
> it. . . . I have to confess, however, that a lot of people in my
> field do think that we're now stopped. It has become
> something of a popular notion to say that the diseases we are
> left with now that we have got rid of the major infections are
> in some sense so complicated and so multifactorial, as the
> term goes—that they have something to do with the
> environment, or have to do with stress and the pace of
> modern living. . . . I simply can't take that point of view very
> seriously—not as long as we are as ignorant about the
> mechanisms of those diseases as we are. . . . Although there
> may be a lot of things going on, there will be one central,
> master mechanism for each of them, which we may be able
> to change when we learn what it is. (Interview. See Bernstein
> 1978, p. 44)

Some thinkers, such as the biologist Paul Weiss, stress that both a "holistic" and a "reductionistic" approach are necessary; he states that they are in a "demonstrable complementarity relation in the sense that either one conveys information which the other cannot supply" (1960, p. 25). With this approach in mind, East Asian medicine can be most interesting to Western observers. It is a medical system in which, while both the ontological and physiological viewpoints can be detected, theoretically the physiological doctrine has remained dominant through the centuries. East Asian medicine is therefore held up as "holistic" and "natural" and has become a popular model for experimentation in medical practice in the West. It is possible that by drawing on both the biomedical and the East Asian medical model we can come closer to a medical system that takes into account "complementary aspects . . . found in every human situation" (Weisskopf 1972, p. 349).

Unfortunately, acupuncture, one small part of the East Asian medical system, is frequently applied in North America today simply as another therapeutic technique in the arsenal of scientific weaponry. Wrenched out of cultural context and subjected to scientific evaluation, acupuncture is apparently still proving effective (Pomeranz et al. 1976; Risse 1973), but scientific experiments with acupuncture and other therapies of East Asian medicine will give us only a limited understanding of the nature of, and reasons for, its use through the centuries. For a more complete picture we must turn to a study of East Asian medicine in its cultural context.

Medical Systems and Cultural Context

Medical systems, like social systems in general, are embedded in a cultural matrix from which is derived the coherent body of ideas of which the system is composed. The practice of all medicine, therefore, including that of industrialized societies, has evolved as a result of its setting in a unique cultural context. Consequently, any attempt to analyze a complete medical system must include not only a description of the social structure, the social organization, and the belief system, but must also demonstrate how this relates, both historically and currently, to the total cultural context. Furthermore, since the actual experience of illness, though influenced by others, is ultimately an individual event, any study that does not consider the relationship of the individual to the social and cultural milieu must be considered incomplete.

Since concepts of health, illness, and disease causation and classification are largely culture-bound, the entire gamut of medical practice is also modified considerably by cultural beliefs; the roles of doctor and patient, the experience of illness, diagnostic techniques, and therapy, including the tools used in therapy, are all modified by cultural values. Medical theory, even that which is scientifically established, is culture-bound in the sense that the questions raised by theoreticians and the methods used to answer them are products of a particular period in history.

It is possible to introduce medical concepts and technology to other cultures, whether it be cosmopolitan medicine to developing countries or East Asian medicine to North America. It is virtually impossible to introduce at the same time the equivalent of the context, both social and cultural, in which those concepts and techniques were originally used. The actual practice of, and meaning associated with, recently imported material is changed considerably. This is true even where doctors go abroad to train in the country of origin of the incoming medical material. The individual doctor may change his beliefs radically, but the system in which he must practice and the attitudes of patients will be important limiting factors on rapid changes in meaning associated with health and illness.

Even where there is a conscious effort from within a society to officially adopt a new approach to medicine, it has been shown that large modifications are made to meet the particular needs and values of the society in question (Sidel and Sidel 1973). By focusing on the variety of ways in which a medical system is actually applied both within and across cultural boundaries it is possible to highlight the values and some of the implicit meaning that people bring to the universal problems of misfortune and suffering.

If medicine is to serve its prime functions of preventing and alleviating suffering, it *must* be culture-bound to some extent. Mary Douglas (1970) puts it thus: "If . . . therapy works it is because the symbols [of medicine] are creative instruments of a particular social structure" (p. 302).

Research both in the medical world (Pelletier 1977) and in the function of symbolism (Turner 1967; Tambiah 1977) confirms this line of argument. The point is stressed that symbolic communication forms a mediating pathway between social and cultural events and psychophysiological reactions. Kleinman (1973a) goes so far as to say:

> The line begins to blur between ordering the experience of illness and shaping the illness per se. I do not mean merely that psychiatric disorders or psychosomatic diseases are in this sense symbolic phenomena, but any disease—smallpox, leprosy, syphilis, hypertension, cardiovascular disorders, cancer, etc.—is in part a cultural construct. Disease derives much of its form, the way it is expressed, the value it is given, the meaning it possesses, and the therapy appropriate to it in large measure from the governing system of symbolic meaning. (P. 209)

East Asian medicine, derived from a totally different philosophical background from that of cosmopolitan medicine and nurtured in a cultural setting in which people understand themselves predominantly in relation to their environment rather than as individuals, gives the opportunity for many insights for the Westerner. We can explore both its strong and its weak points by looking at it in cultural context as a symbolic system as well as an empirical body of knowledge.

Purpose and Setting of the Study

I shall analyze the practice of East Asian medicine in urban Japan in order to demonstrate its degree of adaptation to the cultural ethos of the present day by considering the system from several perspectives: cultural, social, interpersonal, and personal. I shall describe the classical theoretical system and historical background of East Asian medicine in order to compare present-day practice with the traditional, theoretical ideal and also to demonstrate certain continuities in social organization and attitudes that can still be discerned today.

In a discussion of contemporary socialization practices and beliefs and practice related to health care within the family I shall demonstrate some of the expectations that Japanese patients hold regarding the sick role and professional medical care. I shall show how the belief system and the healing processes used in East Asian medicine furnish the type of symbolic communication which anastomoses with the needs of certain patients.

A consideration of some of the problems inherent in the practice of cosmopolitan medicine in Japan will further develop the analysis. With this body of information I shall attempt to account for the resurgence of interest in East Asian medicine in Japan by considering recent changes at both the macro and the micro level of social organization. Finally, the East Asian medical system will be examined as a model for a "holistic" approach to medicine in the West.

Japan provides an extremely important setting for the study of East Asian medicine for several reasons. First, it is a country in which general health standards are extremely high, whose population is stable, and in which the epidemiology of disease allows useful comparisons to be made with patients of industrial societies in the West. Second, Japan's long and voluntary experience of more than a hundred years with cosmopolitan medicine makes it a particularly interesting society in which to study the integration and adaptation of a traditional medical system to the impact of cosmopolitan medical beliefs. Last, it is a society in which virtually all of the population is literate and in which mass media of all kinds are widely disseminated; it is potentially a well-informed population, and there is the possibility, at least, for some educated reflection among the public.

The research was carried out in the city of Kyoto in the Kansai region of Japan. An urban environment was selected because Japan supports a largely urban population today and because historically the complete range of East Asian medicine never did penetrate fully into the Japanese countryside.

The 1972 census of Kyoto city showed a population of 1,419,000. The lower income groups derive their livelihood from employment in light industry and small entrepreneurial enterprises of various kinds of which the silk industry is the most important. There is a high proportion of *burakumin* (the outcast group) and of Korean immigrants compared with other Japanese cities.

Among the middle classes the proportion of white-collar workers is relatively low compared with other major cities, and the proportion of independent businessmen and professional people is rather high. The number of extended families living in traditional Japanese style, frequently with large private incomes, is also higher than in other cities (Statistical Information Bureau, Ministry of Welfare, Tokyo, 1975). Compared with Tokyo and Osaka, Kyoto is regarded by the Japanese as a culturally conservative city, but this is not reflected in current politics—a Communist mayor has held office for many years.

Characteristics of the Medical Systems
and of the Therapies under Discussion

Cosmopolitan medical system: otherwise termed "Western," "modern," or "scientific"; in Japan it is the dominant medical system and is state supported.

East Asian medical system: otherwise known as "traditional Chinese medicine" or "oriental medicine." When dealing with Chinese medicine in Japan I define it as East Asian medicine because it has been uniquely adapted over the past 1,300 years to Japanese cultural conditions while retaining

14

much of its original Chinese flavor. Dunn (1976, p. 135) defines this system as "regional" in that it is applied in several cultural settings and has a long scholarly tradition associated with it. In this respect it can be categorized with the Ayurvedic and Yunānī medical systems. Herbal medicine used in this system is mixed according to prescriptions in the pharmacopoeia of the East Asian medical tradition. Historically animal, mineral, and plant sources were used; today herbal medicine is composed almost completely of plant material.

Folk medical system: medical practice not derived from a scholarly medical tradition and provided by professional or experienced nonprofessional practitioners. Dunn's term for this system is "local." Oral medication is not in the form of individual prescriptions; it consists of one or two ingredients to counteract specific symptoms. Indigenous patent medicine, talismans, and incantations are all part of folk medicine. Moxa (see below) and massage are part of folk medicine when used without reference to scholarly theory. Many, but not all, of these beliefs and practices are indigenous to Japan.

Popular medical system: medical practice carried out among family members or friends without professional sources of advice. Techniques and beliefs are passed on informally from generation to generation.

Medical practitioners and patients state that they can readily make distinctions between these three medical systems and popular medicine, but in actual practice, both historical and current, the distinctions are not clearly maintained.

Frequently Used East Asian Medical Terms

Amma: a massage technique imported to Japan in the sixth century with other aspects of East Asian medicine.

Hari: the Japanese term for acupuncture, a therapeutic technique in which needles are inserted into the body at certain defined points.

Kanpō: means the "Chinese method." It refers to the entire medical system brought to Japan from China in the sixth century. In modern Japan it is also used to refer to the application of herbal medicine, as distinct from acupuncture, moxibustion, and massage. Any clinic that makes herbal therapy the center of its medical system is defined in Japan today as a *kanpō* clinic.

Okyū: a therapeutic technique, known in the West as moxibustion, in which small cones of a powdered herb, mugwort (*Artemisia vulgaris*), are burned on the body at certain defined points.

Shiatsu: a type of massage that was developed in Japan and given its present name in the nineteenth century. Principles from the martial arts are included in its theories.

Japanese Health Standards and Health Insurance Systems

General

Standards of health in Japan are high. Life expectancy is seventy-one and a half years for males and seventy-six for females (Public Health White Paper, 1973, p. 21), longer than in the United States. Epidemic diseases no longer present a major problem, but the death rate from tuberculosis, although dropping rapidly, is still higher than in the United States or Europe. The diseases that produce the highest death rate today are cerebral hemorrhage, malignant neoplasms, especially of the stomach, and heart disease (Public Health White Paper, 1973, p. 27)—a pattern typical for an industrialized society.

For every 10,000 persons in Japan there are 11.6 physicians, whereas there are 12.7 in the United Kingdom and 16.1 in the United States (WHO World Health Statistics Annual, 1971, p. 48). This is considered adequate by WHO standards, although the distribution of physicians is still low in the Japanese countryside. The availability of hospital beds in Japan is adequate: there is a ratio of 12.7 beds per 1,000 population, higher than that in either the United States or the United Kingdom.

The first National Health Insurance program was established in 1938, and this has gradually expanded so that now 50 percent of the population uses this coverage. The program is operated by local government agencies, and the cost of medical treatment is met by a 40 percent contribution from the national government and a 30 percent contribution from the patient, while the final 30 percent is paid for by a contribution from the local government and supplemented by insurance fees of participants. The fees are rated according to local tax payments and property holdings. The average white-collar worker pays about $12 per month insurance fees for a family of four.

This provides complete coverage, including the cost of medication and dental care.

Treatment by participating osteopaths and chiropractors is covered, as is treatment by practitioners of acupuncture, moxibustion, and massage, provided that the insured is referred by an M.D. (Kyoto City Publications, 1974). All out-patient treatment for patients over seventy years of age is free, and victims of certain diseases, which are known as "the thirty hard-to-cure diseases" (these are all diseases for which there is a poor prognosis in cosmopolitan medicine), also receive treatment completely free.

Subsequent reimbursement to physicians is based on a points system. Every diagnostic and therapeutic procedure is allotted a value on a rating scale in which one point is worth 10 yen (3 cents approximately). For example, a venipuncture, 17 points, is worth 50 cents; most injections are rated at 12 points, or 36 cents; a first examination is 90 points, $2.70, and subsequent examinations are 52 points, or $1.56.[3] The doctor must record his every procedure on official forms. There are many complaints about this system from both physicians and patients.

Almost all companies and factories have private insurance systems that provide free medical care for employees and 70 percent coverage for their dependents. Company employees usually use these schemes, while people who are independently employed, unemployed, or retired usually use the national health insurance scheme.

Medical Facilities in the City of Kyoto

Cosmopolitan Medical Facilities The number of doctors practicing cosmopolitan medicine is estimated at 3,280 (Kyoto City Statistical Records, 1973, p. 209) or about one doctor for every 420 people. This is extremely high, because Kyoto not only has a prestigious medical school, but is also a desirable place to live.

Kyoto has 1,628 small clinics and 145 hospitals, only 17 of which are public; a hospital is defined as having twenty beds or more. The number of hospital beds available in Kyoto is thus one for every seventy-two people. Eighty-nine hospitals and 1,277 clinics are owned by doctors. This is a very high figure compared with the United States, and it means that most doctors

3 Based on 1974 rates of exchange.

face all the insecurities of being independent businessmen while practicing medicine. Despite the fact that the clinics are privately owned, all of them must take part in the major insurance schemes, and doctors are not allowed to see patients privately.

As in Japan in general, the cosmopolitan medical facilities in Kyoto appear to be adequate. Most people have a family doctor whom they visit when they first become ill. This doctor usually lives in the immediate neighborhood and knows the patient's family circumstances. He probably owns and operates one of the private clinics described above, and usually the clinic is part of the doctor's own family residence. The family doctor is frequently a specialist in internal medicine, and he will refer patients to the large hospitals for further examinations as he sees fit. There are other specialists who live and work in each area of the city, including surgeons; pediatricians; gynecologists and obstetricians; ear, nose, and throat specialists; eye specialists; and dentists. In one middle-class residential area of Kyoto, in a ward comprising 105 families, there are two specialists in internal medicine, one surgeon, and one dentist; every other type of specialist is obtainable within a five-minute walking distance. Public health centers for free routine X-rays and so on are also readily accessible throughout the city.

East Asian Medical Facilities East Asian medicine—practiced almost exclusively in small private clinics—is not usually covered by health insurance. Only a few practitioners choose to accept insured patients who are referred to them through cosmopolitan medical practitioners. The fees they receive are then determined according to the points system.

In Kyoto approximately 1,800 people practice East Asian medicine, of whom 1,143 hold massage licenses, and 657 acupuncture and moxibustion licenses. There are about 800 East Asian medical clinics in Kyoto (unofficial records, Kyoto City Hall); when compared with the 1,277 cosmopolitan clinics, this means that about 38 percent of all private medical clinics are practicing East Asian medicine.

To obtain a license either in acupuncture and moxibustion or in massage, it is necessary to pass a national examination after completing two and one-half years of study beyond the high school level. Those people holding an acupuncture and moxibustion license who wish to obtain a massage license in addition must study for a further year. The status of the special East Asian medical schools where the students receive their training is equivalent to that of a junior college. Any cosmopolitan medical doctor who wishes to may also practice East Asian medicine without special training.

To practice herbal medicine it has been necessary since 1875 first to take a license in cosmopolitan medicine and then to become attached to a practicing *kanpō* doctor and to learn while working. The number of doctors specializing in the practice of herbal medicine in Japan is relatively low, about a hundred in all, of whom eight are in Kyoto.

With the exception of two recently developed areas of Kyoto, the East Asian medical clinics are fairly evenly distributed within the city, hence are readily available to patients in their own neighborhoods. There is, in addition, a great concentration of massage clinics in the entertainment area.

Some clinics are very modern, others completely traditional, where treatment is performed on *tatami* (Japanese mats). As with the cosmopolitan clinics, most of the rooms are part of the practitioner's private home, but a few are independent structures; some are attached to Buddhist temples, and still others to cosmopolitan clinics.

Just as the physical setting is varied, so too is the belief system of the practitioners. Very few of these clinics provide the complete range of East Asian medical therapies; most specialize in one area or the other.

Folk Medical Systems Apart from cosmopolitan and East Asian medicine, a large proportion of the population of Kyoto has recourse to other methods for dealing with particular health problems. Shintō shrines are still used by all segments of the society, usually in connection with pregnancy, safe childbirth, and mild, early childhood problems. Simple ceremonies are performed at a nominal fee, and talismans are for sale. Some Buddhist temples are well known for the practice of moxibustion in the folk style rather than as part of a complete medical system. Others own famous stones that are said to provide relief for the sick when they are rubbed. Some temples furnish special preparations of food to ward off sickness at certain times of the year. There are also a few female shamans left in Kyoto who deal mostly with cases of spirit possession, as do some Buddhist priests. Participants in Buddhist or shamanistic rituals related to health are primarily from the working classes or small entrepreneurial families. Some of the new syncretic religions, well represented in Kyoto, also focus on healing.

Many older people use popular remedies for self-medication in the home, and this is regaining popularity through the attention drawn to it in the news media. Recently a book entitled *Health through Garlic* was on the best-seller list for six months.

Both traditional and cosmopolitan osteopaths are available, as are chiropractitioners. There are also electrical baths, hot-spring resort areas, and door-to-door salesmen who peddle medicine. The range is seemingly endless but never exclusive, and most people regularly combine the use of several of these systems.

To understand the part that the East Asian medical system plays in this scheme we shall turn first to its philosophical origins and historical development and then to an analysis of several urban clinics.

PART ONE

East Asian Medicine: Its Philosophical
Foundations and Historical
Development

2

Early Japanese Medical Beliefs
and Practices

Heaven and earth and I are of the same root,
The ten-thousand things and I are of one substance.

Seng-chao (383–414),
Chuang-tzŭ, 11

Even while I was getting ready, mending my torn trousers, tying a
new strap to my hat, and applying moxa to my legs to strengthen
them, I was already dreaming of the full moon rising over the
islands of Matsushima.

Matsuo Bashō (1644–1694),
The Narrow Road to the
Deep North

Three distinct composites of beliefs have influenced the state of medicine
in Japan today. They are the indigenous belief system of Shintō, the East
Asian medical tradition, which was officially incorporated into use in Japan
in the sixth century, and the cosmopolitan medical system, which was first
brought to Japan in the sixteenth century by the Portuguese.

The first references to healing occur in the chronicles of mythological and
early historical times. It is recorded in the *Nihongi* (compiled A.D. 720) that
Opo-kuni-nushi united his powers with Sukuna-biko-no-mikoto in order to
construct the universe, and "they also determined the method of curing
illnesses for the race of mortal man and for animals; they also determined

23

magical methods for doing away with calamities from birds, beasts, and creeping things" (vol. 1, p. 122). Opo-kuni-nushi is frequently mentioned in connection with healing practices and is thought to represent an archetypal shamanistic practitioner who combined the use of amulets and ritual curing with the application of herbal medicine.

The *Fudoki* are descriptions of life in the various regions compiled about A.D. 719. The records indicate that among the aristocracy at least, by A.D. 400 or earlier, a shamanistic cult was centered on Izumo. According to Fujikawa (1974, p. 5) the *Izumo Fudoki* contains descriptions of the use of ground seashell against burns; of cattail pollen as an herbal medicine to rub on wounds; of rice wine as a medicine, and of the use of *onsen* (natural hot springs) for therapeutic purposes.

Fujikawa also studied the entire *Kojiki* (compiled A.D. 712) for references to medicines. He found many, including *kuzu* (arrowroot), *shōsai* (Chinese colza, a member of the mustard family), *susuki* (pampas grass), *kaba* (birch), *momo* (peach), *kashi* (oak), *hiiragi* (holly), *fū* (storax tree, from which balsam is obtained), *budō* (grape), and *take* (bamboo).

The early chronicles cannot be accepted as entirely reliable sources on indigenous culture, since they were compiled after Japan was already under strong Chinese influence, but the references to medicine are numerous and all of them are to plants native to Japan. The opinions of Japanese scholars vary, but many of them feel that most of these herbs were being used in Japanese folk medicine, although their method of application may have been modified on contact with Chinese medicine (Tabata, personal communication). There are many plants that are used both in Japanese folk medicine and in *kanpō* today, but their therapeutic function is often quite different in the two traditions (Nishiyama 1963).

Early Japanese beliefs about disease causation are also recorded in the *Kojiki*. These beliefs are central to what was later incorporated into the philosophy of Shintō when attempts were first made to rationalize that religion. Again, using Fujikawa's study on the *Kojiki* (1974, p. 7): "There is no sharp distinction between the gods and man, or between heaven and earth." According to Ono (1962, p. 106), "Man by nature was thought of as inherently good and the world in which he lived was good." Evil came from without, and evil spirits called *magatsuhi* brought retributions, including illness, on man because, while his soul was good, there were times when the flesh succumbed to temptation. This state was seen as temporary, and evil spirits could be removed by purification rites.

A second theory of disease causation was also used: by coming into contact with polluting agents such as blood, corpses, people with skin diseases, and so on, one could get into a state of *ekiakudoku,* which literally means "having a spirit polluted by bad poison." Concepts of communicable and inherited diseases were established early in Japan, for it was believed that such a state not only could bring sickness on the individual concerned but could be passed on to the children.

Katō points out (1926, p. 113) that in the ancient documents the ideas of purity and pollution have highly physical connotations and are in no way of an abstract or a moral nature. According to Blacker (1975, p. 42), becoming polluted is one of "the unavoidable concomitants of the human cycle of life." Accordingly, treatment of disease was straightforward; herbal infusions and hot-spring baths were designed to act as sudorifics, purgatives, or emetics (Tabata, personal communication). In other words, the aim was to drive out the offending material. The medicine was required to be strong and to produce a visible and perhaps violent reaction inside the body, resulting in some form of expulsion. Avoidance of constipation and the practice of regular bathing and gargling are still central to concepts of health in Japan today—the body must undergo thorough and regular cleansing in order to avoid sickness.

A highly elaborate system of avoidance taboos was developed around agents, both tangible and intangible, believed to be polluting. Sick people, menstruating women, women in childbirth, and the dead were categorized as polluted, were feared, and were hedged with avoidance taboos. Because it was believed that people could transmit their diseases to their family members, sickness could potentially lead to public ostracism of the entire family. Shintō priests, concerned with the maintenance of their own ritual purity, did not intervene to help directly in either healing or burial procedures. A sick person therefore became a burden to his or her family; illness was associated with rejection from society, and as such it was greatly feared. It is not surprising, therefore, that preventive medicine, in the form of regular ritual purification ceremonies, has always been central to the Japanese notion of health. Purification rituals occurred at all levels of society, from the two great national ceremonies performed on the last day of the sixth and twelfth months, down to household and individual rites. The national events brought about "expulsion of all forms of defilement and pollution for all persons present and for the nation's people as a whole" (*Engishiki* 1970, p. 84). This is interesting, because people still find it unnecessary to go personally to a shrine or a temple to buy a charm or a talisman today; it is sufficient for a neighbor to bring one back when he goes—none of the efficacy is lost. Social interaction is not required in the avoidance of disease or the restoration of health; rather, mechanical performance of ritual is all that is considered important. If, therefore, having performed regular purification rites, someone should nevertheless become sick, it is regarded as misfortune but not as a result of poor moral or social behavior. Purification ceremonies are those Shintō medical beliefs that have survived and that are practiced most fully today.

From early historical times in Japan, therefore, impurity, uncleanliness, and the occurrence of sickness were inextricably bound up. Shortcomings in the management of one's own body were seen as sources of illness both for the individual and possibly for one's children.

3

Theoretical and Philosophical Foundations
of East Asian Medicine

The Introduction of Chinese Medicine
to Japan

East Asian medicine, known as *kanpō* to the Japanese, first came to Japan primarily in the hands of Buddhist priests and was used to facilitate the spread of Buddhist doctrine. A vast array of Chinese herbs and the techniques of acupuncture, moxibustion, and massage were all introduced by the sixth century, and in 561–562 Chi Chung, a doctor from southern China, brought more than a hundred books on theoretical medicine (Huard and Wong 1968, p. 74).

There was opposition to the introduction of Buddhism and, along with it, East Asian medicine, particularly from some of the powerful families with hereditary rank close to the Imperial family. The Nakatomi and the Imbe, who performed Shintō purification rituals, were especially threatened. Despite this the East Asian medical system soon became widely diffused among the Japanese. Varley (1973, p. 19) states that in the sixth century about a quarter or more of the ruling aristocracy of the time were foreign, that is, of Chinese or Korean origin, and that most of their families arrived during the previous century. These people undoubtedly must have encouraged the adoption of the new medical system. Since Shintō ritualists did not like to act as actual doctors and only took part in healing ceremonies as intermediaries with the gods once they themselves were suitably protected

27

from the threat of pollution, the incoming Chinese and Korean priest-doctors must soon have found many clients.

The medical books that were brought to Japan at this time presented a highly systematized theory of medicine, which the Chinese first started to record on oracle bones in the Shang dynasty from 1700 B.C. onward. The great classics, such as the *Huang-ti Nei Ching* (the Yellow Emperor's Classic of Internal Medicine) and the *Shen-nung pen t'sao* (materia medica of Shen nung), had already been revised several times before they arrived in Japan. The authors of these books, like those of most of the early treatises, are unknown, and the texts were compiled from many sources during the Han dynasty, but by the sixth century the major theories and methods, with some variation, were generally accepted as dogma. Many of these classics are still quoted today in Japan, although with strong reservation at times.

PLATE 1. Performing acupuncture. Fragment from the "Scroll of Diseases" (Yamai no Sōshi), Kamakura period, twelfth century.

Theoretical Foundations of Chinese Medicine

General

Before 200 B.C. in China medical practitioners were shamans, and disease was thought to be caused primarily by unsatisfied ancestors or by evil spirits of various kinds. From 200 B.C. onward, medicine for the upper echelons of society was secularized, and the first texts show a marked Confucian influence. References to the spirit world as agents of disease causation become rare. It is man's duty to keep healthy, and he does this by living according to the rules of society and by taking care of his body in a highly practical way. Through poor diet, lack of sleep, lack of exercise, and so on, or by being in a state of disharmony with one's family or society, the body can get out of balance, and it is at times like this that diseases occur. A "physiological" or "holistic" model emerges as dominant during this period and retains dominance, theoretically at least, until the present century. The classics, however, are textbooks that present the theoretical system of the most influential doctors of their time—doctors who were primarily scholars and not much involved with curing patients. It should be borne in mind that in practice many modifications and local folk beliefs must have been added to the system, and that a broad range of medical practice, from a relatively "true to the classics" style in the court down to an almost complete system of folk medicine used by practitioners who were illiterate, must have coexisted. The bearers of the classics to Japan probably often verbally supplemented the Confucian system, with its heavy sense of personal responsibility for sickness, with some of their own ideas.

As with every other theoretical tradition developed in early China, the concepts of yin and yang are central in medicine. Needham (1962, p. 273) visualizes yin and yang as two forces, but Granet's explanation (1930, p. 146) of these concepts is more general: "Yin and yang may be defined neither as purely logical entities nor as simple cosmogonic principles. They are neither substances nor forces nor genera. To the common consciousness they appear to be indistinctly all this, and no technician would consider them under one particular aspect only, excluding all others." The entire universe, both natural and social, was conceived as being in a state of dynamic equilibrium, oscillating between the poles of yin and yang, and man's body is seen as a

29

microcosm of the universe. Porkert (1974, pp. 9 ff.), in the most comprehensive book to date on theoretical Chinese medicine, feels that both these definitions leave something to be desired. Using a philological and phenomenological approach, he furnishes a most exhaustive explanation. He finds that yin corresponds to all that is "contractive, positive, absorbing into or within the individual, centripetal, conservative and structive" (a word that Porkert creates to include the ideas of completion, condensation, and consolidation, among others). Yang corresponds to things that are "active, expansive, centrifugal, aggressive, demanding and negative." The subtlety of this classificatory system lies in the fact that it is dynamic and not reduced to a static duality. In yin there is always some yang, and in yang always some yin; this is what Porkert terms "qualitative overlaps between yin and yang aspects." He adds that "quantitative gradations of yin and yang may be derived only partly and conditionally from these yin yang polarities." Yin and yang can be diagrammed as the poles of a continuous cyclic alternation. In this model, as in nature, the transitions between the alternate polarities take place gradually and in unbroken progression. All phenomena, including the parts of the body, are assigned yin and yang qualities, and hence man's place as a small part of a great cosmic order is firmly established.

Superimposed on the yin and yang classification system were other ideas about the order of natural phenomena, the most important of which was the Five Evolutive Phases (Porkert's terminology, 1974, p. 43). According to Needham (1962, p. 247), this system was fused onto the yin/yang concept in the former Han dynasty. Porkert defines the five evolutive phases as "stretches of time, temporal segments of exactly defined qualities that succeed each other in cyclical order at reference positions defined in space" (1974, p. 45). He adds that "they typify qualities of energy by the use of five concepts (wood, fire, earth, metal, and water) which, because of the richness of their associations, are ideally suited to serve as the crystallizing core for an inductive system of relations and correspondences." The five evolutive phases occur in several different orders depending on what purpose they are being used for. In medicine the systems shown in Figure 1 are used most frequently.

The cycle depicted by the solid arrows is usually referred to as the "mutual productive order." Each evolutive phase is considered the product

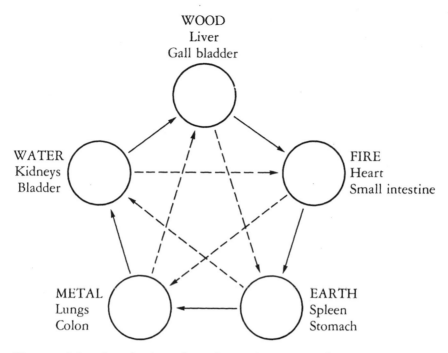

Figure 1. Mutual productive order and mutual conquest order

or child of the preceding one, the mother; that is, the production or stimulation of one element will in turn stimulate the production of the following one in the cycle. In addition, there is a checking sequence, usually called the "mutual conquest order," in which each evolutive phase is thought to limit the action of another in the order indicated by the dotted arrows. Thus, stimulation drives the energy cycle forward, but it is always limited by the checking sequence.

The correspondence system that is derived from the five evolutive phases extends to the entire universe and includes such things as the seasons, atmospheric influences, colors, musical sounds, the planets, the social system, and numerous other topics, all divided into five types related to the evolutive phases. The parts of the human body are similarly divided up, as are various emotional conditions (see Table 1).

This system of correspondences provides a model in which the relationship of the body organs one to another, and to other phenomena both

TABLE 1
Table of Correspondences

	WOOD	FIRE	EARTH	METAL	WATER
Planet:	Jupiter	Mars	Saturn	Venus	Mercury
Direction:	East	South	Center	West	North
Season:	Spring	Summer	Winter	Indian Summer	Autumn
Color:	Blue	Red	Yellow	White	Black
Perverse climates:	Wind	Heat	Moisture	Dryness	Cold
Yin organs:	Liver	Heart	Spleen	Lungs	Kidneys
Yang organs:	Gall bladder	Small intestine	Stomach	Large intestine	Bladder
Sense:	Sight	Speech	Taste	Smell	Hearing
Parts of body:	Muscles Nails	Pulse Complexion	Lips	Skin	Hair Bones
Orifice:	Eyes	Ears	Mouth	Nose	Anus Urinary
Fluid:	Tears	Sweat	Lymph	Mucus	Saliva
Smell:	Rancid	Burnt	Sweet	Fleshy	Putrid
Taste:	Acid	Bitter	Sweet	Piquant	Salty
Sound:	Crying	Laughter	Singing	Sobbing	Groaning
Emotions:	Anger	Joy	Worry	Grief	Fear
Animal (domestic):	Chicken	Dog	Ox	Horse	Pig
Animal (wild):	Tiger	Stag	Bear	Bird	Monkey
Grain:	Wheat	Millet	Rye	Rice	Peas

Source: Table of correspondences in *Japanese Acupuncture*, by Hashimoto (1966).

within and outside the body, are in a complex feedback system. There is a potential for achieving a state of dynamic equilibrium if no strain is imposed on the system. The balance of the cycles are, however, continually disturbed by influences from both outside and inside the body, and these influences become manifest as either a deficiency or an excess of energy. It is believed that the state of imbalance that arises can be detected diagnostically.

In the classical texts two series of "numerical emblems" (Porkert 1974, p. 60) used in conjunction with the five evolutive phases and the yin/yang system were known as the ten celestial stems and the twelve terrestrial branches. By successively pairing all the celestial stems with all the terrestrial branches one can obtain sixty different combinations. Each of these combinations was used as a counter for the years, and after every sixty years the cycle began again. In addition, the terrestrial branches were also used to mark the divisions of the day.

When the Five Evolutive Phase theory and the system of numerical emblems are fused onto the simple yin/yang cycle, then every aspect of the universe from the traditional division of time into sixty-year cycles to the occurrence of ulcers in the human population becomes part of a great, inductively patterned order. This system was used as a basis for divination, including diagnosis of certain medical problems. Since yin and yang are in a dynamic relationship and fluctuate back and forth periodically, there will be times when one or the other is in excess. This fluctuation is predictable when the yin/yang system is used in conjunction with the five-phase theory and the numerical emblems. There are regular sixty-year, annual, and diurnal variations of yin and yang modified by other phenomena, such as planetary movement and the social climate of the time.

Excess of yin is associated with a deficiency of energy, and excess of yang with a redundancy of it, and so, for example, if the year is a yin one, the season winter, and the time midnight, then energy levels will be generally low. The classics describe how these macrocosmic influences affect the body, and both doctors and laymen over the years became extremely sensitive to changes in seasonal and diurnal variation in an attempt to apply some preventive medicine. (For a full and extremely detailed explanation of this system, see Porkert 1974, pp. 55 ff.)

In the East Asian medical model, therefore, man is seen as part of Nature and constantly subject to its forces. On application of this dynamic concept, the patient as a whole person and the parts of his or her body can never be conceptualized in isolation. Furthermore, it is believed that the patient's state is not fixed for the duration of an illness episode, but will be constantly modified by further environmental interactions.

Some of the limitations of this theoretical system are immediately obvious; among others are the original selection of the categories of the correspondence system and the seemingly intuitive assignment of qualities of yin and yang to phenomena. In addition, there appears to have been a preoccupation with categorizing every phenomenon into the system in order to furnish a satisfying and complete method of explaining the entire universe.

At present I wish only to present these data as dogma, as they were brought to the Japanese in the sixth century, and to reserve a discussion of their validity for modern Japanese practitioners until later in the volume.

The Structure of the Human Body

The Chinese idea of the body was always predominantly functional and concerned with the interrelationship of parts rather than with anatomical accuracy. Croizier (1968, p. 26) believes that this was due primarily to a disdain among the literati for working with the hands. The great doctors were scholars, not technicians, and they enjoyed theorizing without testing out their ideas in any systematic way. In addition, Confucianism prohibited any tampering with the human body.

While these factors were undoubtedly important, I believe that the Chinese method of categorization and their world view are also crucial. Unlike the early Greek scholars, the Chinese were interested not so much in causal processes as in the synchronic patterning of things and events. Needham (1962, p. 279) has aptly called this "correlative thinking." He states that, for the Chinese,

> things behaved in particular ways not necessarily because of prior actions or impulsions of other things, but because their position in the ever-moving cyclical universe was such that they were endowed with intrinsic natures which made that behavior inevitable for them. If they did not behave in those particular ways they would lose their relational positions in the whole (which made them what they were), and turn into something other than themselves. They were thus parts in existential dependence upon the whole world organism. And they reacted upon one another not so much by mechanical impulsion or causation as by a kind of mysterious resonance. (P. 281)

With the human body, too, the basic model is not a mechanistic one but one of mutually interreacting parts—the emphasis is on the functional interrelationships between the parts of the body rather than on detailed anatomical accuracy. Holistic thinking rather than linear relationships is constantly stressed, both within the body and in terms of relationships to the macrocosm.

The five principal yin organs were thought of as relatively solid and sac-like when compared with the more hollow and tube-like yang organs. The yin organs are usually translated as heart, lungs, liver, spleen, and kidney, and the yang as the small intestine, large intestine, gall bladder, stomach, and tri-heater system.[1] However, to do the system justice, it is necessary to think in emic terms, that is, in terms of the meaning attributed to these concepts in the classical texts. In fact, included in the idea of each of these organs is a whole functional system that, along with the relevant part of the correspondence system, must be considered synonymously with the organ in question. For example, the idea of the lungs includes not only the lungs themselves but the entire respiratory tract, the nose, the skin, and the secretions associated with these organs. In the correspondence system, the lungs are metal and are thus minor yin, or yin in yang, and are considered female in type. The color white, a piquant taste, a smell of raw or rotten meat, grief, and negativism are all associated with the lungs, and if these phenomena manifest themselves in the patient, they can be used to aid diagnosis.

In the macrocosm the planet Venus is in correspondence with the lungs. A patient will grow worse each noon and get a bit better each afternoon; he should avoid cool food, drinks, and clothing. A lung disease will probably improve during the winter. There are also dream motifs associated with each of the organs, which indicate lack of balance. (See Porkert 1974, pp. 107 ff., for a complete account of all the internal organs and their functional systems.) Other parts of the body were described but were given much less consideration in the classics than those cited above. Exceptions are the meridians and points used in acupuncture, which will be described shortly.

The Chinese postulated several forms of energy of which ch'i is the best known. Porkert (1974, pp. 168 ff.) delineates thirty-two different types of ch'i described in the classics; they refer to energy both in the universe and in the microcosm of the human body. There is thought to be a continual exchange of ch'i between the body and the environment, thus enhancing the view of man as a microcosm. Ch'i circulates through the body in a pre-scribed route, and it is this flow of energy that keeps man alive. It was

---

1 The tri-heater system is yang in nature and is best visualized as the controlling system of all circulating energy in the body. Included in its concept are the endocrine and autonomic nervous system of cosmopolitan medicine and the idea of the sex drive. It does not correspond to any anatomical structure in cosmopolitan medical terms.

believed that at conception *ch'i* was contributed by both parents to the growing fetus, and thus hereditary factors could be accounted for. Imbalances, and hence disease, occur when *ch'i* does not circulate naturally owing to either excessive or insufficient input into the system. However, the nature of all things, including man's body, is one of homeostasis; that is, there is a natural striving to return to equilibrium.

Other forms of energy are cited in the classics, including *hsüeh*, commonly translated as "blood." This is described as a fluid derived from the transformation of energy obtained from food. It is yin in nature and must be in harmony with the other forms of energy, especially *ch'i,* which is yang. The concept of the circulation of blood was known but poorly developed, anatomically speaking; energy and blood were thought to circulate together.

In the *Nei-Ching* (attributed to the Han dynasty 206 B.C. to A.D. 220) appears the first documentation of a series of pressure points at the surface of the body, which, if stimulated, could produce an effect on other parts of the body. It was hypothesized that there must be some form of communication between these points and the internal organs so that blood and energy could be transmitted around the body. These hypothetical channels are usually translated into the term "meridians." There is considerable scientific documentation to show that the pressure points have a distinct electrical resistance and thermosensitivity unlike other areas at the body surface, but there is no scientific demonstration so far of the existence of meridians. It seems best, therefore, to conceptualize the meridians not as permanent structures but rather as fluctuations in the flow of electrical or magnetic energy. There is some disagreement as to how the ancient Chinese themselves visualized the meridians, but in the classics they are always represented as solid lines. The twelve meridians are assigned yin and yang qualities and are associated with each of the twelve primary organs, including the heart constrictor.[2] Energy circulates in the meridians in a specific direction and sequence. There are now in all about 785 recognized points, although the number described in the *Nei-Ching* was only 275. Some are used much more frequently than others to aid in treatment. Each point is assigned a name, which has either a functional or a symbolic significance and which aids considerably in the memorization of the points.

2 There is a sixth yin organ, which Porkert feels was deliberately created at a later date because of a desire for symmetry (1974, p. 147). It is usually translated as the heart constrictor and is generally thought to correspond to the pericardium and the aorta.

There are, in addition, a number of important points not on meridians, and also other minor meridians not in direct association with the main internal body organs. (For a more detailed description of the meridians and points, including a postulated evolutionary sequence for the development of meridians, see Mann 1973 and Manaka 1972, pp. 33–77.)

Disease Causation

The classics state that diseases become manifest when the body gets out of balance and the *ch'i* does not circulate properly. Agents that can cause this are both external and internal. External agents are divided into two kinds, *wai-kan* and *shih-ch'i-ping*. The first term means "induced from without," and the second means "disease dependent on time" (Porkert 1974, p. 55). The second definition is used with reference to epidemic and seasonal diseases, and it was to control and prevent these diseases that the calendar was used in conjunction with the Five Evolutive Phase system. Of the external agents, sudden climatic changes at the end of each season were particularly feared.

Internal causes were attributed to an imbalance of one's emotional state—these emotional states are classified in the correspondence system and therefore act on specific internal organs. There was a second concept, that of dormant *ch'i* (Mann 1973, p. 180), in which it was believed that at certain seasons a noxious substance could enter the body while the resistance was low, remain dormant, and then manifest itself at a later time, particularly after a change of season. This theory presents a striking parallel with contemporary psychosomatic medicine and particularly with research on cancer (Solomon and Amkraut 1972). Last, as was mentioned above, the concept of hereditary diseases was accounted for by the transference of *ch'i* from parents to children.

It should be noted that supernatural agents are not represented as direct factors in disease causation in the *Nei-Ching* or in most of the other Chinese classics. Despite this, medicine to counteract possession is listed in some of the pharmacopoeia. It is probable that few people outside the court were able to accept the *Nei-Ching* in its entirety, and even though the Confucian scholars made great attempts to eliminate all traces of elements that they considered nonrational, belief in spirits as agents of disease causation continued in practice among most of the population.

Theoretically, therefore, sickness in this model is seen not so much in terms of an intruding agent, although this aspect of disease causation is acknowledged, but rather as due to a pattern of causes leading to disharmony. These causes can be at the environmental, the social, the psychological, or the physiological level; some are predictable and dependent on annual and diurnal variations; others are of a more individual nature, though still potentially predictable through the use of the numerological and five-phase-theory charts.

Diagnosis

The purpose of diagnosis is to decide whether the patient's problem is primarily yin or yang in character; whether it has external or internal symptoms; whether it is cold or warm in nature, and whether there is increased (*jissho*) or decreased (*kyosho*) function of the internal organs. In general, the yin state is associated with symptoms of "internal cold" and reduced body function. The patient is limp and requires warmth, and there is no sweating or flush. The yang state is associated with increased function, "external symptoms," and "warmth." The patient will not be still, he feels hot, sweats, is flushed, and is constantly thirsty.

There can be combinations of these yin and yang symptoms in the same patient. For example, a headache and a coated tongue are classified as "external cold surface" symptoms. A reddened tongue with a yellowish coating, thirst, and exhaustion are symptomatic of "internal heat."

There are four standard methods of diagnosis, known as the *shishin*, which include observation, listening, questioning, and palpation. *Observation* includes looking at the skin color and texture, the state of the mouth, nose, eyes, and teeth. The coating of the tongue is given great attention. In addition, the hands and nails are observed. The sound of the patient's breathing and his manner of speaking and coughing are included in the diagnosis by *listening*.

These first two methods of diagnosis were used principally with reference to the correspondence system as an aid in detecting the state of the internal organs. For example, the eyes are in correspondence with the liver, and if they tire easily, and if one feels pricking sensations in the eyelids, and if this is combined with whitish blotches and ridging on the nails, then the doctor would suspect that the liver is off balance.

Questioning is about the family circumstances, habits of exercise and diet, and minute details about the day-to-day rhythm of the patient's body. Part of the reason for this method of diagnosis is to find out how much the patient knows about himself. It also helps the doctor to ascertain what problems the patient is predisposed to.

The fourth method, and the one most highly refined and complex, is that of *palpation*, of which the art of pulse-taking is the most important. Several classical works are devoted solely to this subject. The radial artery is used, as in cosmopolitan medicine, and it is believed that one can determine not only the condition of the heart and aorta but also the state of the other storage and hollow organs. The pulse is taken on the radial artery of both forearms, the doctor placing three fingers on each artery and exerting varying degrees of pressure. Gentle pressure reveals the state of the yang organs and meridians, and heavier pressure that of the yin organs and meridians (see Figure 2). There are numerous types of pulse qualities, some of which Manaka explains in detail (1972, Appendix C).

When the pulse quality is used, the decreased or increased function of each organ, and also tiredness, fever, pregnancy, and constipation, among other things, can be ascertained. In addition to using the pulse the Japanese developed abdominal palpation to a much greater extent than the Chinese as a further method of detecting the state of the internal organs.

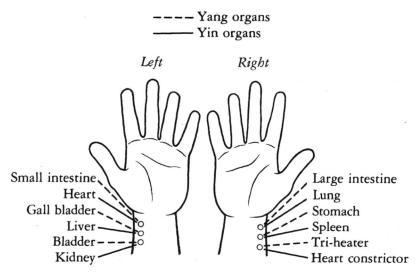

Figure 2. Positions for pulse-taking to determine state of organs

39

Thus, having used the four diagnostic methods, the doctor obtained a whole battery of facts about the patient's state, to which he added a consideration of the current climate, season, astrological conditions, time of day, the patient's age, weight, and bodily constitution before he commenced treatment. Ideally, each treatment for a patient should be regarded as a unique episode, often lasting several hours.

The purpose of diagnosis is not to categorize the patient as having a specific disease but to record his total body state and its relationship to the macrocosm of both society and nature as fully as possible. Diagnosis is of necessity a lengthy process in which the patient must actively participate by contributing considerable information on his or her own way of life.

The techniques of diagnosis rely heavily on the doctor's use of his own basic senses—those of touch, hearing, vision, and to a lesser extent, smell. A diagnosis is then made on the basis of this body of qualitative data obtained through close interaction with the patient.

Treatment

The basic aim of all treatment was to restore balance and harmony to the body, and to achieve this end the doctors used a combination of several techniques, including medicinal therapy, acupuncture, moxibustion, massage, respiratory therapy, and remedial exercises. Ideally, a doctor was supposed to have the ability to practice all methods and to choose whichever was most appropriate to the patient, but in practice many doctors came to specialize in certain aspects of the treatment system.

In the oldest text of the materia medica, the *Shên-nung pên t'sao ching*, compiled in about A.D. 220, the drug classification system is interesting. Ōtsuka (1976, p. 323) believes that it is characteristically Chinese in that man is placed at the center of the system. All medicinal material, regardless of whether it is animal, vegetable, or mineral in origin, is classified into three ranks according to its physiological effect on man. The 365 listed drugs were divided into three groups; 120 were classified as the "upper rank" and were said to confer immortality. The 120 in the "middle rank" were used to maintain health, and the 125 in the "lower rank" were used to cure diseases. This system is influenced by Taoist thought and reflects Taoist disdain for sickness and the quest for immortality. The system continued to be in use in

China until the fifteenth century. Through the years, several hundred more medicines were added to the materia medica, and numerous editions and re-editions of pharmacopoeia were produced. Two other classification systems for the drugs have been in use since early times, and all three systems were used in conjunction with each other.

The *gosei* system is based on the yin/yang theory: all medicine is classified as either hot, cold, warm, cool, or moderate. Cold and cool medicines are used for patients in the yang state who have a fever; examples are rhubarb and adder's tongue, which are cold, and peach seed and oyster shell, which are cool. Hot and warm medicines are used for patients manifesting yin symptoms. Examples are monkshood and dried ginger, which are hot, and angelica, ginseng, and magnolia, which are warm. Medicines classified as moderate are given to patients with neither marked yin nor yang symptoms; for example, licorice.

The *gomi* system is based on the five-phase theory. The five basic flavors in the correspondence system are acid, bitter, sweet, pungent, and salty. All medicine is categorized according to one of these flavors. Thus, medicine with the appropriate flavor will affect the corresponding internal organs (see Figure 3). Examples of an acid medicine are dogwood and Chinese magnolia. Bitter ones are rhubarb and nitrate of soda. Included in the sweet category are licorice and ginseng. Common fennel, lime, monkshood, ginger, dried orange peel, and peppermint are among the pungent ones, and persimmon and *shirao* (a type of fish) are salty.

Before prescribing a medicine, therefore, a doctor has to consider both its quality of taste and its effect on the yin and yang balance of the body. For example, cinnamon is hot and piquant and is effective for respiratory tract problems and helps in the circulation of the blood. Ginseng is cold and sweet and is used to stimulate general body metabolism, especially the appetite, and to settle the stomach.

In actual practice, a medicine is rarely given singly, and a mixture is usually prescribed according to the various symptoms a patient exhibits. In other words, if one has a sore throat with sneezing and a fever, the mixture will be different from that for a sore throat with sneezing and no fever. The combination of the effects of the various medicines in the mixture must be considered, and from experience certain doctors came to prefer certain

41

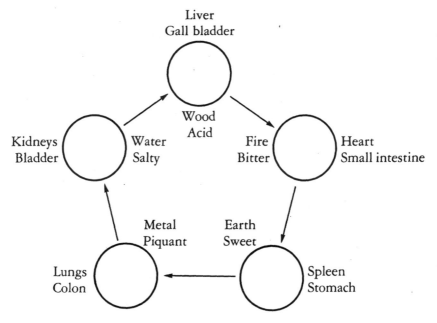

Figure 3. The *gomi* system of drug classification

mixtures, whereas others developed other combinations. The method of mixing medicines became highly complex, and secret formulae were fiercely guarded within the doctors' families. The season and the time of day and even the place for gathering the best wild herbs were all considered very important, and the pharmacopoeia carefully point out these details.

Both acupuncture and moxibustion therapy make use of the meridian and pressure-point theory described above. In the case of acupuncture the instruments used are solid needles of varying gauges and lengths, depending on the age, weight, and constitution of the patient concerned. When acupuncture was imported to Japan in the sixth century the needles were made of gold and silver, with one end thickened to facilitate manipulation. If the diagnosed problem involved one of the internal organs, the appropriate pressure point was selected, and the needle was inserted at that point. If the problem involved superficial pain (muscle, joint, or ligament problems, and so on), the needle was inserted directly into the painful area. The needles can be used either to stimulate or to sedate the body, depending on how they are inserted, manipulated, and withdrawn.

In the application of acupuncture and moxibustion, cosmological and seasonal variations and the time of day were all considered. Treatment could be less effective or even harmful if the timing was off. Calculations were made through the use of the combined charts of numerology and the five evolutive phases. The cycles of production and conquest also had to be considered, since stimulating one organ affected others in the cycle. The order of flow of energy through the body, the pairing of meridians, and a selection from many points all needed careful thought. Before starting treatment a doctor had to consider all these factors and adjust his methods accordingly.

Moxibustion could also be used for the treatment of internal organs by using appropriate pressure points. In general, moxa was thought to act best on yin diseases because it stimulated body function. It was also applied directly in the treatment of boils, abscesses, warts, and so forth. Being hot, moxa was classified as yang and therefore was considered especially suitable in the treatment of women, who are thought to be predominantly yin in type.

Massage therapy, *amma,* was applied either therapeutically or for general toning of the body. As a therapy its effect was considered lighter than acupuncture. Use was made of the pressure points, and techniques were employed to either stimulate or sedate the body as it was thought necessary.

Other therapeutic techniques introduced to Japan at this time included remedial exercises and respiratory therapy, which has much in common with the techniques of yoga. Their application in Japan was not widespread, however.

Therapy is designed to stimulate the patient's body in an effort to regain its equilibrium. But, because of the dynamic nature of the model, perfect health is a hypothetical state that can never be fully maintained, and in medicine, therefore, *perfect* health is not the ultimate goal of either patient or doctor. The aim is one of achieving the best possible adaptation to the total milieu that can be expected. Therapy is not designed as an attempt to dominate the forces of nature. Health and ill-health are both seen as natural and as part of a continuum and are not viewed as a dichotomy.

Because of the nature of the model, the patient cannot be readily labeled and fitted into a relatively unchanging category of disease—ideally each patient should be regarded as a unique case presenting a vast array of variables to be taken into account. The classics indicate that in actual practice there probably always was a tendency to classify according to patterns of symptoms, both major and minor, that occur with great frequency, but a thrust for precise classification and labeling is not present.

The dynamic nature of the model becomes apparent once again in attitudes toward therapy: ideally, the state of the patient should be checked several times a day and treatment adjusted accordingly, as the diurnal cycle progresses and modifies the total picture. Moreover, it is thought that diseases change with time and that all patients initially exhibit predominantly yang symptoms, if only for a brief period, but gradually change so that yin-type symptoms become prominent. Therapy should be modified as these changes occur. In addition, human beings individually have a tendency to be yin or yang in type, and as the life cycle progresses, everyone, whether predominantly yin or yang, changes toward the yin part of the cycle. In treatment these variables should also be taken into account.

Preventive Medicine

It is usual for systems of medicine that emphasize theories of balance to stress preventive measures, and traditional East Asian medicine is no exception. Because many diseases are expected to arise as a result of an inevitable lack of harmony with the environment at times, and because the macrocosm is viewed dynamically with predictable alternations in the yin/yang cycles, it is natural to try to compensate for the lack of equilibrium that is bound to occur. It is generally accepted that in China doctors refused patients once their condition reached a certain point of severity. The *Nei-Ching* puts it this way:

> To administer medicines to diseases which have already
> developed and to suppress revolts which have already
> developed is comparable to the behavior of those persons
> who begin to dig a well after they have become thirsty, and
> of those who begin to make their weapons after they have
> already engaged in battle. Would these actions not be too
> late? (Veith, trans., 1949, p. 105)

It is frequently claimed that the doctors in China were reimbursed only while their patients stayed well and that payments stopped once they became ill (Mann 1973, p. 221). This claim is probably exaggerated, but the emphasis on preventive medicine was certainly great.

Comparison of East Asian and Shintō Medical Beliefs

This account of the theoretical system is presented in a simplified form; in both theory and practice there were many elaborations and variations in use. For the Japanese, this highly systematized medical system, couched in Confucian, Taoist, and Buddhist terms and presented in Chinese script, must have been a source of great controversy and discussion.

In fact, the medical practices of the early Japanese seem to mesh closely with the Chinese tradition at some points. The concept of preventive medicine is common to both traditions, and in both systems the individual was required to take positive steps to maintain his health. Like the Chinese, the Japanese believed in communicable and hereditable diseases, and the external agents of disease causation in the Chinese system could have easily been redefined as objects causing pollution. Attitudes toward causality are therefore fairly compatible, with the exception of the concept of spirit possession, which doctors of the East Asian tradition theoretically did not recognize. Patients with this problem, therefore, made use of Shintō and Buddhist priests, both of whom provided shamanistic types of rituals, talismans, and herbal medicines for therapy. The incoming Chinese medicine did not, of course, provide means to combat highly acute and epidemic diseases. Shintō and, less frequently, Buddhist ritual that was used to prevent epidemics persists until the present day; the *Gion matsuri* in Kyoto is one of the best surviving examples.

It is in the realms of therapy and attitudes toward patients that Chinese medicine and Shintō beliefs are very different. In East Asian medicine, therapy is mild, designed to help the body itself restore equilibrium; the patient is considered in relation to his total environment, and the healing process involves social participation. In contrast, Shintō therapy is strong, designed to purge; the patient is isolated from his group until such time as he should recover. These two systems of belief still operate in Japan today.

Early in Japanese history Shintō came to have the function of dealing with community problems of preventive medicine and with possession. Buddhist priests and a few secular doctors using a mixture of folk and East Asian

45

medical ideas dealt with the problems of individual sickness for the majority of the population, while the limited number of secular doctors at court and among the aristocracy practiced a relatively classical style of East Asian medicine. But none of these medical spheres remained unaffected by ideas from other segments of the population, and before the tenth century a complex, pluralistic medical system was well established in Japan.

Philosophical Foundations of East Asian Medicine

The philosophies of both Taoism and Confucianism contributed greatly to the development of early Chinese medicine. Of the two, Taoism is the most influential, and according to Needham (1962, p. 34), the origins of proto-scientific thought can be seen in the Taoist belief system as early as the second century A.D.

Two types of practice developed: one was a highly individualistic ascetic form in which one of the principal aims was to achieve immortality on earth; the other was a more popular form of Taoism in which many shamanistic elements were incorporated and in which the art of healing was developed. For all Taoists the Tao, or Way, was synonymous with the order of nature—it was the means of explaining how the universe worked. They devoted themselves to a study of nature, which gave rise to a tradition of close observation of all phenomena and eventually to some scientific explanation. Emphasis was on the unity of nature, on equality, and on the importance of all phenomena for their contribution to the total pattern of things.

The doctrine of yin and yang first appears in the appendix to the *I Ching* ("The Book of Changes") which Needham (p. 274) dates as early as the third century B.C. Both Confucianists and Taoists used this doctrine as a system to account for change and for movement in space and time. Unlike Western concepts of dualism, at no time was the yin/yang system equated with ideas of good and evil—both elements are essential for harmony.

The origin of the five-phase theory is usually attributed to Tsou Yen, who was the founder of a school of thought called the Yin-Yang Chia, which evolved from about 250 B.C. onward. Unlike contemporary Taoists of his time, he moved in court circles, and thus the five-phase theory and the elaborations built on it became widely known. The Taoists were attracted to the theory, for it allowed them to account for qualitative changes of all phenomena in a highly elaborate way without relinquishing their theories of unity in the natural order. Needham believes that Tsou Yen and his school also developed theories of calendrical science and alchemy (p. 239), both of which were to influence medicine. Through the years more elaborate systems were added onto the original five-phase theory, and the cyclical recurrence of the elements became highly stylized. Geomancy, divination, astrology, physiognomy, and chronomancy (designation of days as lucky and unlucky) all depend on the five-phase theory, and much of this material became incorporated into early medical practice.

It was the popular Taoists who largely developed theories about diagnosis and treatment that would later contribute to the art of healing itself. Through their contacts with shamans and the ordinary people they did much to spread some aspects of these theories widely. The ascetic Taoists, on the other hand, in their search for immortality, stressed the practice of techniques that would later be incorporated into a system of preventive medicine. Their most important contributions were in the fields of alchemy and nutrition. In their search for a drug to confer immortality the Taoists systematically studied plants, animals, and minerals and their effects on man.

The Taoists were frequently in opposition to the hierarchically organized, dominant Confucians. Like the Taoists, the Confucians used the yin and yang theory and the five-phase theory, but they stressed that not only nature but the social order was part of the system and used these theories to explain change in the social system. In addition, they stressed the connections between a well-functioning social system and a healthy body. As the system was interpreted at its extreme, any misbehavior on the part of the Emperor and his entourage was supposed to influence the working out of the cosmic order and thus bring not only the state but the whole of nature, including individual men, into a state of disharmony.

The Confucian tradition probably provided the impetus to compile the first books on medicine. By the late Chou (700–206 B.C.) there is evidence for a distinct secular medical tradition (Croizier 1968, p. 15), and during the early Han (206 B.C.–A.D. 220) the first purely medical books compiled by professional doctors appear.

Thus, at a very early date, a high tradition of medicine was established, which had been fostered by Confucianists, court Taoists, and secular doctors. The adherents all used the same basic theoretical system of beliefs, but the potential for different rival factions to develop was great. Furthermore, popular Taoism coupled with shamanism enhanced the spread of ideas from the literate to the folk tradition.

At the end of the first century, Buddhist monks started to come to China from India, and from the second century onward some Buddhist texts were available in Chinese. While Buddhism is essentially an "other-worldly" type of religion when compared with Confucianism or popular Taoism, in its later formulations the Mahayana doctrine came to stress that the relief of pain and suffering in this world was the duty of its adherents. It was thought that disease was primarily caused by *karma*, that is, it was a retribution for wrongs committed in previous lives. Preventive medicine is therefore not stressed, since suffering is unavoidable, but the practice of healing was a virtue that became a central function for the priests. In China, as in Japan, it was the Buddhists who built the first hospitals and administered herbs together with amulets and talismans to people of all classes.

Huard and Wong (1968, p. 34) believe that asceticism, practiced by both Buddhists and Taoists, aided the adoption of the medical system by the Buddhist priests; but the function of asceticism for the two groups is quite different. The Taoists sought to nourish their *ch'i*, to make their bodies strong in order to obtain a clear understanding of this world, which was all important to them. The Buddhists, on the other hand, were attempting to escape this world of illusion, to transcend things of a materialistic nature, and consequently gave little thought to the physical body. The philosophies are quite unlike each other, and probably the Buddhist adoption of the medical system was largely for pragmatic reasons.

While the Buddhists did not accept the Chinese theory of disease causation, as was shown above, the efficacy of the therapeutic system does not depend on an understanding of the specific internal problem as it often does in cosmopolitan medicine. The doctor simply has to acknowledge a lack of balance in the patient, diagnose the places where this is manifest in the body, and proceed from there. The prescription of treatment is not affected by the assignment of responsibility for the lack of balance to *karma*, bad spirits, the weather, diet, emotions, or any other factors. Curing of disease, however, is only part of the system. In the classics, preventive medicine and the elimination or avoidance of causes of disease were considered to be as important as the removal of symptoms, if not more so. Buddhist priests practicing medicine may have been very weak in the application of this part of the system, and it is they who are largely responsible for the spread of East Asian medicine outside of aristocratic circles in Japan.

4

History of East Asian Medicine in Japan

One of the results of successful military expeditions to Japan from Korea in the fourth century was that during the ensuing period there was much cultural contact—the Chinese script was introduced and, later, Chinese books were imported by scholars and priests. The arrival of the first Korean doctor in Japan is recorded as A.D. 414, when he was summoned to attend the reigning emperor. In A.D. 458 another Korean doctor set up his practice in Naniwa in Osaka, and from that time on all his descendants became doctors (Fujikawa 1974, p. 4).

Later, in the reign of the Emperor Kimmei (540–571), many more secular doctors, diviners, and numerologists were summoned to the court. Most of the earlier doctors, however, had been priests. When the Chinese were united under the Sui dynasty in 601 and Buddhism was officially declared acceptable, this provided a great impetus to the spread of Buddhism in Japan and with it other aspects of Chinese culture, including medicine. When the Taiho code, modeled after the Chinese institutions of the T'ang dynasty, was compiled in 702, it included a provision for the establishment of a ministry of health. The ministry was composed of the following specialists: one minister of health; one vice-minister; one secretary; one senior assistant; one junior assistant; ten physicians; one doctor of medicine; forty students of medicine; five acupuncture practitioners; one doctor of acupuncture; twenty students of acupuncture; two massagers; one doctor of massage; ten students of massage; two magicians; one doctor of magic; six students of magic; two herbalists; six students of herbal lore, and some nonacademic staff members (Ōtsuka 1976, p. 326).

One of the most important subdivisions of the ministry was devoted to the study of natural phenomena; its purpose was to help the government in making political decisions. It was called the *ommyō-ryō,* or the "Bureau of Yin Yang." Its staff consisted of doctors, masters of divination, doctors of astrology, chronology, and calendar-making. Thus the Japanese aristocracy became familiar with the intricacies of Han Confucianism, including the yin/yang theory, the five-phase theory, and numerology. In adopting the political structure of the Chinese, the Japanese had to attempt to understand the philosophy that justified the system, so that when this same philosophy appeared in the medical literature and in other scholarly books the Japanese were presented with a satisfying, unified, and orderly system for explaining all phenomena, which must have seemed highly plausible.

With the introduction of Chinese herbal medicine came the new difficulty of obtaining the raw materials. Because of climatic differences much of the Chinese plant material cannot be cultivated in Japan, and thus trade was established early. The Tōdaiji-shōsōin, a temple in Nara, still has a collection of herbal medicine presented to it by the Emperor Shōmu in 756. All sixty of the herbs were analyzed, and it was found that they were all imported from China or ever farther afield.

From that time until the present day the spread of *kanpō* in Japan has always been limited by the lack of availability of raw materials. The doctors in the major urban areas were able to remain relatively true to the classics and to prescribe according to the traditional pharmacopoeia, but apart from these privileged few, doctors always had to make do with mixtures of folk medicine and true *kanpō.*

By the eighth century, therefore, Chinese medicine was being studied and used by the aristocracy. In theory, the Chinese examination system was adopted, but as the Japanese historically put more stock in rank than in examinations, entrance to the medical high school that was established at Nara was limited to students from high-ranking families of the aristocracy. Provincial schools were also set up for the benefit of sons of people in local government. Hereditary families of secular doctors and acupuncturists were soon established at court. Among the ordinary people the practice of Chinese medicine was spreading through the work of Buddhist priests, but at this level of society the theoretical framework was probably often lacking.

Until the end of the tenth century all written material was in Chinese, but in 984 Yasuyori Tanba dedicated the first medical text in Japanese to the reigning emperor. This text shows little original Japanese thinking, but it gives a clear picture of the complexity of the belief system of the time. It is based primarily on T'ang dynasty documents, and the topics covered include acupuncture and moxibustion; diseases of the storage and transportation organs; skin diseases; eye, ear, and tooth problems; abscesses and tumors; pediatrics; obstetrics; sexual hygiene; respiratory exercises; nutrition; herbal medicine; massage; details on how to sleep and work, what clothes to wear, and what type of housing to live in; alchemy; and the treatment of cases of possession. The book shows an interesting synthesis of Buddhist ideas with the Taoist-Confucian tradition. The causes of disease are explained as disturbances in the balance of the four elements of the Buddhist tradition (fire, water, air, and earth), and the human body is thought to be composed of these elements. Amulets and charms are recommended for therapy in addition to the other techniques.

During the Kamakura period (1192–1333) there was a tendency, as in other aspects of Japanese culture, to try to strike out independently of Chinese influence. The flourishing Zen sect of Buddhism sent several priests to China, who brought back the latest books, but these books were interpreted and even openly criticized by the Japanese. During this period when political power was transferred to Kamakura, the Taihō code was abolished and medicine at the court went into a decline. It was the priest-doctors and some of the lower-ranking secular doctors attached to feudal lords who tended to provide the forces for change and innovation.

As the fortunes of lords and samurai rose and fell during the Muromachi period (1336–1568) so did that of the doctors, since they were usually attached to feudal domains. Like the samurai, many doctors took to the road, or else they tried to establish their own entrepreneurial practices. The traveling doctors carried reduced equipment and used simple techniques. Sometimes they teamed up with prostitutes and with *yamabushi* (ascetic mountain priests) who could practice divination, in order to attract clientele more readily. These doctors abandoned the classics completely and developed highly pragmatic, simple theories, which were handed down orally. During this period the Zen priests continued to make contact with China, and they brought back the classics of the Yuan and Ming dynasties. Apart from some variations in theories of disease causation, these books still contained the same basic theories as the early classics. The pharmacopoeia were enlarged and included medicine from the Indo-Iranian tradition.

The Development of Factionalism

In the Azuchi-Momoyama period (1569–1600), during which Buddhism was oppressed, cosmopolitan medicine was introduced by the Portuguese. At this time Dosan Manase became the leader of the most important faction of traditional medicine in Kyoto. He established a school where he taught both medicine and Confucianism, despite the fact that he had studied Buddhism for twelve years. He was totally opposed to the practice of medicine by priests and planned to replace them with well-trained secular practitioners (Huard and Wong 1968, p. 78). He also helped to spread the use of acupuncture and moxibustion. Manase is representative of the influential neo-Confucianist philosophic approach, and this movement in medicine simply reflects the general swing at this time in other areas of Japanese society toward a neo-Confucian outlook. The school that Dōsan Manase founded is called the *goseiha*, and its texts are considered by modern scholars to be of a highly abstract and theoretical nature (Ōtsuka 1976, p. 328), although, as Ōtsuka points out, the doctors still continued to value their own practical experience and were not tied blindly to theories. In this school the mixing of medicine became highly refined. The basic emphasis was on treating the whole man and on removing all symptoms, both major and minor. The aim was to build up the patient's own body resistance, to provide time to recover slowly and with no great shock to the system. Mixtures of up to twenty medicines were frequently used, but the total quantity was small, and the overall effect on the patient was very mild.

Manase also emphasized and encouraged virtuous and benevolent behavior between doctor and patient and insisted on strict secrecy among pupils regarding the techniques of the school (Bowers 1965, p. 8).

One hundred and fifty years later, in parallel to the new movement in Confucianism pioneered by Jinsai Ito, there emerged a reform school of medicine, the *kohōha*, founded by Geni Nagoya (1629–1696) and Gonzan Gotō (1659–1733). The *kohōha* advocated a return to the true classics of medicine, that is, to the original publications of the Han dynasty, and in particular to the thoughts of Chang Ching-chung and his most important work, the *Shōkanron* (Chinese: *Shang han lun*), a treatise on fevers first published about A.D. 200. This book became the bible of the *kohōha* group, and its theories of treatment were applied to all types of diseases, whereas the Chinese had limited its application to diseases which they diagnosed as being caused by outside influences only. There are 113 prescriptions in the *Shōkanron*, most of which are still in use today. The principal theory in the book states that all fevers progress through six stages and that each stage has characteristically different symptoms. In the initial stages of the disease, the patient is in a yang state; after passing through three yang stages of lesser intensity, the patient enters the three yin stages. (For a description of the characteristic symptoms of these stages, see Chapter 3, and for a more complete description, see Ōtsuka 1976, p. 324.) Therapy should be adjusted according to which stage of the disease the patient is in. The six disease stages are known as the great yang, intermediate yang, final yang, great yin, intermediate yin, and final yin. In the yang state the patient's natural resistance is strong and he must be given yin type of medicine. In the yin state his natural resistance is low and he is given yang type of medicine.

Keisetsu Ōtsuka, a practicing *kanpō* doctor, believes that the main reason the *Shōkanron* was so attractive to the Japanese is that it is straightforward and easy to read, compared with other classics. Relatively little space is devoted to theory, and emphasis is on treatment. Above all, the number of medicines used is limited, and to the Japanese, always short of raw materials, this must have been most attractive.

There was no parallel movement to the *kohōha* in China, and this school, along with gathering influences from the West, provides the basis for the modern syncretic type of East Asian medicine that is characteristically Japanese. Tōdō Yoshimasu (1720–1773) is the most influential figure in the *kohōha* in the Tokugawa era. He was opposed to the speculative tendency of the *goseiha*, and he believed that actual practice and firsthand observation were essential. His most famous theory is the *manbyō-ichidoku-setsu*, in which he states that all diseases result in the production of "poison" regardless of the origins of the disease. He developed a highly complex abdominal palpa-

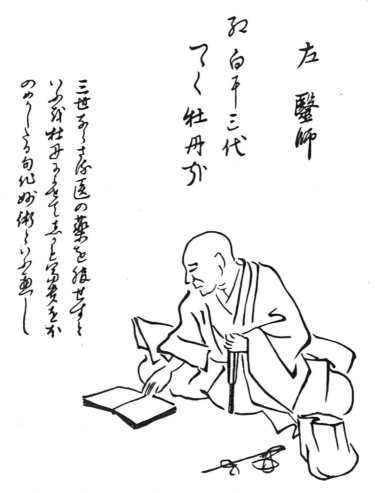

左 醫師

弘 白平三代

てく牡丹か

三世そくさ作医の薬を後せすく

いう分牡丹うら至て五うと写麦をか

のかうくる句化ぬ衛よいう志し

PLATE 2. Doctor attired in the clothes of a priest, Edo period.

tion technique to locate the poison. This is still characteristic of Japanese traditional medicine today, though it is applied to detect muscle tension and is frequently used in preference to taking the pulse. The *kohōha* medicine is stronger than that of the *goseiha* and is usually limited to a maximum of five ingredients. The main purpose is to expel the poison, and for this purpose many laxatives, emetics, and sudorifics are used: influences from the Shintō belief system are apparent in Yoshimasu's thinking.

A *kanpō* doctor living in Kyoto expresses the difference between the *kohōha* and *goseiha* medicine in the following way: the *goseiha* doctors are

PLATE 3. Doctor preparing a prescription, Edo period.

trying to eliminate all symptoms and treat them all with equal attention. "Consider a photograph of a wedding party in which the sharp focus on the bridal couple is sacrificed somewhat in order to have all the relatives clearly in the picture too—this is similar to the action of the mild herbal medicines of the *goseiha*. If, on the other hand, the bridal couple is kept in sharp focus and the relatives are somewhat out of focus, then this is similar to the techniques of the *kohōha*, who are more concerned with the elimination of the principal symptom."

Tōdō Yoshimasu was opposed to all theories that he regarded as speculative, including not only the five-evolutive-phase theory but even the yin/ yang doctrine, which does in fact appear in the *Shōkanron*. Yoshimasu's followers, however, later modified his ideas and reverted partially to the yin/ yang theory, but have always been against the five-phase theory.

Recent commentators feel that Yoshimasu's approach is very close to that of cosmopolitan medicine. He felt that his main purpose was to treat the disease rather than the whole patient, and he even recommended using one specific medicine for a specific disease. These ideas are clearly at variance with the theories of both the Ming dynasty Chinese and the *goseiha*, as the approach is basically reductionistic and "ontological" rather than holistic. Yoshimasu also stated that if the patient died, it was the work of the gods (*kami-sama*) and not part of the doctor's responsibility. These and other ideas of Yoshimasu run contrary to the Confucian system of beliefs in which he was schooled as a high-ranking member of the samurai class.

Many doctors at this time were drawn toward *rangaku* (the school of Dutch medicine established in Japan), which also stressed practical experience and tried to reject speculation. The doctors interested in *rangaku* came principally from the *kohōha*, but most of them, though drawn to Western surgical techniques, continued to use the Chinese system for internal medicine.

The emperor in Kyoto and the *shōgun* in the capital, Edo, had their personal doctors, who were permitted to be carried in a litter (a privilege for those of very high rank) when they traveled. From these men evolved a group of scholars who later gave up the practice of medicine entirely and devoted themselves solely to the study of theoretical issues and to classification systems.

There was regional variation in the body of material taught in the schools: in the central Kansai region, including the Kyoto schools, for example, theory of the *goseiha* was emphasized, whereas in Kyushu and in and around Edo (Tokyo) the ideas of the *kohōha* and of *rangaku* held sway. Graduates from schools representing rival factions remained competitive and aloof, and there was little exchange of ideas between them.

From the Edo period (1600–1867) onward many private medical schools were established, and each feudal area also had an official school, which picked the best students from the samurai class. The samurai themselves came as patients to these same schools. Study of the medical classics and of Confucian theory was stressed, and licenses were issued to all students upon graduation.

It was possible to achieve samurai rank and prestige by becoming attached as a physician to a feudal lord. Graduates from private schools, even if not from the samurai class, could improve their social status in this way. Like the priesthood, medicine was a good profession for the second and third sons of samurai and was also an excellent means of social mobility for the merchant and even the peasant class if they had talent (Mitsukuni Yoshida, personal communication).

In each province there was fierce competition to become attached to a lord upon graduation from medical school. One way to succeed was to produce many publications. The production of books at this time expanded enormously, and in the area of medicine most of them were highly practical and stripped of all but the most essential theory. In the later medical publications the incorporation of cosmopolitan medical concepts is frequent. Japanese scholars believe that copies of the *Nei-Ching* and other highly theoretical works were probably restricted to use in court circles and in the most powerful temples. In the provinces the use of a straightforward, readily obtainable book, like the *Shōkanron,* spread rapidly, and each feudal lord built up his own library of medical books from among the new works produced by his best doctors. The new ideas in these books were carefully guarded from outsiders, and doctors vied to sell themselves and their books at high prices.

Despite Confucian influence, until the Edo period most medical books included chapters on possession, divination, cosmology, physiognomy, and so on. From the middle of this period (c. 1700), these references are radically reduced. Fate and the spirit world now play no official part in disease causation.

Access to licensed doctors was limited to the aristocracy, the samurai class, and wealthier residents residing in the capital of a feudal domain. For the poor merchant's benefit and for village residents, unlicensed doctors continued to practice a blend of *kanpō* with folk medicine, and in the temples some priests carried on their tradition of healing despite official opposition; these practitioners paid little regard to theoretical trends in the literate tradition. During this period certain temples gradually came to specialize in a particular treatment rather than attempting to act as general physicians. For example, some temples of the Shingon sect on Koya mountain became, and still are, famous for their moxibustion techniques.

Up until the Edo period almost all doctors learned massage (*amma*), since it provided a practical way of becoming familiar with the pressure points of the body. Among the merchant classes in this period, *amma* took on a second function, that of being used for relaxation and leisure. It became customary for blind people to provide this kind of massage, and they formed themselves into an immense guild for this purpose (Casal 1962, p. 233). They had to pass examinations and were graded and paid according to their ability.

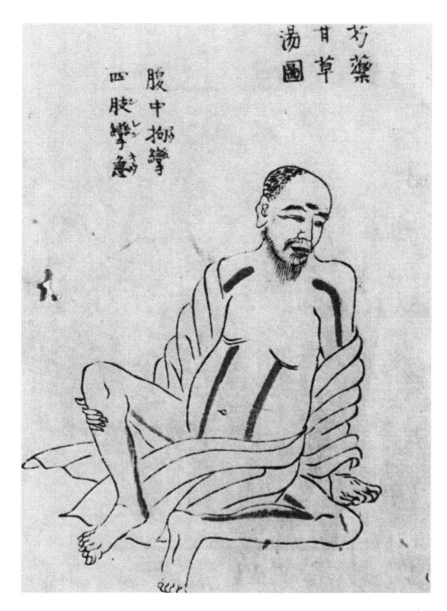

芍
甘草
湯圖

腹中拘攣
四肢攣痛

PLATE 4. Diagram to aid in diagnosis, from a Japanese text, *Fukushō Kiran Yoku*, compiled in the Edo period. This text specializes in abdominal palpation techniques.

咳嗽喘將昼

心下有水氣

小青龍湯圖

PLATE 5. Diagram to aid in diagnosis, from a Japanese text, *Fukushō Kiran Yoku*, compiled in the Edo period. This text specializes in abdominal palpation techniques.

In the mid-seventeenth century an enterprising blind man, Waichi Sugiyama, decided that the blind could do acupuncture, and he started a school to train blind students in this art. He used only very fine gold and silver needles and developed a special tube into which the needle was inserted. This tube acted as a guide to facilitate the insertion of the needle and is still widely used in Japan today. It is recorded that Sugiyama cured the *shōgun* Tsunayoshi Tokugawa of a serious illness (Huard and Wong 1968, p. 80). Some historians believe that in the teaching of blind students the body of knowledge had to be reduced as much as possible and that this was in part the reason for the appearance of so many highly simplified and practical books.

As blind people became associated with the practice of *amma* and acupuncture the prestige accorded to these treatments fell because the status of blind people, despite Sugiyama's success, was generally low. The higher-class urban *kanpō* doctors mostly came to specialize in herbal medicine. Some retained the arts of moxibustion and acupuncture, but almost all of them gave up massage. In the classics, the Chinese stress that a doctor must be able to integrate all types of treatment in order to handle all patients adequately, but in the Edo period the Japanese chose to ignore this.

At this time in the province of Etchū, which now roughly corresponds to Toyama prefecture, the *daimyō* decided that one way to help the revenue problem in his agriculturally poor district was to make use of the mountain herbs that were readily available and to develop a patent medicine industry. The dried herbs were made into pills and powders and peddled around Japan; small shops were set up along the Tōkkaidō, Nakasendō, and other great highways and in the cities. In an era when, owing to the political system, the amount of travel was enormous, these salesmen must have done a great deal of business and functioned to reduce some of the anxiety related to travel. Good doctors were still scarce, and self-medication was often necessary. The peddlers came only once a year and returned a year later to collect their money and any unused medicine. This custom is continued in contemporary Japan. A whole cult grew up around the buying and selling of medicine, and the production of the type of paper it was wrapped in, the boxes it was stored in, and the medicine containers that samurai carried with them everywhere became art forms in their own right. This of course put up the price and added to the prestige value of the medicine. A high regard for expensive, well-packaged medicine is often still present in Japan today.

The introduction of smallpox vaccination by the *rangaku* school in 1824 was a great blow to the *kanpō* doctors, and even before the Meiji Restoration fairly widespread education in cosmopolitan medicine had begun. Some *kanpō* doctors from both the *goseiha* and the *kohōha* decided to combine forces in an attempt to combat the inevitable. In 1869 a decision was made to officially adopt the German system of medical education, but by 1873 there were 23,000 *kanpō* doctors and only about 520 registered cosmopolitan doctors. In 1876 the government passed a regulation that all physicians were required to study Western medicine, but the practice of *kanpō* was not forbidden. Some doctors, particularly sons of *kanpō* doctors, returned home after their training and continued to practice only *kanpō*. In 1879 one of the leading *kanpō* doctors became the emperor's doctor, and this temporarily improved their status.

Finally, in 1883, the regulations regarding the practice of *kanpō* were made extremely rigorous, and although the system has never been totally outlawed, its practice was greatly inhibited. The *kanpō* doctors appealed the government decision once in 1885 but were unsuccessful. At this juncture many of the doctors who were not from influential families decided to try their hands as pharmacists and set up shops where they sold both imported Chinese medicine and Japanese folk medicine. There was some rather unsystematic oppression of these activities also.

According to Nakagawa (personal communication), the standard of cosmopolitan doctors was at first very poor, their fees were exorbitant, and the schools were hastily organized. Western drugs were extremely expensive, and the quality was often in doubt. This period too must have influenced the Japanese in their attitude toward self-medication. Many popular books were published on preventive medicine, describing exercises, breathing techniques, and diet. Books on popular, simplified, home-style *kanpō* and folk medicine became very fashionable. Avoiding illness and the doctor became an ideal. It was prestigious to have a well-stocked medicine box, especially if it contained a few highly valuable cosmopolitan drugs.

While the expense of cosmopolitan medicine inhibited its growth, other factors encouraged its spread. There were constant epidemics of smallpox, cholera, and typhoid among the population. Leprosy was also common, and tuberculosis was rampant (Takenaka 1959, p. 37). The value of techniques of vaccination soon became apparent, and in the field of public health, progress was also rapid. With the onset of the Russo-Japanese war in 1904 the position of cosmopolitan medicine was consolidated when it was used in surgery and for the treatment of war wounds. The rapid adoption of the new system must also be attributed to the fact that it was not imposed on the Japanese by an outside, alien force, as is frequently the case in other countries.

When cosmopolitan medicine was adopted by Japan as the official medical system, therefore, it was superimposed upon extremely complex, pluralistic, traditional systems, systems with long historical roots and deeply meshed with other aspects of Japanese culture. The threat posed by cosmopolitan medicine served to unite kanpō doctors, who were able for the first time in several hundred years to overcome the rifts caused by professional factionalism. But the split between kanpō doctors, who were drawn mostly from the upper echelons of society, and the practitioners of acupuncture and massage, associated with middle and lower classes, was too great to be bridged.

The teaching and practice of acupuncture and massage was nevertheless deeply affected by cosmopolitan medical beliefs, as we shall see. Practitioners of East Asian medicine of all kinds have been continually forced in the years since the Meiji Restoration to reevaluate their position toward and their relationship with cosmopolitan medicine.

This rapid survey of Japanese medical history illustrates several important points regarding social organization in general and also attitudes toward classical medical theory that are still part of East Asian medical practice in contemporary Japan.

The development of competitive factions in the business world and within professions is highly characteristic of Japanese society both historically and today (Nakane 1970, p. 48), and the medical world was no exception. Since the relationship between factions is one of rivalry, a competitive attitude is fostered. This atmosphere encourages secrecy and a lack of willingness to share ideas across factional boundaries; it also encourages innovation and hence specialization. With medical specialization comes a tendency toward reductionism, which is readily seen in the books produced during the Edo period. In fact, the style of many of these books is remarkably similar to some of the manuals on acupuncture being produced in China today for use by paramedicals: they are concise, pragmatic, and cheaply produced, and they focus on the techniques of treatment for the removal of symptoms and little else. In Edo Japan many students could be funneled rapidly through the schools, but they would, upon graduation,

63

become apprenticed to experienced practitioners and would thereby gain the bulk of their knowledge, including the secret, special techniques of their master, on which the group relied to bring them success in a competitive climate.

There were other pressures that encouraged reductionism: first, since Tōdō Yoshimasu and later his son were leaders of one of the most important and influential factions during the Edo period, their reductionistic approach became widely accepted. Second, for most doctors, access to the limited editions of the comprehensive classical texts was impossible, and many of them did not read well. Furthermore, the political climate was such that doctors were frequently on the road working in a rather makeshift manner. Finally, the raw materials necessary to perform a full range of classical East Asian medicine were rarely available. All these factors encouraged doctors to be pragmatic and experimental rather than devoted to classical theory and practice. This enhanced pluralism, competition, and innovation in medical practice, trends which are still at work today.

Revival of *Kanpō*

In 1910 Keijuro Wada published a book stressing the superiority of *kanpō* over cosmopolitan medicine, and a few doctors were influenced by him. These doctors had to practice without the benefit of any advertisements.

Since the end of World War II, interest in *kanpō* has accelerated. On March 12, 1950, the Society for Oriental Medicine was founded. It publishes a journal and has about a thousand members today. There are many major research institutes where pharmacognosy is studied, the most important of which is in Toyama University.

In Dr. Yasuo Ōtsuka's words, "The new generation of *kanpō* doctors is no longer weak, since all the practitioners have studied and practiced modern medicine and have found themselves somehow dissatisfied with it." He feels that the doctors have a good theoretical and practical background from which to make constructive criticisms of cosmopolitan medicine.

The Meiji government at the Restoration chose to retain the practice of acupuncture and *amma* and established a system whereby students could study for a diploma that would allow them to practice acupuncture, moxibustion, and massage but not to administer medicine. Schools equivalent to junior colleges were established, and graduates were able to practice, but the financial rewards were low. Today in Japan there are approximately forty thousand registered practitioners of acupuncture, moxibustion, and massage. They must attend a three-year course and pass a state examination to obtain a license.

Research by physiologists into acupuncture and moxibustion was started early, for it was felt that the meridian system could be readily explained anatomically. This research has continued without interruption, except for the war years, but progress has been extremely slow. Certain physiological changes have been definitely established in the body on the application of acupuncture, moxibustion, and massage, and there is general agreement that the pressure points do indeed exist. Much ink has been spilled on the subject of meridians, however, and scientists—Japanese, European, and American—and practitioners alike are at present divided on the question whether they exist. Even those who accept their existence argue about whether they constitute part of the autonomic or the central nervous system or whether they are not anatomical structures at all but rather nonspecific pathways along which electrochemical changes take place.

Research into herbal medicine has proved even more frustrating, and because of the complex nature of the medicines involved, until very recent years it has been limited to the isolation of specific alkaloids. In 1885 ephedrine was isolated from *Ephedra vulgaris* by Nagayoshi Nagai, and since then the principal components of most of the herbs used in *kanpō* have been isolated. The physiological actions of the herbal mixtures in the human body still have to be analyzed—even today mixtures with up to ten unrefined herbs are frequently used, making the problems of analysis difficult.

In 1914 the Kitasato Research Institute was built in Tokyo to house medical research projects. In 1973 work started on a new branch of this institute, to be devoted entirely to research into East Asian medicine. The building was opened in the fall of 1974 and comprises six floors of completely up-to-date research laboratories. For the first time since the Meiji Restoration the government has showed support for East Asian medicine by providing funds for this institute. Among many other topics around which research is focused, that of diseases caused by industrial pollution is one of the most important.

65

In the spring of 1976 tbe Japanese government made an extremely significant step toward the reestablishment of the status of East Asian medicine: a law was passed that allows certain herbal prescriptions to be obtained under the National Health Insurance system. It was reported in the *Asahi Shinbun* that it was *Kanpō Gannen* (the first year of the reign of *Kanpō*).

PART TWO

Attitudes toward the Body in
Health and Sickness

5

Early Socialization

On the Day of the Dog in the fifth month of their pregnancy,
my patients bring me a special maternity *obi* that they have
bought at the shrine. I examine them and then I wrap the *obi*
around them for the first time. By this act the women know
that they are already halfway to motherhood and they are
psychologically prepared for the future.

A Kyoto Obstetrician

We have considered the long tradition of pluralistic medicine in Japan and
the variety of theoretical perspectives associated with it. Now we shall turn
to contemporary attitudes toward health and illness in order to try to
understand a little of the expectations that people hold regarding the sick
role in Japan.

Attitudes toward the body and the experience of both health and sickness
are learned during socialization. Child-rearing techniques are in turn influenced by what Whiting (1961, p. 356) has termed "maintenance systems":
the economic, political, and social organization of a society, that is, "the
basic customs surrounding the nourishment, sheltering, and protection of its
members." Whiting's model shows the relationship thus:

Maintenance systems	→	Child training	→	Personality variables	→	Projective systems

By "projective systems" Whiting means religion, art, folklore, and other
"expressive," as opposed to "instrumental," aspects of culture. He demon-

strates that this process is not unilinear and that each system feeds back into all the other systems to form an integrated whole. Medical systems are a special case in that they are both a "maintenance" and a "projective" system. In situations of culture contact when a new medical system is incorporated into a society, it is primarily medicine as a "maintenance system"—that is, its techniques and its educational and organizational aspects—that is adopted. The "projective" aspect, including beliefs both lay and professional about the expression and experience of illness, can only be adopted very gradually, for this involves a complete restructuring of socialization patterns and also of other parts of the "maintenance" and "projective" systems.

Influences from Shintō, East Asian, and cosmopolitan medical theory can be detected in socialization practices in Japan, and this accounts partially for the wide variety of attitudes toward health and illness that exist today. A brief survey of current socialization practices in middle-class Japan provides some insights into attitudes toward the body and expectations regarding medical care. The concepts discussed below represent the ideal and are not necessarily always lived up to. As Vogel pointed out (1968, p. 280), an overwhelming number of books on child-rearing are published in modern Japan, but there is not one standard text that most mothers turn to. The result is that informal advice from mother, mother-in-law, and friends is highly valued. Vogel makes the important point that with modern technology in every home, and with the advent of the nuclear family, most middle-class wives are free to devote themselves wholly to child-rearing, since very few of them choose to be employed. Child-rearing is a highly valued occupation, and Vogel demonstrates how competitive women in this role can become. Among middle-class families, therefore, the ideal close mother-and-child relationship can be attained more readily than in prewar days, when the young mother had less time for her baby because of the demands on her time for household duties and because of the presence of her mother-in-law. The data available on socialization are limited in that they are derived largely from urban middle-class families, and mothers in lower-class families do not have the freedom to spend so much time with their babies. They are, however, aware of the concepts presented below, even if they have little opportunity to put them into practice. The day-care centers where many babies from lower-class families are placed try consciously to live up to middle-class values. They are legally supposed to provide one adult for every five babies, and therefore theoretically each child can get a great deal of attention.

Nonverbal Techniques of Nurturance

When a Japanese baby is born, relatives should be sent some especially prepared food, symbolizing that one more member has been added to the primary group. Despite the increase in nuclear families, birth is still often thought of in terms of its meaning for the extended family, and the baby will be socialized to think of itself initially as part of its group rather than as an individual.

Infants are regarded as naturally passive, gentle, and dependent beings who must be molded to fit the norms of society; to call someone's baby *sunao* (gentle, meek, compliant) is considered highly complimentary. It is the mother's responsibility to instill correct values through love and quiet but persistent manipulation of the child; recourse to aggressive or blunt techniques of control are highly discouraged. Lengthy verbal explanations are not considered necessary, for the child will learn best by imitating those around him and by receiving rewards for good behavior. It is common to see a mother or even a teacher actually physically putting the child through the desired procedure or else demonstrating what is wanted, largely nonverbally.

Caudill (1976, p. 166) shows convincingly that by three or four months of age infants in Japan and the United States are already responding in characteristic ways to the different styles of care-taking employed by their respective mothers. While American mothers encourage their babies to be vocal and physically active, Japanese mothers aim to soothe and quiet their children. The maintenance of the "natural" state of the infant, its gentleness and passivity, is thought to be best for the continuance of health. It is also considered to be the most receptive state, in which all the necessary learning for the future will take place. The Japanese mother therefore holds, rocks, and lulls her infant much of the time; unlike an American mother, she rarely chats to her baby, nor does she position it apart and opposite to her but most usually keeps it on her back or in her arms. Ideally, in middle- and upper-class families small babies in Japan should frequently be in contact with another human body, but recently carrying a baby on one's back has come to be considered old-fashioned by some mothers, and plastic baby-seats are in wide circulation. Nevertheless, inside the house, especially that of an extended family, the infant spends much of its time in someone's arms, including those of its father when he is present. Motor and speech development has been shown to be slower than in the United States, possibly as a result of these practices.

Compared with an American mother, the Japanese mother spends more time with the actual care-taking of the baby. She rocks the child to sleep, changes its clothes, diapers, and bedding frequently, washes the baby, wipes off sweat, and subjectively checks its body temperature several times a day. The child is often disturbed by others in his sleep, and according to Caudill this is the origin of much of the unhappy vocalization that he noted in small Japanese babies. The mother's response to crying is to increase her rocking and lulling and to offer the baby the breast or bottle frequently throughout the day. A highly negative view is taken of anyone's leaving a baby to cry.

Children up to five or six years of age may be given the breast by either mother or grandmother to calm them, particularly after an unpleasant event such as a visit to the doctor. Failing this, they will receive candy. Presents to small children are usually in the form of candy or other similar treats (Vogel 1968, p. 234). The extent to which this custom is practiced is attested to by the rows of black stumps of milk teeth visible in the mouths of many children under five.

Caudill and Plath (1966) also studied sleeping patterns in Japan and found that the majority of children sleep with either their parents or their grandparents until they are about twelve years old, not because of overcrowding, but by choice. This custom is now changing somewhat, but small babies, even today, rarely sleep alone. Some parents compromise by putting the baby in a separate room in which they have installed an intercom device so that they can listen to breathing patterns while the baby sleeps. Bathing is also communal: children bathe with one of their parents or their grandmother, who holds a baby closely throughout in order to avoid accidents in the deep bath.

The maintenance of a calm emotional state in children is therefore aided by physical proximity and oral gratification but not very much by verbal interaction. Tangible rewards for good behavior are more frequent than lavish verbal praise. Caudill (1976, p. 168) puts it this way:

> In America, the mother views her baby, at least potentially, as
> a separate and autonomous being who should learn to do

and think for himself. For her, the baby is from birth a distinct personality with his own needs and desires which she must learn to recognize and care for. . . . In Japan, in contrast . . . the mother views her baby much more as an extension of herself, and psychologically the boundaries between the two of them are blurred. . . . Because of the greater emphasis on the close attachment between mother and child in Japan, the mother is likely to feel that she knows what is best for the baby, and there is no particular need for him to tell her what he wants, because, after all, they are virtually one.

Dependency is subconsciously valued and encouraged in Japan so that group loyalties will take precedence over individual aspirations in adult life. As Caudill points out, one striking example of acknowledgment of the close tie between mother and child is the custom of keeping the umbilical cord in a box inside the family home until the child becomes an adult. When the World War II survivor Sergeant Yokoi was rescued from the Philippine jungle in 1973, he was reduced literally to a handful of possessions, and the umbilical cord that was given him by his mother on his departure for the war was one of them. Although today most deliveries are in hospitals, the mother is presented with the cord as she leaves the hospital with her new baby. Forms of punishment furnish another example of attitudes toward dependence: one of the worst kinds of punishment for a Japanese child is to be made to stand outside its house in the street, to be separated from its family—a striking contrast to the American child who is shut in. In Japan, punishment is separation from nurturance; in the United States it is separation from freedom and individuality.

Caudill's study includes a detailed analysis of interaction between two-and-a-half-year-olds and their mothers. He finds that at this age there is not a significant difference in the two societies in the total amount of time mother and child spend together, but that American children of two and half "do more total body management for themselves than Japanese children." It is in the activities of going to the toilet, bathing, washing, and going to sleep that the Japanese mother remains highly involved with her child. My observations in a Japanese nursery school used mostly by lower-middle-class families support the work of Caudill. Feeding was not included in Caudill's analysis, but my experience is that much more time is spent by the Japanese mother than the American mother in the preparation of food for her child and in making sure that it is nutritionally balanced. It is customary for nursery schools in Kyoto to present parents with a detailed daily account of everything the child has eaten. The report also includes a minute description of the child's behavior, sleep, and excretory functions. It is assumed that the mother will want the details in order to keep "in tune" with her child, and she in turn must fill out a form with similar information for use by the teachers the next day.

The child, therefore, gradually becomes aware that its body processes and everything that enters and leaves its body are being carefully monitored by its mother, and it is trained to take over these functions from her. This regular monitoring of the body results in a great sensitivity to bodily functions and an ability on the part of most people to discuss their own bodies in a rather objective way without embarrassment.

The effects of climatic changes on the body are also carefully controlled: children are taught that they must pay attention to the weather, particularly at the change of seasons, and appropriate clothing is chosen with care. The tendencies of the child's body to be susceptible to particular constellations of environmental conditions are noted early by the mother. Certain foods, types of weather, and so on produce mild alterations in the body, which would pass unnoticed by most American mothers. The Japanese mother types her baby as prone to mild illness under particular conditions and avoids them insofar as possible.

Patterns of Responsibility

From the age of four years onward children in middle-class families are generally trained to develop an inner calm and stability. The expression of strong emotions, particularly anger, is discouraged. Correct posture, neatness of dress, and tidying up of toys are all encouraged. Japanese children of this age are markedly different from their middle-class American counterparts. Their appearance is neater and cleaner; they passively accept tidying up of their bodies and clothes several times each day; they are willing to put on clothes selected by their mothers; they generally leave their shoes in orderly rows when they enter a house; and often their first impulse when presented with several similar toys, such as model cars, is to line them up in neat rows.

PLATE 6. Buying aloe. The caption says: "Aloe, a substitute for the doctor."

At kindergarten, all children use three or four different types of regulation bags and boxes to keep aprons for art work, spare shoes, lunch, and other items in order. Children and parents comply willingly with these rules and feel acutely embarrassed if they do not conform. Traditionally, this type of training was regarded as development of *ki* management: only in a calm, balanced, and healthy state can one expect to learn well. Today most mothers do not explicitly use the word *ki* when asked why posture training and so on is important; instead they use the term *seishin jōtai* (mental state), stating that care of the body, attention to one's appearance, and an orderly life all help to develop a calm inner or mental state, which is reflected not only in one's social relations with others but in one's health. The child is therefore gradually trained to be personally responsible for his body's functioning, his emotional state, and his immediate surroundings, all of which are seen as interrelated. Most informants of all ages recall their mothers' warning that sickness stems from poor *ki* (*yamai wa ki kara*).

More important still, children are taught that failure to be responsible will reflect upon the family and can lead to suffering for those one loves. As DeVos (1973) states:

> The traditional Japanese mother's strongest weapon in
> disciplining her child is the very self-sacrifice with which she
> dedicates herself to her offspring. She tends to "suffer" her
> children rather than to forbid them or inhibit their behavior
> by resorting to physical punishment or verbal chastisement.
> The child learns the vulnerability of the loved one and is
> frightened by his own capacity to injure. Bad behavior can
> inflict irreversible injuries upon the very person whom one so
> badly needs; one can make another ill. The mother who
> exhausts herself on behalf of her child is a source of potential
> guilt that a Japanese child so brought up cannot escape. The
> converse is also learned. A Japanese child learns: "I can
> control by my own suffering someone bound to me. My
> illness or death can cause unhappiness, an unending guilt in
> another." (P. 479)

Sickness in a child, as one practicing acupuncturist pointed out, signals failure on the part of the mother to a large extent; the attitude of this acupuncturist was confirmed by all types of doctors interviewed. For an adult it can reflect a failure in one's personal responsibility for keeping in good health by not having maintained a careful watch over the effects of the environment on the body, or by not having maintained good social relationships with others and hence having become vulnerable to disease.

The Need to be Nurtured

There is a second constellation of feelings associated with illness which also stems from an extremely close mother-child relationship and the resulting dependence. The Japanese term *amaeru*, best translated as "a desire to presume upon another's love," is central in this respect (Doi 1973). In return for hard work, responsible behavior, and submission of self, one can be assured of care and attention regarding all one's personal needs. In times of stress—and illness is just such an example—it is acceptable to become highly dependent on the group, to *amaeru*. As a chance to escape temporarily from the pressures of society, mild sickness can be rather welcome. To elicit reactions on the topic of illness, Caudill (1962, p. 115) used a picture of a man lying on a *futon* (Japanese mattress) and being taken care of by a woman. Responses to the picture, where the man was seen to be enjoying sympathetic concern and a chance to *amaeru*, were mostly that it gave a "good feeling." Minor illness can have what Caudill termed an "ego-syntonic" quality. Moreover, the responses indicated further that illness is a chance for nonverbal communication between people. Following is an excerpt from a story given about the picture:

> Japanese won't express their feelings such as "I love you" or
> "I like you" or "I dislike you" or that sort of thing in words.
> Rather than using words, they often show their feelings in
> their behavior, and sick time is a very good time for this. It is
> the one time you can show in action how much you love the
> other. (P. 119)

The communicative nature of sickness was confirmed by my informants: one young man stated that "there is no point in getting sick in the dormitory" (many unmarried men live in a dormitory supplied by their company), "but at home it is pleasant to 'amaeru' sometimes." Another man, a physiolo-

77

gist, said, "Some Japanese believe that illness is a favorable opportunity because it is an indication of disorders in life. Illness gives people a chance to stop and think about life and death, and being human, and things like that."

Visiting friends and relatives who are sick in hospital (o-mimau) is a social obligation taken seriously in Japan. As Lebra (1976) puts it:

> The sick person, particularly if hospitalized, draws the
> attention of his friends and colleagues. The hospital room,
> with the patient surrounded by sympathetic visitors, becomes
> a place for confirming and restoring group solidarity. The
> desire for belongingness and togetherness is well gratified.
> The patient's dependency seems to strike a sympathetic cord
> in people who might be indifferent otherwise. . . . It appears
> that one person's obvious need to amaeru has aroused in
> another the wish to amayakasu [to accept and nurture
> dependency needs]. In Japan, sickness, enabling such free
> exchange of emotions, should be observed in light of its
> social significance. (P. 64)

Mild illness as a means of nonverbal communication therefore reinforces the interdependency and solidarity of the group. Feeding, bathing, and massaging are activities that also function in this way. Inside the home it is usually the young wife who massages her husband and also his parents if they live in the same house. Children are massaged after a long evening of homework. When the wife feels in need of a massage she usually persuades the children to oblige. Hard work can leave the body out of balance and is frequently acknowledged as one of the major sources of illness. The act of massage inside the family symbolizes one of the core values of Japanese society: one works hard for the primary group and suppresses individual needs, but this same group will provide nurturance to its individual members in the form of security, trust, and care for the body. Communal bathing, massage, and eating are some of the ways this care is most frequently expressed—the conflict of individual needs versus group demands is gently eased in the family circle. Ten years ago, it was still common practice for many middle-class wives to dress and shave their husbands as further proof of care.

Mild illness, therefore, with its affirmative qualities, can potentially be accepted without guilt. This is further enhanced by traditional East Asian beliefs about preventive medicine: mild problems must be treated carefully, and balance must be restored, otherwise something much more serious could develop—"A cold is the origin of ten thousand diseases" (*kaze wa man byo no moto*), so goes the old adage.

The enjoyment of mild illness and feelings of responsibility not to become ill are of course in conflict, and these two attitudes apparently symbolize the conflict of all societies, that of the individual and his needs versus responsibility toward the family and society. Sickness can serve in a way to indicate just how hard one has been working for the sake of the group—imbalances have arisen owing to excessive strain. The sick role can be seen as a welcome relief from responsibility, a time for taking stock, and a chance for insights and psychological growth. As the author Ishikawa wrote in his diary (1956):

> I want to be sick. For a long time this desire has been lurking
> in my head. Sick! . . . A free life, released from all
> responsibilities! Sickness is the only way we have to obtain
> peace of mind. (P. 221)

A Japanese proverb expresses the same desire another way: "Only a fool never catches a cold."

Dependency and the Female Role

The concept of *amaeru* is initially centered on the mother-child relationship, and later in life both wife and mother are nurturant figures. The question arises as to what women who have also been indulged as babies, though less so than boys, do with their dependency needs. While sickness in a man is viewed primarily by both sexes as a time for restoration of family unity, the experience of illness for a woman is quite different. Responses to TAT (Thematic Apperception Test) cards (DeVos and Wagatsuma 1973, p. 131) show that both men and women are worried about the occurrence of sickness in a woman. Most of my informants stated that "wives must not get sick" or that "women have to keep going even when they feel tired." There is little leeway in the Japanese family system for a young woman to be overtly, emotionally dependent. She must nurture her husband, her children, and her parents-in-law through illnesses, but when she herself becomes ill there is rarely a role reversal. Rather than suffering the indignity and the unbearable sense of obligation incurred by being dependent on her husband's family, most young middle-class women, even today, opt to return to their own parents if they become more than mildly ill. It is only with their own mothers that they can escape normal social restrictions sufficiently to relax and recover. The same is true after childbirth, when it is usual for a young woman to return from the hospital to her own mother for a month or two; even when one is part of a nuclear family, this is the custom. Sickness in a woman, therefore, disrupts family unity and is associated with separation. That this lack of opportunity to *amaeru* is a source of stress is acknowledged by most people, including doctors, who see women as more vulnerable than men to sickness. Under these circumstances it is not surprising that the women interviewed consistently responded that they pay more attention to preventive medicine than do their husbands, and that they usually try to relax quietly by themselves when they sense minor changes in body function, which are interpreted as early signs of symptoms of illness. Although lower-class women have less opportunity to actually do this, it was held up by them as the most suitable kind of behavior. At the interpersonal and personal levels, therefore, responses to the occurrence of illness may vary, depending on whether the patient is male or female.

Society and Health

The close relationship in the primary dyad of mother and child in Japan is the paradigm for all group behavior in adult life. The use of fictive kinship terms between superiors and inferiors in many groups confirms that this is so. As Reynolds (1976) puts it:

> The superior member of the dyad has the responsibility of
> protecting and rewarding the inferior member and the
> privilege of demanding services and esteem in return. The
> social inferior must be sensitive to the desires, attitudes, and
> moods of his superior. Simultaneously, the inferior must be in

PLATE 7. Morning exercise at the local fire station.

control of his own behavior (and one step further, his psychological state) so that he does not alienate his superior and thus bring down punishment or withdrawal of rewards. The inferior's alertness, plus several indirect means of communicating his needs to the superior, usually nets him satisfactory material and self-esteem rewards. (P. 105)

In return for the dedication and hard work received, business concerns and industry throughout Japan implicitly acknowledge partial responsibility for the maintenance of a worker's health and for the occurrence of illness (Rohlen 1974b, p. 45). Organized group exercise, which is customary throughout the day in business enterprises, is performed not simply to raise morale but to restore balance to the body and therefore incidentally to increase productivity. Moreover, sick leave is extremely generous by American standards. The usual policy in big business is to allow up to six months sick leave on full salary; after that, the biannual bonus *may* be cut and the salary *may* drop by about 15 percent. Each employee's case would be appraised individually. There is government support for families in difficulty through the occurrence of illness. Employers feel strongly that only by helping an employee feel psychologically at ease and in good health can they expect good work. Furthermore, the achievement of harmony (*wa*), which is a stated goal of most Japanese groups (Rohlen 1974b, p. 47), can only be fulfilled with healthy, actively contributing group members. It is noteworthy that many company employees in Japan do not take their allotted vacation from work, because of their sense of dedication, and that these same men take all their annual sick leave because only thus can they rest and recuperate without a sense of guilt.

People who are independently employed and who do not enjoy the security of belonging to a business organization report a higher interest and active participation in all types of medical systems and in religious activities related to health care. Their situation is similar to that of a housewife in that illness for them poses a threat, in this case financial, to family security. Therefore, they use a variety of techniques to try to avoid illness, and on becoming ill, visit the doctor with great frequency.

6

The Interrelationship of Socialization Practices and Medical Beliefs

Socialization and East Asian Medical Beliefs

Having been trained to be sensitive to his or her body's functioning, a Japanese, on a visit to the doctor, usually has numerous subjective symptoms to report. Normally reserved people, when asked about themselves, will pour out information making discrete distinctions between different body states. For example: the stomach can feel heavy (*omoii*), leaden (*omoikurushii*), sour (*muneyake*), nauseous (*hakike*), or painful (*itai*), to name a few of the distinctions. Arms and legs, or the whole body, can be heavy (*omoi*), languid (*darui*), tingling (*shibire*), or chilly (*hie*). These distinctions can be made without hesitation by most people.

Furthermore, probably as a result of their mothers' attitudes toward them as children, people classify themselves as a "type," such as "easily tired" (*tskareyasui*), "of chilly disposition" (*hieshō*), "given to sweating too much" (*takanshō*), "of allergic disposition" (*allerugi taishitsu*), "of nervous temperament" (*shinkeishitsushō*), or an invalid or weak type (*sembyōshitsu*). Some people still use the yin and yang distinction and label themselves *insei* (a yin type) or *yosei* (a yang type). One's basic type is thought to be unchanging and attributable to hereditary or karmic factors. It is necessary to be in possession of this knowledge about oneself in order to practice preventive medicine and to provide useful information for a conscientious East Asian doctor to work with.

When informants were asked to give definitions of the nature of health, many of their answers reflected East Asian medical beliefs to a remarkable degree:

> People who have something wrong with them tend to be pessimistic, but on the other hand some sick people have a strong enough will to recover.
>
> (Male company employee, 26)

> Health is the original state in which we conform to the absolute laws of the Universe. But we do not need to become gloomy when we get sick—we can recover harmony by using our natural energy.
>
> (Male company employee, 25)

> Health is having no defects in either the mind or the body. Real health does not exist on this earth and so everyone lives their life seeking it forever.
>
> (Female student, 24)

This last quote is very close to that of the official definition of the World Health Organization: "Health is a state of complete physical, mental and social well-being and not merely the absence of disease or infirmity." This definition is taught to students in many Japanese high schools, but my informant has made an interesting modification to the second part of the quote.

The Concept of *Ki*

Ordinary people today do not know the East Asian medical origins of the concept of *ki*, nor do they use the word in quite the same way that East Asian doctors do. Nevertheless, the concept has pervaded the Japanese language and culture and appears in numerous everyday words. Doi (1973) and Rohlen (1974a) deal with this topic in detail. The concept is used particularly in association with expressions dealing with emotion and temperament. Doi (p. 109) points out that *ki* implies that human emotions are in a constant state of change and flux. Examples of its use in everyday speech are these: *ki no okii*, literally, having a large *ki*, means "to be generous"; *ki ga shimazu,* literally "*ki* sinks," has the meaning "to be disappointed"; *ki ga kawariyasui,* "easily changed," means "to be unsettled" or "fickle"; the literal translation of *ki ga fusagu* is "a choked up *ki*" and means "to be listless" or "discouraged"; *ki no hayai,* literally "a fast *ki,*" means "to be excitable."

Change in a person is seen as transient, oscillations about a hypothetical norm, which is a state of balance. The image of a human being is of a relatively fixed container, a body type, largely determined by hereditary constitution, around and in which a dance of the exchange of energy is ceaselessly enacted—a view influenced by and close to East Asian medical beliefs. Health and ill health are both normal, the body continually moves in and out of both states, which are intimately related to a dynamic image derived from *ki.* Good health, *genki,* literally means "original *ki*" but also implies a steady flow of *ki; kigen* means health and also tempo or mood. The general word for ill health is *byōki* or "sick *ki.*" Linguistically, as Rohlen and Doi point out, illnesses can be divided into three major types: those that are "from *ki*" (*yamai wa ki kara*) produce physical manifestations in the body; illnesses "of *ki*" (*ki no yamai*) produce predominantly psychological symptoms and include depression, obsession, neurosis, and hypochondria; finally, illnesses in which "*ki* has changed" (*kichigai*) refer to psychotic problems. In modern Japan, new words borrowed from English are also in current use for the last two categories, but the original Japanese is most revealing about attitudes toward these problems. As long as *ki* is simply off balance and not actually changed, it is believed that therapy will restore health. Once *ki* is actually changed, there is no hope—there is no therapy in the East Asian medical system even today for psychosis, and historically priests dealt with this type of problem.

Informants cannot express themselves easily with reference to their feelings about *ki.* Nevertheless, as was discussed above, people are socialized, albeit implicitly, to manage their *ki* satisfactorily and to understand the indivisibility of the environment, emotional states, and physical states. For patients who accept this concept, therapy must therefore facilitate restoration of *ki* management either directly or indirectly—something that East Asian medicine aims to do by supplying a physiological stimulus to set the process in motion.

Hara, the Center of the Body

It is well known that Japanese people suffer inordinately from stomach problems and that when they contract cancer it is frequently in the stomach. Diet certainly is a contributing factor to this problem, and so possibly is genetics, but there are other points to consider. The abdomen, *hara*, in Japanese, has long occupied the place corresponding to that of the heart in Western culture.

Historically, yoga-derived breathing techniques were brought by Buddhist priests from India to China, where they were fused with similar Taoist beliefs. These breathing techniques were used both in meditation and as part of East Asian medical therapy, the principle in both cases being to sit in a relaxed way, concentrate on a spot (*tanden*) two inches below the navel and perform abdominal breathing. Statues of Buddha in meditation provide the finest examples of this technique. *Tanden* is thought to be the center of gravity of the body, and when breathing and concentration are performed correctly, it is a source of great strength, and the flow of *ki* will be at its best. Both *tanden* and the whole abdominal region, known as *hara*, thus came to be of central importance to the Japanese.

In traditional East Asian medicine, the five-phase cycle is often drawn so that the element earth is placed at the center of the other four elements. The body organs related to earth are the spleen and the stomach. An influential school of thought was formalized in the Ming dynasty, which held the belief that if the stomach and spleen were treated therapeutically, then all the organs of the body would automatically be harmonized. The spleen and stomach of traditional East Asian medicine were not confined to the anatomical structures of cosmopolitan medicine, but taken together they constituted much of the abdominal area. Early medical beliefs, therefore, reinforced the importance placed on the abdominal area, and it is interesting to note that pharmacopoeia, both old and new, have listed more kinds of stomach medicine than anything else.

During the Edo period, with its emphasis on the cult of the samurai and a fostering of the martial arts, the cultivation of *hara* was further developed. A good samurai practiced the art of talking from his abdomen, and his true emotions were also believed to originate there. The position in which a warrior or a soldier was thought to be most prepared for action was in a stance with abdomen out and shoulders unobtrusive—the reverse of Western ideas. It was believed that a man with *hara* could truly transcend himself both physically and spiritually. At this time *seppuku*, or in vulgar terminology *harakiri* (the art of cutting the belly), as a means of suicide reached its peak. The equivalent act in the West would be to tear out one's heart to demonstrate the depth and sincerity of one's emotion.

As with the concept of *ki*, so with *hara*, many everyday terms related to the expression of emotion are used in the Japanese language. For example, the literal translation of *hara ga tatsu* is "*hara* stands up," which means "to be angry"; similarly, *hara no okii* translates literally as "*hara* is big" and means "to be generous"; *hara o kimeru*, literally "*hara* is decided," has the meaning "to make up one's mind." Some expressions that convey the idea that *hara* is the emotional center of the body are as follows: "He is an honest man in his *hara*," that is, "at heart" (*kare wa hara no naka wa shojiki na hito desu*); "his mouth and his *hara* are different," which means "he says one thing and means another" (*kare no kuchi to hara to wa chigau*); to have a black *hara* means "to be black-hearted," "evil," or "wicked" (*haraguroi hito*).

Japanese people today show great concern about their abdominal regions. In modern Japan, the classical concept of *hara* has become blurred with that of the cosmopolitan medical concept of stomach (*i*). The psychological and symbolical significance of *hara* and of the classical East Asian medical terms for the abdominal region have subconsciously been transferred in the minds of many Japanese to their anatomical stomachs, where their concern is manifest in the form of diseases of all kinds. Stomach diseases are more feared than any other because it is believed that if the stomach is functioning poorly the whole body will be out of balance. In 78 percent of my informants, mild tension first becomes manifest as a stomach problem. Concern with this part of the anatomy is demonstrated in several ways; for example, many men wear a *haramaki*, a six-inch-wide wool or cotton band, around their upper abdomen to keep that region at a constant, warm temperature. Even in the Tokyo summer the *haramaki* is prevalent. Mothers are careful to keep the abdomens of their children at a constant temperature. A second example is the folk belief that if one cleans out the navel a stomach ache will result. Twenty people out of thirty questioned on this topic all confirmed the

87

belief, and fourteen of them never clean their navels for this reason. A culture-bound syndrome furnishes another example: "dropped stomach" (*ikasuishō*) is a problem in which the stomachs of nervous people can become permanently distended, causing feelings of discomfort. In an extreme case the stomach may descend into the pelvic region, and this has been confirmed by X-rays. The problem seems to be related to eating rice but is not totally explainable in this way. Finally, small children are threatened that if they behave badly the thunder demon will come and steal their belly buttons.

These customs and others derived originally from ancient philosophical and medical beliefs have a profound effect on attitudes toward the body which affect the epidemiology of disease in Japan today.

Socialization and Shintō Beliefs

The continued contribution of Shintō values to modern Japanese culture tends to pass unrecorded and underestimated. It has been described by Bellah (1970, p. 126) as the "ground bass of rather naive communal religion: functional, affirmative, this-worldly." While beliefs arising from Chinese- and Buddhist-derived philosophy tend to emphasize unity, harmony, and balance, Shintō-derived ideas often act in opposition to these tenets. The concept of pollution, with its implicit dualism, is central in this respect. In line with the thinking of Douglas (1966), Japanese people symbolically demarcate areas that are considered "outside," dirty and potentially dangerous, from others that are denoted as "inside," sacred and clean. This is true of social relationships, of the use of physical space, and of attitudes toward the body. The child must be taught to make a clear distinction between relatives, both fictive and real (*miuchi*), and outsiders (*tanin*). The strict code of behavior required with relatives, including the application of concepts of *giri* and *enryo* (Benedict 1946; Doi 1973), social sensitivity to the needs of others, and the use of languages of respect is not required with outsiders. Close dealings with strangers are in general avoided. The separation of inside from out is reinforced every time someone takes off his shoes (the least-cared-for article of clothing in Japan) to enter a house or private building. In a similar vein, on returning from school or work one customarily washes one's hands and by so doing washes off the dirt of the outside world.

PLATE 8. Festival at Shimogamo shrine, Kyoto, originally to ward off the plague. Participants must wade through sacred water to cleanse themselves.

Children are frequently made to gargle, both at home and in kindergarten, after play in the school yard. The purpose is to expel dirt before it enters the body proper.

Inside the house, cloths used for cleaning are carefully separated so that each cloth has only one specific function. Exchanging a cloth used in cleaning the sink for one used for wiping off the stove or the kitchen table is a cause for great concern. Boundaries have become confused. Informants state specifically that their concern is not about bacteria but about something else, which they can only describe as "dirt." Fear of "dirt" is also the reason for strong sanctions against finger-sucking and nail-biting in children—it is not because the habit is thought childish. Children are frequently warned not to touch things and are admonished against exploring the environment, because it is "dirty" and "dangerous."

Traditionally, childbirth and menstruation were hedged with Shintō-derived taboos, which are still practiced in isolated areas of the countryside. A woman undergoing either of these events was considered polluted and made to live separately from the rest of the family, or at least to eat separately for a required number of days. She did not prepare food for anyone during this time. Some women today still consider themselves to be "dirty" when menstruating. Underwear worn at these times is usually washed separately from other clothing. Some women still feel the need to isolate themselves while menstruating, and all working women have a right to two extra days a month off work with no questions asked. It is interesting to note that members of women's liberation movements in Japan are adamant about retaining these privileged days and feel that American women are unliberated in this respect.

Ambivalence toward menstruation is expressed in other ways: of ten informants between the ages of twenty-five and forty, not one had been informed by her mother about the approach of menstruation prior to its occurrence. Japanese mothers go to great lengths to teach their children many other small details related to health matters that Americans would find quite unnecessary. Once menstruation has actually started, the parents are usually embarrassed but joyful. In spite of its abhorrent nature, it heralds the childbearing ability and hence the marriageability of a girl and therefore must be celebrated as a family event. Red bean rice should be prepared and sent to the relatives, and the girl and her parents enjoy a special meal at home. Psychological concern about menstruation is expressed in the form of pain and cramps—something which every informant said she suffered to a great degree. The varieties of medicine for menstrual and gynecological problems are exceeded only by the number for stomach problems.

Illness was also a state that was considered polluting, according to Shintō beliefs, and thus it called for temporary separation and even ostracism from the group. Certain hereditable diseases came to be particularly feared because marriage to someone thus "contaminated" meant defilement for one's family and children. Before marriage today an investigation is still usually carried out into the background of the prospective marriage partner (Hayashida 1975). Inquiries include questions regarding the occurrence of any tuberculosis, mental illness, contact with atomic bomb radiation, or color blindness in the family under investigation. Should this be the case, negotiations would cease. Several of my informants indicated that some types of cancer have recently been added to the diseases that cause ostracism.

The frequent use of a gauze mask to cover the mouth and nose when one has a cold is justified in terms of protecting others from infection. It can also serve to signal one's polluted state and allows one to stay in society, though suitably demarcated. Concern with keeping clear boundaries between inside and out still seems to be important and to have social consequences for one's group as well as individual effects in cases of failure.

Therapy based on Shintō beliefs was designed to purge and expel the pollution. For this reason baths that induce sweating are today thought to be therapeutic and not simply relaxing. Informants state that by sweating in a bath, "dirt" from inside the body can be eliminated. Most people in Japan bathe at least every other day.

Dramatic, radical, and painful forms of therapy are all popular in Japan under certain circumstances. One should not mutilate the body, according to Shintō or Confucian beliefs, yet extensive surgery is practiced in Japan today (see, for example, Yoshida and Yoshida 1976), and until very recently, moxa was often burned to leave extremely obvious scars. The subconscious need to eliminate things that are offensive or "dirty" as radically and as fast as possible could explain this behavior. Such scars are considered highly disfiguring, but they also symbolize that "once I was dirty but now I am clean." Better to be disfigured and remain part of one's group than to be thought of as polluted and thus risk ostracism. Some women even undergo an operation to remove their sweat glands, so great is their fear of appearing dirty to others. The obsessive reactions of *shinkeishitsu* patients in which they show excessive concern about body odor and sweating probably also have their origins here.

During early socialization in Japan today young children internalize many Shintō-derived values; they are taught to fear dirt and to make clear distinctions between what is clean and good and what is dirty and bad. I never once heard a mother teach her child about bacterial theories of infection. It is only later, in school, that children are taught ideas derived from cosmopolitan medicine.

Although today, with the exception of bathing, the therapy of cosmopolitan medicine has ousted most of Shintō-derived therapy, I believe that, under the stress of acute, serious, or shame-inducing illnesses, cosmopolitan therapy is often used in conjunction with a symbolic system derived from Shintō beliefs, for it is in times of stress that values internalized and related to the deep affective states of early childhood come to the fore. Under these circumstances disease becomes a threat to group solidarity and as such is feared. The dualistic idea of good versus bad, and beliefs about the irreconcilability of opposites become dominant, and there is a desire to drive out or eliminate the intruding "dirt." The therapeutic techniques of cosmopolitan medicine appear very powerful under these circumstances.

Socialization and Cosmopolitan Medicine

From the age of four onward children are taught simple principles of anatomy, physiology, biochemistry, and hygiene in kindergarten and at all later levels of the school system. Most urban children today become familiar with cosmopolitan medicine through regular visits to their pediatrician and by periodic health checks held at the schools. A healthy teenager will be aware of the existence of East Asian medicine because of advertising and through the family but will probably have no contact with it in a clinical setting unless he or she sustains an accident while participating in a traditional sports event. Many sports coaches are trained in traditional osteopathy and massage. For the majority of young people in Japan today cosmopolitan medicine is thought of as the only really viable medical system, and this viewpoint is usually sustained until some member of the immediate family contracts a problem that cannot be cured or is not recognized by cosmopolitan medicine. Informally, inside the home, however, influences from traditional sources can be seen on health practices, so that those who turn to East Asian medicine in a clinical setting usually feel readily at ease with what they find.

Use of Preventive and Therapeutic Techniques within the Family

Fifty families were selected for interviews in two different parts of Kyoto in connection with health practices inside the home. Half of the families regard themselves as middle to upper middle class, the other half as lower class. In every family the mother regarded herself as being responsible for the maintenance of the health of all the family members. The results of the interviews are summarized in Table 2.

Figure 4. Elementary principles of anatomy, physiology, biochemistry, hygiene, as taught to children in kindergarten

PLATE 9. Eating boiled radishes at the local temple. Sutras are written on them to preserve health.

Every person interviewed was familiar with moxa, which grows naturally all over Japan. Not only the ancient pharmacopoeia but literary works of all periods make reference to it, from Murasaki Shikibu's eleventh-century *Tale of Genji* onward.

Inside the home today the use of moxa is restricted almost exclusively to older women and men and to young children. It is rolled into tight little balls the size of a pea and placed on the painful spot or on particular pressure points used in East Asian medicine. Half of the informants could name several pressure points, and several of them had learned them from television programs. The moxa is ignited with a stick of incense and allowed to burn until it just singes the skin. It is most frequently used for shoulder stiffness (*katakori*), a widely recurrent chronic problem in Japan, or else for lower-back pain or general fatigue (Lock 1978).

Traditionally, moxa was used as a form of chastisement for young children. Every informant over forty years of age recalled its being used in such a

TABLE 2
Regular Use of Preventive and Therapeutic Techniques in the Home

	UPPER MIDDLE CLASS N = 25	LOWER MIDDLE CLASS N = 25
Moxibustion	10	21
Massage	15	13
Herbal medicine from a pharmacist	21	12
Folk medicine (herbs)	18	14
Patent medicine	19	14
Tonics and/or vitamins	4	12
Synthetic drugs (nonprescriptive)	23	25
Care with diet	11	11
Care with exercise	2	5
Bath thought of as therapy	18	21

way on their siblings if not on themselves. Only three families continue to use it thus today. In cases of enuresis it is burned on the buttocks; the belief is that the pain will shock the child and cause a change in its behavior, and also that the moxa will have a therapeutic effect on the physiology of the body, in this case the kidney function.

When very young children are exhibiting many temper tantrums they are said to have a worm, *kan no mushi*, which is causing their misbehavior. In these cases the moxa is usually burned on the *gōkoku* point between the thumb and the forefinger so as to cause pain but no scarring. The child can be taken to a Shintō shrine to have the worm "sealed" (Wagatsuma 1970, p. 58), and there is a shrine in Kyoto that specializes in this practice, or it can be done at home. In Kyoto there is also an M.D. who specializes in treating babies suffering from this problem with moxibustion. Another possibility is to give the child patent medicine made in Toyama especially for this purpose. Five families had children whom they diagnosed as suffering from *kan no mushi;* three of the children had been given patent medicine and two had had moxa burned on them. I found no informants, even those who took their child to a shrine, who actually believed in the traditional concept of *kan no mushi*. Instead, it was acknowledged that some children are excessively irritable and fussy, and the usual explanations offered for this condition were hereditary or dietary imbalance. Pediatricians, practitioners of East Asian medicine, and many noninvolved parents usually offered a different explanation: they believe that the problem almost invariably arises as a result of the disposition of the mother rather than of the baby. While the baby's heredi-

95

tary constitution may play some part, what *they* felt to be most relevant is the way the mother handles her child. Nervous and fussy mothers predictably have babies with *kan no mushi,* and its prevalence in Japan is attributed to the extremely close mother-child relationship during early socialization. When moxa is used for treatment, whatever explanations are given for the origin of the ailment, it is expected to induce physiological as well as behavioral changes in the body. The use of moxa is therefore associated in the minds of many older Japanese with their childhood and with the inducement of behavioral changes that restore good family relationships.

All the families use massage occasionally, but only twenty-eight receive it regularly from other family members. Massage-sticks, somewhat like a stick for hitting a gong, can be purchased at the stalls near Shintō shrines on festival days and are used to beat the tension out of one's own back muscles. Half of the lower-class families were in possession of these sticks.

Among the twenty-five upper-middle-class families half the sample said that they had read books or articles on the topic of East Asian medicine in the recent past. In this group particularly there was a renewed interest in the use of herbal medicine with the express purpose of avoiding illnesses that would entail a visit to the cosmopolitan doctor and hence the ingestion of synthetic medicine.

The most popular preparations used in the home are designed to be preventive rather than curative, and older women in possession of recipes are in great demand in their neighborhoods. The Japanese are well known for strongly disliking garlic in cooking, but their interest in health is marked enough to overcome this dislike. Garlic has been proclaimed a health promoter, and half of the families interviewed have recently started to use it regularly. One man eats two raw cloves at breakfast every day in order to promote sweating and thus help maintain good health—Shintō-derived ideas seem to apply here.

Herbal medicine is associated strongly with food, and informants frequently point out the plants growing in their garden or on sale at the greengrocer's shop. While some preparations must be made especially, many can be taken as part of a well-balanced diet. *Shiso* (beefsteak plant, *Perilla nankinensis*), rhubarb, peppermint, fennel, and cinnamon, among many other examples, are used regularly.

Most popular medical ideas about herbal medicine are probably not derived directly from the East Asian medical system (Nishiyama 1962), but there is a classification of food into pairs that should not be eaten together (*kuiawase*), and this *may* be due to influences from the yin/yang theory, in which all foods and medicines are classified as yin or yang and a balance of both kinds must be taken to maintain health. The lists of unsuitably paired foods are obtainable today with the packages of patent medicine sold from door to door by the Toyama medicine seller, and they also appear in the almanac that indicates lucky and unlucky days and is issued at the major shrines. Although all the informants had heard of these food restrictions, only two were ever observed: watermelon and *tempura* (fried fish) do not mix and produce a stomach ache, and eel, if eaten with dried salty plums (*umeboshi*), will give food poisoning. A complete list of *kuiawase* appears in Table 3.

TABLE 3
Foods That Should Not Be Eaten Together (Kuiawase)

COMBINATIONS	EFFECT
Mushrooms (*shiitake*) and spinach	Food poisoning
Clams and mandarin oranges (*mikan*)	Food poisoning
Rice boiled with red beans and blow fish (*fugu*)	Food poisoning
Carp and mustard plant (rape seed)	Hemorrhoids
Horsemeat and yams	Round worms
Noodles (*soba*) and freshwater snails (*tanishi*)	Stomach ache
Raw plums and brown sugar	Food poisoning
Watermelon and *tempura* (fried food)	Stomach ache
Mushrooms (*matsutake*) and clams	Stomach ache
Peppermint and potato	Food poisoning
Quail and mushrooms	Food poisoning
Loquats and red beans	Stomach ache
Duck's eggs and yams	General debility
Catfish (*namazu*) and pork	Food poisoning
Leeks or scallions and honey	Hysteria or cramps
Pork and freshwater snails	Baldness
Crab and persimmons	Food poisoning
Herring roe and bear's gall	General debility
Noodles (*soba*) and dates	Stomach ache
Corn and freshwater snails (*tanishi*)	Diarrhea
Eels and dried plums (*umeboshi*)	Food poisoning
Eggs and garlic	Food poisoning
Bamboo shoots and brown sugar	Stomach ache

Source: Almanac for 1974, obtainable at the Fushimi Inari shrine in Kyoto.

97

Thirty-three of the families keep a stock of patent medicine, which salesmen from Toyama replenish twice a year. The most popular medicines, in the form of powders, relieve headaches, stomach aches, general fatigue, and menstrual cramps.

A large proportion of the families interviewed, fifteen in all, continue to practice palmistry (*tesōmi*) and related forms of divination, which were originally allied with the East Asian medical system. The observance of unlucky directions (*hōgaku*), also derived partially from traditional East Asian medicine and used as a preventive technique, is practiced by twenty-seven of the families. The most common practice is to avoid sleeping with one's head in a northerly direction (*kitamakura*). Informants state that they do not really believe these old ideas but that they feel uncomfortable if they are not observed.

Not a single family uses religious ritual in lieu of a visit to a doctor to solve their medical problems, though all but five of them believe that the use of religious ritual can help psychologically to relieve tension, and they put this belief into practice (see Table 4).

During pregnancy forty-eight out of the fifty mothers interviewed had paid regular visits to the Shintō shrine. On the Day of the Dog in the fifth month of their respective pregnancies they each had purchased a special *obi* (sash) to wear under their outer garments. It is thought to function as a means of holding the baby firmly in place; to stop it from moving around too much *in utero;* to stop it from growing too big, thus allowing for an easy delivery; and to keep the abdominal area warm and the mother therefore free of illness. The women had each taken the sash, purchasable only at a Shintō shrine, to their obstetricians. The doctors, after making their routine examinations, had wound the *obi* around the women with supportive reassurance that this was a sensible thing to do. Twenty-eight of the mothers had also taken herbal medicine throughout their pregnancies to ensure a safe and easy delivery.

Every family except two has a cosmopolitan style of family doctor and a medicine cabinet stocked with synthetic medicine for colds and stomach problems, and excesses from old prescriptions.

Table 5 shows the use of East Asian medicine in a clinical setting. An affirmative answer means that at least one member of the family interviewed used a traditional clinic for more than a single isolated visit. Out of the fifty

TABLE 4
Use of Religious Ritual in Connection with Illness

	UPPER MIDDLE CLASS	LOWER MIDDLE CLASS
Visit to a shrine	12	19
Visit to a temple	1	11
Use of shamans	0	7
Safe birth ritual (Shintō)	23	25
Religious ritual in the home	20	25

families there were only five whose members had never made use of this system. In general, the lower-middle-class families have more acquaintance with traditional clinics and particularly with those that provide acupuncture and moxibustion.

In summary, informants over forty, and in particular the women, are most familiar with traditional medical ideas. Conflicting ideas about health beliefs are often expressed within a family, but people do not see traditional and cosmopolitan medical beliefs as mutually exclusive. Some people lean more toward one system or the other, but very few rely totally on one system, and a large number of informants expressed a renewed interest in traditional health beliefs and practices. Socialization practices tend to reinforce the acceptance of pluralistic ideas with regard to health and sickness. Young

TABLE 5
Use of East Asian Medicine in a Clinical Setting

	UPPER MIDDLE CLASS	LOWER MIDDLE CLASS
Acupuncture	4	11
Moxibustion	6	10
Shiatsu	3	4
*Honetsugi**	4	7
Amma	11	15
Kanpō	2	0
Prescribed herbal medicine	9	8

Honetsugi is the art of bone-setting in the East Asian style. Analysis of these clinics was beyond the time limitations of the present study.

people under the age of twenty-five have usually had few experiences of illness other than problems of infection. They associate traditional medicine with middle-aged and old people and think almost exclusively in terms of cosmopolitan medicine. Potential feelings of anxiety during pregnancy and childbirth, feelings of responsibility while raising a family, or the personal experience of a chronic medical problem stimulate a greater interest in traditional medical beliefs, and the ready acceptance of pluralistic ideas becomes more pronounced among middle-aged and older people.

The following passage from Tanizaki's *The Makioka Sisters* (*Sasame Yuki*) reveals the clash of different beliefs regarding health matters within one family. The setting is in Osaka just before World War II, but it could well be representative of a postwar family in which some members prefer cosmopolitan medical ideas while others have reverted to, or have always remained more interested in, traditional ideas. Teinosuke is arguing with his wife, Sachiko, over the treatment of their daughter, Etsuko, who has been diagnosed as suffering from nervous prostration (*shinkeishitsushō*). He feels that Sachiko and her sister are at fault for being too old-fashioned in some ways and also for having misunderstood the application of modern Western-derived ideas. Teinosuke, on the other hand, takes a point of view derived from traditional East Asian medicine when he states that an ordered life above all else will prevent disease:

> They were wrong to be so noisy about antiseptics and
> sanitation and to pay no attention to order and discipline.
> They must begin immediately to order the child's life.
> So Teinosuke argued, but his recommendations had little
> effect. To Sachiko it seemed that one as strong and healthy as
> Teinosuke would never understand the feelings of one like
> herself, so quick to catch each passing ailment. To Teinosuke
> it seemed that the chances of catching a disease from
> chopsticks were one in ten thousand, and that this constant
> disinfecting only lowered one's resistance. When Sachiko said
> that grace and elegance were more important for a girl than
> his "order," Teinosuke answered that she was being old-
> fashioned, that the child's habits and play hours should
> follow a strict pattern. Teinosuke was a barbarian who knew
> nothing about sanitation, said Sachiko; Sachiko's methods of

disinfecting were ineffective in any case, answered Teinosuke. What good did it do to pour hot water or tea over chopsticks? That would kill no germs. . . . Sachiko and Yukiko misunderstood Occidental ideas of sanitation and cleanliness. . . .

One day [Teinosuke] saw Etsuko at play. . . . Taking a worn-out hypodermic needle, Etsuko gave her straw-stuffed doll a shot in the arm. What a morbid little game, Teinosuke thought. That too was the result of a dangerous preoccupation with hygiene. Something must be done. (P. 118)

Etsuko is able to find a hypodermic syringe in the house because prior to, and just after, the war many middle- and upper-class families gave themselves regular injections of vitamin B. Springtime was known as the season of "B-shortage," and beri-beri was a much feared disease. Two families interviewed still keep syringes in the house for this purpose, though most prefer to take pills today. Injections are considered much more powerful than pills, but there is no longer a fear of beri-beri.

The health-related activities of four Kyoto families presented in detail below highlight some of the material under discussion and demonstrate the wide variety of attitudes and activities that can be met with in modern Japan.

Since the days when Tanizaki wrote *The Makioka Sisters* people no longer think so consciously of sanitation and hygiene as being "occidental" and new, but conflicts in ideas regarding health-related activities occur in many families, nevertheless. Ultimately, however, it is almost always the young mother of the household who makes the final decisions about what should be done. When in doubt she turns to her female friends or her mother or mother-in-law for advice. Since women are more conversant with traditional medical ideas, and since they reside in residential areas where traditional practitioners of all kinds are readily available, it is likely that they will encourage their family to use the traditional system at times.

Mrs. Fujiyama runs a small tea-selling business in the front part of her house.[1] This has been the major source of income for the family since her husband suffered a cerebral hemorrhage five years ago. Her husband receives

---

1 Fictitious names are used throughout the book for all informants.

a disability pension, and both her children have recently graduated from school and can now earn some money, which makes the financial situation a little easier.

She says that when her husband had his hemorrhage they were "treated very badly" by the local hospital, which did not send an ambulance for several hours under the pretext that it was broken down. She states that if she had paid her doctor or the hospital some money at the time, the ambulance would have come right away. Mrs. Fujiyama believes that if her husband had been taken to the hospital right away and massaged professionally, or if she herself had massaged him at the time at home, he would not be paralyzed down his right side as he is today. She feels strongly that her husband's misfortune is something that could have been avoided and that she is to blame for it.

After her husband returned from a six-week stay in hospital her family doctor made a house call every day for several months; this was gradually reduced, and now he never visits the family. Her husband takes no medication, because he is concerned about possible side effects. Mrs. Fujiyama called in a masseuse (*amma*) to the house every day for two months after her husband returned from the hospital, but eventually the masseuse asked to quit because the patient did not enjoy the visits. Her neighbors told her that the best thing for paralysis was to drink an extract of unripe persimmon juice while receiving regular massage treatments, but her husband refused the medicine after trying it a few times. Some months after her husband returned from the hospital, Mrs. Fujiyama started to consult regularly with a fortune-teller (*uranaishi*) at a local Shintō shrine in an effort to find out if anything could be changed in their lives to help matters. She was particularly concerned about having had a new room added on to the house just before her husband's illness occurred. The carpenter had paid no attention to directional lore (*hōgaku*) and had built the room facing in the wrong direction. The fortune-teller hinted at the danger of ignoring directional lore, and eventually Mrs. Fujiyama became so worried that she had the new room torn down. Her brother and sister told her she was being silly and ordered her not to go back to the fortune-teller again. Shortly after, another very small new room was built on the second floor of the house as a study for the children. Mrs. Fujiyama's daughter became mildly ill after she started to use the room, and Mrs. Fujiyama went to talk to her brother and sister about what should be done. Although the matter was discussed very carefully, no agreement could be reached and the room is still there today but is used only for storage purposes.

With regard to herself, Mrs. Fujiyama feels that she is generally healthy. She has a minor ailment in that when she sews her arm goes numb (*shibireru*), and she believes that the origin of this problem is a faulty electric fan. When she plugged the fan in one day she received an electric shock, and she states that she has had problems with sewing since that time. She went immediately to a neighborhood lady to receive moxibustion. She continues to do this regularly; she says she likes it and that the lady takes small presents but no money. She took her husband along for moxibustion once, but he didn't like the pain of the treatment and never returned. At the same time she went to her family doctor and received a short course of injections. She also went regularly to a special bathhouse nearby where electric currents are passed through the water to help relax the body. She says that her arm is getting better but that she worries about it because it is a problem with "the nerves," and she doesn't know where it will pop up next.

Mrs. Fujiyama describes herself as "*insei*" (a yin type) and says she tries to eat accordingly. She prepares mushrooms (*shiitake*) almost every day for the family meals. The family takes patent medicine for headaches and stomach problems.

Mrs. Fujiyama used to go to the Shintō shrine regularly to pray for good health, and she bought talismans to keep in the house. Since her husband's illness she has given that up and now prays to the ancestors. She has also joined Myohōkai, one of the new syncretic religions in Japan, but says she is only half-hearted about it. She brings home special teas regularly from both shrines and temples to try to help her husband, but she is gradually resigning herself to the fact of his permanent disability. Although Mrs. Fujiyama feels somewhat resentful toward her family doctor and cosmopolitan medicine, she does not reject it. She relies heavily on positive support from her relatives and neighbors to help her cope with a stressful situation about which she harbors many feelings of guilt. She is willing to try any kind of treatment or take any action that she feels might help relieve the burden.

The Gotō family lives in a small, clean house in a middle-class residential neighborhood. Mr. Gotō is an employee of an insurance company, and he

103

lives with his wife, their three children, and his mother. None of the family has ever been seriously ill, and Mrs. Gotō deals with all mild problems by going to the pharmacist to buy some medicine, except in the case of the youngest child, now two, whom she takes to the doctor at the first sign of any problem. She likes her family doctor very much and has gone to him regularly for ten years. He will make house calls if a child has a high temperature, and he prefers to prescribe pills, which Mrs. Gotō likes, rather than shots. All the family take vitamin pills regularly every day, and in addition the children are given cod liver oil in candy form.

Each time she was pregnant Mrs. Gotō took herbal medicine; she was frightened of taking synthetic medicine, because of the thalidomide problem. She says that the herbal medicine prevented colds and other minor ailments, and she liked it despite its bad smell. She believes that a good diet is essential for maintaining health and serves raw vegetables every day. She also makes plum wine and eats large quantities of seaweed. She is especially concerned with the vitamin content of foodstuffs.

Old Mrs. Gotō likes moxibustion, and her daughter-in-law burns it on her back regularly. Young Mrs. Gotō has never tried moxibustion. Her eldest daughter gives her massage regularly for shoulder tension. She also uses the massage machine at the public bath when she goes there once a week. She doesn't want to go to a professional masseuse regularly, because she believes that it can become habit forming. While she was pregnant Mrs. Gotō visited the Shintō shrine regularly and used the maternity *obi* despite the fact that her husband thought it was nonsense. She prays regularly to the ancestors for good health. When Mr. and Mrs. Gotō built their house, Mrs. Gotō consulted a fortune-teller and a specialist in directional lore, "so as to feel at ease," and she always tries to do important things on "lucky days" (*taian*). Mr. and Mrs. Gotō both consider East Asian medicine old-fashioned and state that cosmopolitan medicine meets all their needs. If their lives should be disrupted by chronic illness in the future, however, Mrs. Gotō is well aware of several sources of alternative medical care.

Mrs. Kimura lives with her husband and two children in a middle-class neighborhood. Her husband is a schoolteacher, and the family are practicing Buddhists. Mrs. Kimura says that her husband leaves rice and water in front of the *kamidana* (household Shintō shrine) and the *butsudan* (place for the ancestral tablets) each morning, and that he always leaves his driving license inside the *kamidana* as a form of protection.

Mrs. Kimura believes that sensible diet is the basis of good health. (For example, at home the family uses honey instead of sugar and eats only food with no additives.) She is very careful about this, and her family has never suffered any major medical problems. She also states that if an illness occurs it is one's own responsibility (*bioki ga okoru no wa jibun ni sekinin ga aru*), meaning that one has not taken sufficient personal care.

The Kimuras do not have a regular doctor, and state that they would use cosmopolitan medicine only in case of an emergency. Mrs. Kimura says she doesn't trust cosmopolitan doctors much, that they give too many injections and do not listen to the patient's problems. "All they do is use a stethoscope and try to cure you with one shot; how can any doctor possibly cure a patient with one shot?"

For mild problems Mrs. Kimura makes her own preparations rather than using either medicine from the pharmacist or patent medicine. She prepares hot noodles for a mild fever to induce sweating, and she makes *tamagozake* (egg in sake) for a head cold. The family takes ginseng tea regularly, and she makes the children take twice as much just before exam time.

As a general preventive measure, Mrs. Kimura uses a lot of garlic, green onions, mushrooms, and salted plums (*umeboshi*) in the family's diet, and she also keeps a stock of garlic wine (*ninnikushu*) and plum wine (*umeshu*) in the house. In the summertime she takes especial care regarding the abdominal region; she states that "many diseases originate in the abdomen" (*manbyō o naka kara*), and she encourages all the family to wear either a cotton or a wool band (*haramaki*) around their abdomens in the hot weather. She believes that expression of envy and anger can make one ill and encourages the family to be calm and content at all times. She also encourages the family to exercise regularly.

Mrs. Kimura was told at her local parent-teachers meeting that she is too old-fashioned, but she says that she doesn't care what people think and that preventive medicine is vital. Although she has not used either acupuncture or moxibustion, she keeps a massage machine in her house for problems of shoulder tension. Mrs. Kimura takes her role in looking after the health of the family very seriously. She reads books on herbal medicine, home remedies, and first aid and believes fervently that a healthy family is the key to a good life.

Mr. and Mrs. Kakihara live with their children and his parents in a small, cramped house. Mr. Kakihara works in a company that makes locks and keys, and his wife works in the Nishijin textile industry as an unskilled laborer.

Mrs. Kakihara says the family has two regular doctors because her mother-in-law and father-in-law prefer different practitioners. When there is a mild problem in the family she goes to her local pharmacist, who decides what medicine she should buy. If someone has a high fever, they visit the doctor for a shot "because shots work faster than medicine." Mrs. Kakihara says she trusts the doctors and is totally satisfied with the service the family receives. She formerly used some herbal medicine but gave it up, and her father-in-law tried moxibustion once but discontinued it. Although the family takes no special care over food, exercise, or any other form of preventive medicine, the children give their grandmother a regular massage for muscle tension.

The family takes part in religious observances only occasionally and has never visited a fortune-teller or similar type of specialist. Mrs. Kakihara did not buy a special *obi* for pregnancy; she says she was interested but just never found the time to do it. She doesn't like keeping talismans of any kind in the house because she would have to "treat them properly."

In conclusion, the variety of health-related practices in Kyoto is very striking. Interest in traditional forms of medicine, or a lack of interest in it, seems to occur in both lower- and upper-middle-class families. Where there is an interest in traditional ideas, the upper-middle-class families tend to be more concerned with diet and herbal medicine; among lower-middle-class families interest in fortune-telling and directional lore is more prevalent. Knowledge, if not experience, of all types of traditional health practices is still well known, and even young people, especially those who live in an extended family, will be exposed to these ideas to some extent. Family members help one another regularly to restore and maintain good health.

When a health problem does arise, choices of ameliorative action are discussed among family members, including, at times, relatives living in separate households.

We shall now turn to the clinical setting where traditional medicine is practiced and look first of all at the patients and their medical problems, expectations, and experiences.

PART THREE

The East Asian Medical System
in Urban Japan: *Kanpō*

7

A *Kanpō* Clinic: The Patients

> We Orientals . . . find beauty not only in the
> thing itself but in the pattern of shadows, the
> light and darkness, which that thing produces.
> Junichiro Tanizaki,
> *In Praise of Shadows*, 1934

Ways to the *Kanpō* Clinic

Patients have a choice of many kinds of traditional medical clinics in
Kyoto. Through data on small samples of people at a variety of clinics I shall
attempt to show why they selected the traditional medical system in the first
place and why they selected a massage clinic, for example, rather than an
acupuncture clinic, and what kind of experience they underwent when they
got there.

Mr. Wada was born in Toyama city near the Japan seacoast. A few years
after completing high school, he moved to Kyoto, where he was apprenticed
in a small watch-and-clock repair business. He is now sixty-four, owner of
the same business where he has worked all his life, and classifies himself as
middle class. He has a wife and three grown children and says that they are
all practicing Buddhists.

For seventeen years Mr. Wada has had recurrent stomach ulcers. During
the first twelve years of his illness he went periodically to his local Western-
style hospital for treatment, where he received both in-patient and out-
patient care. Mr. Wada was frightened of the idea of surgery, and each time
that his ulcer recurred he was warned that surgery was probably inevitable if

PLATE 10. The waiting room of the *kanpō* hospital.

he couldn't change his way of life sufficiently to avoid getting sick. He began looking around for other kinds of medical treatment, and one day he happened to read an article in the *Asahi News* (the newspaper with the largest daily circulation in Japan) about *kanpō*. He became interested in the possibility of treatment with herbal medicine and found out the address of a *kanpō* clinic from the telephone directory. When he arrived for his first visit he was surprised to find a modern building; like the majority of urban Japanese, he had an image of East Asian medicine as old-fashioned and conservative. He was even more surprised to find several young doctors and nurses and modern equipment.

The clinic Mr. Wada selected is set in the eastern hills of Kyoto, and the present building is only five years old. Practical, spotless, and tastefully designed, it provides many amenities to put the patients at their ease, such as piped-in music, color television, a chatty monthly journal put out by the doctors, and a Japanese garden to view from the waiting room.

The clinic is a small, flourishing family business founded in 1936 by a now semiretired doctor, rather well known in the Japanese medical world. His son-in-law is the present director of the clinic, and there are four assistant doctors, all of whom with one exception are either a son or a son-in-law of the two senior doctors. All the doctors are M.D.'s and were graduated from the prestigious Kyoto University medical school. The senior doctor says the principal reason he founded the clinic was that he cured his son, then a child, of chronic asthma by using herbal medicine.

The facilities and reputation of the clinic have increased over the years, and today there is a capacity for twelve in-patients and up to one hundred out-patients per day. Clinic hours are from 9 A.M. to 4 P.M. six days a week. Apart from the doctors, the professional staff consists of six nurses, two dieticians, three pharmacists, two laboratory technicians, an X-ray technician, and one licensed acupuncturist; all the doctors also practice acupuncture and moxibustion themselves. There is a well-equipped laboratory and an X-ray machine in the building. This clinic has two subsidiary branches, one in Osaka and one in Tokyo.

All treatment at the clinic is private, and the average cost is between seven and eight dollars a visit. For in-patients the cost is about eight dollars a day for a shared room, including meals, with an additional small fee for herbal medicine.

Examination of a Patient

There is no appointment system, and patients wait for from twenty minutes to—on busy days—an hour to see the doctor. Mr. Wada well remembers his first visit to the clinic. Though he felt nervous, his confidence was boosted by the pleasant surroundings and the modern, clean appearance. He waited about thirty minutes and was then ushered into a private changing-room, where he slipped into a clean *yukata* (cotton kimono). When his name was called he entered a spacious room where he underwent the standard preliminary examinations conducted by a young doctor, who wore the familiar white coat of his profession and had a stethoscope protruding conspicuously from his pocket.

Mr. Wada was questioned, listened to, and examined for thirty minutes. Apart from basic life-history material, the entire examination was repeated

113

each time Mr. Wada came to the doctor—usually once a week and for more than a year's duration.

The following details are recorded on all patients whatever their problem: family and work situation; age; body type; bone structure; state of the skin in detail, especially the face and palms of the hands (principally to ascertain dietary deficiencies or excesses, water retention, and nervousness); whether the tongue is in a yin or a yang state; condition of the nails (to aid diagnosis of dietary imbalances); the taste in the mouth; appetite; stools and urine (routinely tested in the cosmopolitan style); sleep habits; headaches; heavy head; dizziness; heart tremors; ringing in the ears; heavy or dull legs; shoulder stiffness; dryness of the mouth; sweating; night sweating; fluid intake; state of the lymph glands, tonsils, and adenoids; favorite foods; alcoholic intake; and intake of sweet things. This is followed by an examination of the back for muscle tension. Auscultation of the chest is then performed with the use of a stethoscope.

Next, the pulses are taken in the East Asian style while the patient sits quietly. Then, as he lies on a couch, his blood pressure is taken, and the doctor palpates his abdomen: first in the cosmopolitan style, with the patient's legs flexed, he feels for any enlargement of the internal organs, and then in the East Asian style, with the legs extended, he feels for increased or decreased areas of muscle tension and fluid retention. This aids the doctor in deciding whether the patient is basically in a yin or a yang state. Finally, pain associated with pressure points on the meridian system is noted. Elaborate notes and diagrams are made on the diagnostic forms, which are printed partly in German and partly in Japanese. The objective is to use both a cosmopolitan and a traditional East Asian system of diagnosis. The parts of the form that refer to cosmopolitan concepts are printed in German (the major Western source of influence on Japanese medicine was Germany), and the parts that refer to East Asian concepts are printed in Chinese ideograms.

Establishing a single, precipitating cause of disease is not the sole purpose of the examination; another objective is the detection of points of imbalance in the body and its relationship to the total environment. Throughout the examination the doctor chats with the patient; there is no evidence of time pressure. He explains in simple terms any unusual findings and then emphasizes that the therapy will merely be a boost to start the healing process, which may take a long time. Basically, the body will heal itself, but the patient must cooperate by changing anything in his environment that is upsetting the balance. It was explained to Mr. Wada that he would have to have some laboratory tests made and an X-ray picture taken and that it might be necessary for him to come to the clinic as an in-patient for a while. He was given acupuncture treatment, and he finally went home with a supply of herbal medicine, each dose sealed in a small packet and ready to be taken with either food or beverages.

Mr. Wada was initially hospitalized at the clinic for four weeks, during which time he received only herbal medicine, acupuncture and moxibustion treatments, and a carefully controlled, cosmopolitan type of diet. He was discharged once his X-rays revealed that only scar tissue remained, and he came regularly to the clinic as an out-patient for several months. Then, he says, he started to feel so good that he stopped taking the medicine and started to drink *sake*. At about this time his business life became stressful, and the ulcer flared up once more. X-rays and a biopsy were taken, and although cancer was ruled out, the doctors told Mr. Wada that the lesions were so severe that although they were not sure whether they could cure the ulcer with herbs, they would give it a two-week trial period. Herbal medicine, acupuncture, and a cosmopolitan type of diet were administered, and regular laboratory tests were performed. The ulcer responded, and after three months Mr. Wada was discharged and expects to continue coming regularly to the clinic as an out-patient for many months.

Mr. Wada says he especially likes the combination of science and traditional techniques at the clinic. Treatments are expensive for him, but he feels that it cannot be helped. He comes once a week and it takes a total of three hours traveling time, which he says is a strain, and he worries about his business while he is away. The doctors have met and talked to Mr. Wada's wife; she has received written instructions regarding his diet, and she has been taught how to do moxibustion at home. After nine months of treatment as an out-patient, Mr. Wada says that he is feeling good. He believes that his illness is due to a combination of genetic, dietary, and stressful factors. He feels that he can keep up his new dietary habits, including abstinence from alcohol, and he also believes that his business with all its insecurities will always cause him to worry and that this situation cannot be avoided. Although Mr. Wada does not believe that he is necessarily cured forever, he feels much more relaxed than formerly because he thinks he can avoid surgery and, even more important, because he is concerned about the long-term ingestion of synthetic drugs, which he now never uses.

While Mr. Wada was an in-patient he shared a room with Masao, an eleven-year-old boy, whose father is a mailman and who lives with his family in the countryside about a hundred miles from Kyoto. When he was ten years old, Masao was diagnosed as having nephrosis and was hospitalized near his home for four months. After a brief period as an out-patient he entered the same hospital for another six months and was given hormone treatment. The obesity, moon face, and loss of appetite characteristic of this treatment soon developed, and as his prognosis was rather poor, the family doctor suggested to the boy's father that he might consider the *kanpō* clinic. Despite the journey, Masao was brought to Kyoto and remained in the clinic as an in-patient for a total of one year. The hormone treatments were gradually reduced, and herbal medicine and moxa were administered each day. Regular laboratory tests were performed. Protein excretion and the obesity lessened, but when the hormones were stopped completely the protein loss increased again. The process of gradually reducing the hormone level was repeated several times, but it was not until the fourth trial that the kidney function remained good with only herbal medicine. Gradually the kidney function returned to 75 percent of normal, and no further improvement can be expected. The obesity is markedly reduced, and Masao's appetite is generally good. Masao has been sent on to another hospital, which specializes in children's nephrosis, where he will continue to receive only herbal medicine provided his kidney function remains stable. At this second hospital he will have school work to do and friends to play with—the doctors agreed that the *kanpō* hospital was not a good environment for him. Masao expects to return home shortly and to be able to carry on a normal life with only slightly less physical activity than most children. He said he liked the doctors in the *kanpō* clinic and that he enjoyed being able to help the nurses in their work. He particularly liked being able to help make his own medicine (which, unlike most medicine in the clinic, had to be prepared especially for him from raw materials). Toward the end of his stay in the hospital, a large stock of medicine was made for Masao without his help, so that his mother, who would have to administer the medicine in the future, would not have to spend a lot of time preparing it. Masao was upset because he would no longer be able to take part in the preparation of his medicine after he left the hospital, and when the new batch of medicine was tried out in the *kanpō* clinic just before his discharge, his kidney function suddenly dropped and protein loss increased. It stayed that way until the original medicine, specially prepared with Masao's help, was reintroduced, when his kidneys improved again. Masao's mother was taught how to make the original medicine starting from the raw materials.

The *kanpō* doctors used this example to stress the point that there is a large psychosomatic component in the illnesses that they deal with. They believe that patient involvement in the treatment process is an important part of therapy, and they consciously spend a lot of time developing trust and rapport with each patient.

Mrs. Morita was an in-patient at the hospital at the same time as Masao and Mr. Wada, but she had her own private room. Though she was born in the countryside, she has lived in Kyoto all her married life. She is fifty-nine and lives with her husband and a married daughter and her family. Her husband is a company executive, and Mrs. Morita states that the family is probably upper middle class. She says they have a general belief in the Jodo sect of Buddhism but never take part in any religious rituals. Mrs. Morita has been suffering from rheumatoid arthritis for twenty-six years; she cannot walk easily, and her hands are very deformed. She describes the origin of her sickness in the following way: "Twenty-six years ago on a cold, cold New Year's Day, I went to Koyasan [the spiritual center of the Shingon sect of Buddhism] to see the temples. I wore new *zōri* [straw sandals] and they were still very stiff. It was snowing and really cold. When I came back, my legs swelled up and my feet started to hurt. That was the beginning of this illness—and it was because I didn't take care and allowed myself to get too cold."

Mrs. Morita went to her family doctor and took medication for many years. The problem seemed to be under control until four years ago, when it suddenly flared up again and her hands became particularly swollen and painful. She was an in-patient in a Kyoto hospital for awhile and then continued visiting her family doctor and receiving medication, when a friend introduced her to the *kanpō* clinic. After reading many articles about the side effects of modern medicine she was very concerned about having to continue to take it, possibly for the rest of her life, and so she came eagerly to try herbal medicine.

Mrs. Morita says she developed great faith in the *kanpō* doctors, and after coming regularly to the clinic for two years she felt much better and decided not to come any more. A few months later her leg swelled up again, and within the space of a few weeks she could not walk at all. Mrs. Morita was admitted as an in-patient to the hospital and had been in a private room for four months when she was first interviewed. She had a *tsukisoi* (a personal attendant) who lived in the room with her day and night. Therapy comprised herbal medicine, acupuncture, and moxibustion, and she had tiny balls of gold taped in place where the joints were swollen. Mrs. Morita said she was not in pain any more, and she demonstrated that she could walk again, though not freely. The senior, semiretired doctor came and talked to her regularly and explained why she must keep up treatments, even if she was feeling well. After five months as an in-patient, Mrs. Morita was discharged, and the doctors made regular house calls for several more months until she was well enough to visit the clinic as an out-patient. She expects to continue treatment for the rest of her life, and like Mr. Wada, she is delighted that her illness can apparently be controlled by using medication that she regards as "natural" rather than by taking strong drugs on a regular basis. Although Mrs. Morita feels that treatments are expensive, she says she can manage without much difficulty. She has failed to persuade her husband, a mild diabetic, to transfer to the *kanpō* clinic.

Mr. Ishi is twenty-nine, is a high school graduate, and works in a dyeing company. He has been married for one year and lives separately from his parents. He has no special religious beliefs. In order to do his work Mr. Ishi has to sit in one position all day, and he has developed lower-back pain. He also has mild stomach problems, tiredness, and depression. When Mr. Ishi first noticed the back pain he went to his local doctor, who looked only at his back, he says, and not at his whole body. He had X-rays and injections, and was told after a few visits that there was nothing wrong with him and that he was neurotic (*shinkeishitsu*). He tried several other cosmopolitan doctors, with similar results, and then a friend introduced both Mr. Ishi and his wife to the *kanpō* clinic. Mr. Ishi comes as an out-patient whenever he can get the time off work, about once every two weeks. He receives acupuncture to take away the lower-back pain, and herbal medicine for his depression and stomach. The *kanpō* doctors believe that all the symptoms including the mild neurosis are interrelated and must be treated as such. They agree that he is indeed *shinkeishitsu,* but they go on to say that he has functional symptoms that must be removed. Mr. Ishi says he trusts the *kanpō* doctors completely, they look at him carefully, care about him, and explain things well. The expense is a problem, but Mr. Ishi thinks it is worth it. After six months of treatment Mr. Ishi said he feels a bit better but that his working conditions are difficult. Both he and the doctors believe that no marked improvement will occur unless these conditions are changed—he works an average of ten hours a day with only a few brief intervals from his desk.

Mrs. Hamada is also twenty-nine years old. She has suffered from rheumatism since her early twenties and has taken medication regularly for seven years with only sporadic symptom relief. She came, rather unwillingly, to the *kanpō* doctor on the recommendation of her mother, who takes herbal medicine on a regular basis. Mrs. Hamada thinks East Asian medicine is old-fashioned and expensive and that it requires too much active participation on the part of the patient. She continued to receive acupuncture treatments and herbal medicine for about six months on an out-patient basis, once more with only sporadic relief of symptoms, and then decided to return to her family doctor. She says she probably won't try East Asian medicine again and hopes that soon there will appear on the market some new drug that will cure her of her disease. She believes her illness is partially due to her genetic constitution and partially due to a kind of "chemical imbalance."

Some important generalizations can be made from these case histories, with regard to the practice of *kanpō.* First, there is a very lengthy time commitment both as an in-patient and in the number of visits as an out-patient, which doctors and patients accept as necessary. Second, there is flexibility in treatment plans for patients, as was documented in Mr. Wada's and Masao's cases; psychological well-being of the patient during treatment is the major consideration in modifying plans, within the limits of what is considered good medical practice. Third, both traditional and cosmopolitan concepts are applied during examination and treatment, but actual therapy is limited to the use of traditional techniques wherever possible. Fourth, although attention is paid to social and psychological factors as contributing to the patient's illness, no attempt is made, as in Mr. Ishi's case, for example, to change these factors. Last, family involvement in treatment is rather limited, and when it does occur it is usually in connection with medication and dietary issues.

Kanpō Clinic Patients: General

The cases discussed above exemplify experiences and attitudes that are common to other patients at this clinic. A total of fifty patients—twenty-seven females and twenty-three males—were selected for interviews while they waited to see the doctor. All ages are represented, including babies and young children. Patients over fifty are most numerous and proportionately the same as at small cosmopolitan clinics.

The sample is predominantly urban by birth (74%) and even those of rural origins come mostly from villages very close to an urban environment. The level of formal education is high, and all the patients with six years or less of education are over sixty years of age, with one exception, a Korean. Most patients think of themselves as middle or upper middle class. All the housewives are married to business or professional men. Only four of the patients could be classified as lower class, and they come from families in unskilled trades. They received reductions in fees at the *kanpō* clinic.

The patients' high levels of education (see Table 6) and income (see Table 7) are explained partially by the fact that the clinic does not participate in a health insurance system. It is viewed from the outside as a rather expensive clinic set in a wealthy part of the city. But, among the fifty patients, only fifteen responded that paying the bills was difficult, and many of these pointed out that because their conditions were chronic, the continuous expense of drugs (even with insurance coverage) adds up to as much as the entire cost at the *kanpō* hospital. Because of the fashionable setting, the large, foreign cars waiting outside for some of the patients, and the meticulous formal language spoken at the clinic, most less well-educated patients would not feel comfortable here regardless of the financial aspect. Residence patterns are typical for Kyoto: twenty-eight patients live in a nuclear household and twenty-two reside in an extended household.

The sample does not show more affiliation to religious groups than is usual in Japan (see Table 8 and Japan, Ministry of Education, 1971), and the

TABLE 6
Education of Kanpō *Clinic Patients*

EDUCATION	MALE PATIENTS	FEMALE PATIENTS
Primary school graduate	1	3
Middle school graduate	4	6
High school graduate	4	11
College or university graduate	14	7
Total	23	27

use of East Asian medicine cannot be correlated with special religious beliefs or practices. The use of home remedies and preventive medicine is not significantly different from its use in the families reported in the previous chapter (see Table 2).

Comparisons of this sample with patients attending other East Asian clinics and also with patients attending their cosmopolitan style of family doctor indicate that it is not unusual in any way, except for the levels of education and income mentioned above. Moreover, these patients do not take part particularly in traditional aspects of Japanese life—only five of the patients are highly involved with other forms of traditional Japanese culture.

Medical Problems

On average, 550 patients attend the clinic each month. The medical problems are of all kinds. All the categories of disease shown in Table 9 are represented in my sample of fifty patients. The number of chronic diseases is extremely high, and all but three of the informants had been ill, though not

TABLE 7
Occupations of Kanpō *Clinic Patients*

OCCUPATION	MALE PATIENTS	FEMALE PATIENTS
Professional	5	0
Business, senior executive level	5	0
Housewife	0	19
Independent entrepreneur	4	2
Skilled trades	6	0
Unskilled trades	3	1
Teaching, private or part time	0	5
Total	23	27

TABLE 8
Religious Beliefs of Kanpō *Clinic Patients*

RELIGIOUS BELIEFS	NUMBER OF PATIENTS
Practice of Buddhist ritual	15
General belief in Buddhism but no practice	9
Christian	2
Practice of Shintō ritual	27
No religious belief	24

Note: Many people believe in or perform both Buddhist and Shintō ideas and ritual.

necessarily continuously, for more than one year. Ten had been ill between six and ten years, and eight for over ten years.

Ninety-five percent of the new patients each month have been to a cosmopolitan style of hospital first. When they fail to receive a satisfactory cure or are rejected by cosmopolitan doctors—because they are classified either as incurable or as having no problems—they then try the *kanpō* clinic. About five patients each month are referred back from the *kanpō* clinic to other hospitals. Referrals are made only when either surgery or intensive psychiatric care is considered necessary. Terminal cancer patients are retained and given acupuncture treatment for relief of pain.

Over half of the fifty patients interviewed were surprised to find such a clean and modern building; they said their image of *kanpō* as old-fashioned was now completely changed. The entire sample said that they trusted the doctors completely. Nineteen of the patients added that they believe that

TABLE 9
Principal Conditions Treated at the Kanpō *Clinic in One Month (May)*

CONDITIONS	PERCENTAGE
Neuralgia, lumbago, and arthritis	17.0
Bronchial problems, including asthma and rhinitis	15.0
Digestive problems, including ulcers	14.0
Mild problems such as shoulder stiffness, headaches, and tiredness	11.0
Problems of the circulatory system	10.0
Urology, including nephrosis and nephritis	9.0
Dermatitis	8.0
Other	15.1

Note: Figures are from unofficial clinic records. The categories are those used by the clinic.

their family doctor is as good as the *kanpō* doctors but that cosmopolitan medicine just could not handle their problem. All of the patients agreed that the *kanpō* doctors spend much more time with them, and this they felt was highly advantageous. Several informants went on to note that the total time spent is often longer in the cosmopolitan system, but that it is taken up with impersonal laboratory tests and in going from one department to another.

Many of the patients have been coming to the clinic for an extremely long time (Table 10). Treatment of chronic diseases with herbal medicine takes many months and requires a long time commitment from the patient. Patients rarely complained about this; rather, they emphasized that visits to the clinic had been incorporated into their way of life and made them more thoughtful and responsible about their health. However, painful symptoms can usually be removed at once, and the patient soon feels that some progress is being made.

The following are some typical comments from the patients: "These doctors look at me carefully, and they listen to what I have to say." "In an ordinary hospital it's like being on an assembly line." "Herbal medicine has no bad side effects." "I like the combination of science and herbs." "Western medicine got one part of me better and another part got sick." "Here they treat me like a whole person and not like a machine." And from an in-patient: "I feel like one of the family." Adverse comments from four patients who stopped coming to the clinic focused on the expense and the length of time of the treatment with little improvement to health.

The clinic is well known, and a few patients come from outlying areas of Kyoto and even from the distant countryside. Referrals are predominantly

TABLE 10
Duration of Visits to Kanpō *Clinic*

LENGTH OF TIME	NUMBER OF PATIENTS
Over 10 years	3
2 to 4 years	10
1 to 2 years	8
6 months to 1 year	11
1 month to 6 months	12
Less than 1 month	4
Clinic used permanently as substitute for family doctor	2

from satisfied patients, and the clinic is full to capacity on most days. Some cosmopolitan-style family doctors have good relationships with this clinic and refer patients to it (Table 11); these patients are usually suffering from chronic diseases of several years duration. The clinic does not maintain a close relationship with any other East Asian medical clinic in Kyoto, and patients are never referred on to, or received by referrals from, other East Asian clinics. The doctors do, however, have close relationships with other *kanpō* doctors, and there is a constant exchange of ideas among them.

Because the *kanpō* doctors are M.D.'s and because they combine the use of cosmopolitan medical theory, technology, and classical East Asian medicine, the majority of the patients put themselves completely in their hands and do not visit any other doctor for the duration of their sickness. Most patients believe that chronic diseases are best handled by the *kanpō* doctor and that acute ones should be taken to the cosmopolitan doctor (Table 12); in the future they would select the doctor on the basis of self-diagnosis into these categories.

Answers to the question "Why do you think that you became sick?" (see Table 13) demonstrate the belief among the majority of patients that the environment—social, psychological, and physical—can affect one's health. Further inquiry indicated that every one of the informants was apparently well aware of bacterial, viral, and simple physiological explanations for the various diseases in question, but not one of them chose to give their answers in these terms. All of the informants emphasized that the functioning of mind and body are inseparable and that they mutually influence each other.

The answer "not keeping the rules of life correctly" was given only by people over forty years of age, and when they were asked to expand the idea,

TABLE 11
Introduction to the Kanpō *Clinic*

METHODS OF INTRODUCTION	NUMBER OF PATIENTS
From friends who had been patients or knew patients	23
From relatives	12
From family doctor	7
Read about the clinic in mass media	4
Friends of the *kanpō* doctors	2
Kanpō clinic has always been family clinic	2

TABLE 12
Management of Illness in the Future

Patient's Action	Number of Patients
Visit cosmopolitan doctor first	7
Take a chronic disease to the *kanpō* doctor and an acute one to the family doctor*	29
Take everything except surgery to the *kanpō* doctor	11
Take everything to the *kanpō* doctor	3

*The acute/chronic dichotomy was made by the patients themselves *(kyūsei/mansei)*.

the response was that one should keep in harmony by eating, sleeping, and exercising carefully and by keeping up good relationships with the people around one. Excesses should be avoided.

Every patient said that his or her family was in agreement with the visits to the clinic, although there had sometimes been dissension at first, and that there was cooperation at home regarding diet and so on. In serious cases the doctors had had personal contact with the family, and written instructions on dietary matters are frequently issued for the whole family.

In summary, the principal reason for the selection of the *kanpō* clinic is dissatisfaction with the cosmopolitan medical system by patients suffering with chronic problems, whether these are incapacitating or simply minor functional disorders. The patients have usually tried the cosmopolitan medical system first, and when they receive little or no relief, or are rejected by the cosmopolitan doctor, they turn to East Asian medicine. The majority of

TABLE 13
Origin of Illness

Patient's View of the Cause	Number of Patients
Personal or environmental stress	24
Lack of care with diet	6
"Not keeping the rules of life correctly"*	7
Climatic influence	4
Hereditary constitution	8
Traffic accidents	2
Environmental pollution of specific origin	1

Note: Some informants gave more than one response.
Kisoku tadashii seikatsu o shinakata.

patients have little or no previous experience with *kanpō* in a clinical set-ting—before coming to the clinic their opinion was that it was "old-fash-ioned"—and patients may persist with cosmopolitan medicine for years before they are introduced to the clinic. *Kanpō* is therefore not an alternative that many potential patients are aware of—it is used initially by most people as a last resort when in desperation they will turn to something new, al-though this pattern seems to be changing as the clinic becomes better known. Having found the clinic, most patients feel that something is being done to help them. Only one patient out of the sample of fifty had stopped coming when a checkup was made after a six-month interval, and three more after a twelve-month interval, for reasons of dissatisfaction.

Before discussing further implications of these data, I shall present the beliefs and attitudes of the *kanpō* doctors in order, first, to demonstrate how closely their practice conforms to that recommended in the classical texts, and second, to see how well it conforms to patient needs and expectations.

8

A *Kanpō* Clinic: The Doctors

Attitudes toward Traditional Concepts

The forerunners of the doctors in this clinic were members of the *goseiha* based in the Kansai region. Compared with present-day *kanpō* doctors who practice in Tokyo, the Kyoto doctors are considered rather conservative. In Tokyo many *kanpō* doctors run their private traditional practice in conjunction with a second practice in a cosmopolitan style of hospital. They have rejected much of the classical teaching still accepted by the Kansai doctors and usually do not practice acupuncture at all. However, in the face of opposition from the cosmopolitan medical tradition, factionalism in *kanpō* circles is almost completely overcome and has been replaced by cooperation for the mutual cause, so that *kanpō* doctors all over Japan participate in an active, close-knit organization.

At the annual conference of the Japanese East Asian medical society held in Kyoto in 1974, the senior doctor at the clinic where I studied stated that his continuing objectives are to combine the best facets of both cosmopolitan and East Asian medicine. Broadly speaking, this means that the doctors hold cosmopolitan beliefs about the cellular level of disease causation, use both cosmopolitan and East Asian methods of diagnosis, and use a totally traditional system of therapy.

The *kanpō* doctors believe that the Taoist approach to nature is basically correct and that man should aim to keep his body in balance by trying to sustain a state of adaptation to the environment.[1] Avoiding excesses, eating a

1 The actual language of the *kanpō* doctors, a mixture of scientific and traditional concepts, is retained throughout this analysis.

PLATE 11. Pharmacy of the *kanpō* hospital.

largely traditional diet, and exercising regularly are all considered important. There is no such state as perfect health, because the model of man's body and its relation to the environment is a dynamic one, and though small fluctuations occur constantly, they are not regarded as ill health. Large fluctuations must be treated therapeutically, and the principal aim of all therapy is to restore balance, or a state of dynamic equilibrium. The doctors agree that man is like a microcosm of the universe; they point out that the molecules and compounds of organic chemistry are common to both man and the rest of nature. Their approach is an ecological one in that they believe that nature in general functions as a homeostatic system and that this is also true within the human body. Therapy, that is, intervention by man, should therefore be as light as possible, for it is simply a boost or a catalyst to help nature take its course. Wherever possible therapy should also be as "natural" as possible—that is, simply correcting the diet is the ideal therapy, whereas introducing strong drugs, which are not normally metabolized in large quantities by man, is not held in high regard. The heavy metals of the ancient pharmacopoeia, which were prized as an aid in attaining immortality, have been eliminated.

The doctors use the concept of yin and yang, and they accept the ideas postulated in the *Shōkanron* (Chinese: *Shang han lun*), a treatise on fevers, regarding the progression of diseases from yang to yin (see Chapter 4). They vary their prescriptions accordingly, so that a case of tonsilitis with no fever will receive a mixture of medicines different from that for a case of tonsilitis with fever, even if the infecting bacteria are the same. As the disease progresses and as the manifest symptoms change, so is the prescription changed. Ideally, a patient should be checked on several times a day.

In the case of chronic diseases they do not refer to the *Shōkanron* (the progression of diseases from yang to yin is not considered generally applicable to chronic problems today); they ascertain whether the body is exhibiting an increased or a decreased function by using the abdominal palpation techniques developed in the Edo period in Japan.

The doctors visualize people as basically yin or yang types, but they do not accept the division of the entire body into yin and yang parts except insofar as it is helpful as a classificatory system to refer to certain meridians. They believe that all people become progressively more yin and less yang as they get older, and they take this into consideration during treatment (in general, older people are given therapy that has a mild action). They also believe that annual and diurnal changes occur in the yin/yang balance and that ideally some patients should be treated in the morning, whereas others would respond better in the evening, but in actual practice it is usually impossible to adjust for this.

On the whole the doctors believe that the correspondence system (see Chapter 3) is oversimplified, but they do use it in a general way at times to help in diagnosis and in therapy. For example, a red skin color is associated with heart disease, and a whitish skin color with respiratory problems; tired eyes or pricking sensations in the eyelids are often associated with liver problems; the state of the tongue is used as an aid in diagnosing heart problems; the state of the skin and nails, persistent tastes in the mouth, and so on are all noted, though diagnosis is never made from these observations alone.

Use is also made of the Five Evolutive Phase theory in the application of acupuncture and moxibustion, but the doctors state that the classical cycles are much too abstract and idealistic and only of use theoretically. They say that it is usually impossible to manipulate the flow of energy inside the human body in the complicated ways suggested by the classics. However, the doctors state that the principle often works in a very general way; for example, if the lungs are weak, the kidneys (which follow the lungs in the medical cycle of the five evolutive phases) will usually show a weakness too, and similarly, if the kidneys are off balance, then the liver will often also be off balance. Since one of the principles is to try to give as little treatment as possible, especially in the case of weak patients, the doctors often, for example, insert the needles only on the lung meridian when they are trying to restore balance in both the lung and the kidney meridians, and they state that if they check the pulses afterward they find that indeed both the systems have been affected by the treatment.

Use is never made of the numerical emblems and the charts developed to help predict the occurrence of epidemics and seasonal diseases. The doctors state emphatically that this system is nonsense; yet, perhaps partly because of its influence on the behavior of Japanese people since the Heian period, the doctors, like most Japanese, are highly sensitive to the importance of the effects of climatic and seasonal changes on the human body. They pay particular attention, for example, to seasonal variation in the occurrence of chronic diseases, such as ulcers, which tend to flare up in the spring, and to the effect of the climate on the way in which pain is sensed in certain diseases, such as rheumatoid arthritis. A distinction is made between several types of headaches, depending on the environmental conditions under which they occur. The doctors state that, although cosmopolitan medical practitioners are sometimes sensitive to these variations, they do not adjust their treatment accordingly, as is done in the East Asian system.

In summary, the doctors' principal complaints about the classical belief system are that it is vague and open to numerous interpretations; that it became associated with divination and therefore with what they see as irrational elements; that the classics themselves were reworked again and again over the years by doctors who were not practitioners but simply scholars; and that therefore the system gradually became abstract, too complex, and altogether unwieldy in actual practice. A typical comment by many of the doctors who were interviewed can be summarized as follows: "The Chinese are very philosophical; we Japanese are practical people, and we had to simplify the classics to make them useful for us." Nevertheless, they retain a dynamic concept regarding the relationship of man to the environment and of the nature of the disease process.

The doctors believe in *ki*, and one of them stated: "It definitely exists, and I visualize it as some sort of electrical, magnetic, or thermal energy system, which is not bounded by the human body but probably changes potential as it moves from one environment to another. Inside the human body it may be closely related to the autonomic nervous system, but it is not fully explained in this way."

Causes and Diagnosis of Disease

On the whole, specific, cellular level, explanations for the causes of disease are drawn primarily from cosmopolitan medicine, which the doctors acknowledge is greatly superior to East Asian medicine in this respect. Explanations for the patient's benefit, however, put stress on all possible factors and are not limited, for example, to bacterial invasion as the answer. The patient's "why" questions are answered very fully, and it is stressed that bacteria do not usually constitute a threat unless the body is already predisposed to infection due to environmental, hereditary, dietary, or emotional factors. Similarly, while the doctors are actually relieving the pain, they help the patient establish reasons, such as climatic factors, stress, and tension, in addition to the actual functional problem in the body, for the present state of ill health. The explanation for disease is always given in terms of the "whole man" and his relation to the environment.

The doctors say that both cosmopolitan and East Asian techniques of diagnosis are essential and are directed toward different ends. The cosmopolitan style of diagnosis is a technique designed primarily to aid in establishing causes of disease at the cellular level. East Asian diagnosis (see Chapter 3), on the other hand, provides a method of describing the present state of the entire body and establishes how one part of the body or the environment is affecting other parts of the body. The doctors believe that, in order to catch as many diseases as early as possible (their ultimate aim), they must use both a reductionistic and an inductive approach. The cosmopolitan, reductionistic approach is most useful for acute, localized bacterial infections and for problems of mechanical failure. The East Asian, inductive approach is particularly useful in cases of chronic problems, in which the entire body is gradually brought out of balance, and for all problems at an early, nonspecific state of development. This distinction is not exclusive, however, and they believe that both systems should be applied to all patients.

The function of diagnosis is therefore, first of all, to eliminate the possibility of problems that need surgery or of contagious bacterial infections that cannot be handled at the clinic. For this, cosmopolitan diagnosis is used; with the East Asian diagnostic system it is possible to detect that, for example, the stomach is not functioning well, but it is impossible to ascertain if this is due to a malignant growth or simply to a small ulcer. From this point on, diagnosis is basically East Asian in technique and is used to decide if the patient is exhibiting yin or yang symptoms, increased or reduced body function, and to amass as much information about the body as possible.

In order to make a traditional diagnosis and to administer acupuncture and moxa, the doctors think in functional, inductive terms and of the interdependence of parts of the body. When they state that a patient has a weak respiratory system they mean that the whole complex of lungs, skin, nose, throat, bronchial passages, parts of the nervous system, and some aspects of the immunological system are not functioning well. Similarly, in the liver system they include the idea not only of the liver itself but some of the lymphatic system, part of the hormone system, particularly in relation to sexual functioning, part of the circulatory system, part of the autonomic nervous system, part of the immunological system, and part of the functioning of the eyes. Therapy is directed at restoring balance throughout the entire system. The doctors accept the tri-heater system and the heart constrictor system (see Chapter 3); they use the meridians and pulses related to these systems of diagnosis and therapy.

Labeling the patient's problems with the name of a disease is not important, but it is used, the doctors say, because it is convenient, first, as an aid during the clinical discussion of cases, and second, because patients want to be given some kind of scientific label for their problem.

Traditional practitioners believe that by using the East Asian system they can catch potential problems earlier than by using laboratory techniques: by taking the pulses they can detect small functional changes in the body before they are quantifiable through blood or urine tests and before microscopic cellular changes take place. The pulse diagnosis is combined with close observation of changes at the body surface, and treatment is prescribed accordingly. Thus, the doctors are frequently treating minor functional changes that have no name in cosmopolitan medicine, diseases in which the patient's chief complaints are tiredness, headaches, occasional dizziness, numbness, and so on.

The doctors have no scientific explanation for the mechanism of the pulses as they are recognized in traditional medicine. They state that with experience one can definitely feel the different pulses and can also feel that the quality has changed after treatment. They also believe that the pulse quality varies with the season and diurnally, but they state that some of the minute differences in pulse types which the Chinese classics claim to be able to differentiate are doubtful. The pulse is important in the application of acupuncture and moxibustion. A doctor who only uses herbal medicine needs simply to know the general constitution of the body (*karada no taishitsu to honshitsu*), whether the patient is in a yin or a yang state and whether he has fever, vomiting, diarrhea, and so on; the state of each individual organ ascertained by taking the pulse is not so important.

Treatment

The ultimate aim of treatment is to restore balance to the whole body system. The doctors believe that specializing in one aspect of the therapeutic system is not adequate and they do not believe that removing the principal complaint is sufficient. Dietary advice is given to most patients and is considered of fundamental importance for good health. The doctors believe that changes in dietary habits, particularly since the end of World War II, have been so drastic that the body constitution of the Japanese has been unable to adapt satisfactorily in so short a time and that this is the cause of many minor illnesses. In addition, the doctors believe that the Japanese do not yet know how to eat a balanced Western kind of diet and that this compounds the problem.

Dietary advice is based on the classical theories of balancing yin and yang foods, but the doctors do not present their ideas in the classical terminology. They talk in terms of vitamins, carbohydrates, proteins, and so on, and they believe that a diet balanced in the classical way will also provide a scientifically nutritious meal. Patients are told to avoid excesses of every type of food, to try to eat fruit and vegetables that are in season, and whenever possible, to avoid artificial preservatives.

If health cannot be restored by simply adjusting the diet, then combinations of herbal therapy, acupuncture, and moxibustion are used. The doctors agree that massage is also useful, but mostly for mild problems, and they do not in fact practice it.

133

Specific advice on exercise is not usually given to patients—the doctors say that everyone knows that exercise is good for them and that they should try to fit it into their daily lives.

No synthesized medicine is ever used unless a patient has already been receiving massive doses of hormones or antibiotics when he arrives at the clinic. In these cases the doses are reduced gradually and doses of herbal medicine are slowly increased. No vitamins or tonics are ever used. It is believed that a well-balanced diet can supply all the basic needs of the body.

One of the doctors explained his ideas about the differences in Western and Eastern approaches to therapeutic systems in the following way: "It is like the difference between the knight and the samurai. A knight must never retreat, he attacks with all his might until the enemy is destroyed. A samurai, on the other hand, learns to bend before an opponent, he allows the opponent to advance, but he is watching for a 'weak' point. He then induces the opponent to destroy himself by luring him off balance, and in his weak position one small blow from the samurai is all that is needed to finish the contest." This, of course, is the basic principle for many of the martial arts in Japan and for handling disputes in interpersonal relationships. That it is applied to problems of sickness is not surprising.

Herbal Therapy

Most of the herbs have to be imported from mainland China even today because, despite extensive experimentation, the Japanese cannot reproduce the natural ecological environment of many of the herbs well enough to grow plants with the right proportions of active principles in them. This means that supplies are limited and expensive. The kanpō doctors are in a dilemma: the more patients they get, the more acute becomes the problem of supplies. Furthermore, the Chinese have noted the increased interest in herbal medicine in Japan recently, and prices have gone up to as much as ten times their original cost in the last three years.

The dried material is tested roughly on importation to assess whether the main active principles are present in sufficient quantities. The doctors say that in practice the effectiveness of each batch of herbs varies considerably and that the accurate chemical analysis required to allow them to control for this would be very time-consuming. They are not worried by this variation, however, because they are administering mild doses over a long period of time, and some variation in the strength of each dose is therefore not very significant. They state that the time of day and the season in which the herbs are gathered is very important to ensure that the correct proportion of active principles are present, and that the classical texts seem to have been very accurate in this respect.

The clinic stocks about six hundred herbs of which around three hundred are used frequently. Although it is stated that the medicine is prescribed individually for each patient, most of the herbs are in fact premixed, as they have been since classical times, into prescriptions which have been handed down through the years in the pharmacopoeia. The prescriptions are designed to cure not specific diseases, however, but rather, sets of symptoms, so that two patients with, say, asthma, will receive either a similar or a different prescription, depending on their individual pattern of symptoms. As the course of the disease progresses, and as the symptoms change, so is the prescription changed as the doctor sees fit.

The doctors keep the yin/yang distinction in their heads carefully all the time when prescribing medicine, and a patient in a yin state will receive a mixture that is predominantly yang, and vice versa. It is believed that if one administers a yang type of medicine to a patient who is in a yang state, it can be extremely dangerous and the patient could die. The reverse is not true. A yin type of medicine given to a yin patient will simply not be efficacious. Many mixtures are neutral, and these are given to patients who do not exhibit strong symptoms one way or the other. The *gosei* system is therefore acknowledged and preserved by the doctors. The *gomi* system (see Chapter 3), on the other hand, is used only implicitly. Herbal mixtures are prescribed for their action on a certain body system, but they are never classified today according to their "flavor." The dosage is modified according to the patient's age, body weight, and constitution, and a particularly weak patient will receive very mild doses. Small, mild doses of medicine taken four or five times a day are thought to be better than larger doses taken less frequently.

It is believed that herbal medicine is like traditional food in that both are derived directly from nature, and no sharp distinction is made between the two—they are quantitatively but not qualitatively different. Similarly, no sharp distinction is made between food and poison. The chief complaint against synthetic medicine is that it is made in a laboratory and that the doses are extremely strong for the human body. Imbibing artificially purified and concentrated materials of any kind is considered very bad. Recent experiments with herbal medicine have indicated that the purified active principle is less effective as a medicine than is the crude extract because the trace elements, and other molecules considered unimportant to date, play a vital role on ingestion and provide a limiting effect, so that the reaction in the body does not go too far and cause unwanted side effects (Sakaguchi 1963). Crude extracts of some herbal mixtures have also been shown to have antibacterial properties (Kyōgoku et al. 1973).

The doctors state that of all the East Asian therapeutic techniques herbal medicine is the most profound and has the most long-lasting effect on the body; they believe that in some cases, if the treatment is continued long enough, they can change the basic constitution of the patient and enhance antibody production permanently, so that in allergy-prone patients the reaction is no longer produced even in the presence of the precipitating antigen.

In the *kanpō* clinic under study the crude plant extracts are prepared as tiny granules and stored as such. The actual prescription for a patient frequently makes use of as many as five or ten herbal extracts, which are mixed by the clinic pharmacist and poured into airtight cellophane bags so that each bag holds one dose of medicine. It is thus very easy to take. Other *kanpō* clinics make it a policy to issue the prescription to the patient in its original plant form. They believe that the patient's daily active involvement in the preparation of his or her own medicine is part of the healing process and that the vapors given off during the preparation of the extract are highly therapeutic—this, of course, is particularly true in the case of respiratory problems.

Acupuncture and Moxibustion Therapy

The needles used in acupuncture are made of stainless steel and are of varying gauges and lengths. They are inserted by hand with the guide tube (*kudabari*) developed in Edo Japan to help the blind practice successfully. After insertion the needles may be left in place for up to ten minutes. No electrical acupuncture is ever used. The aim is to avoid all pain during treatment (usually this is completely successful) and to give as mild a stimulus as is possible and still be considered effective. Patients sometimes experience tingling sensations or feelings of numbness. They may become mildly euphoric after the treatment. Sometimes the needles are manipulated by hand while they are inserted at certain pressure points; but the doctors do not believe, as it is stated in the classics, that if they manipulate it one way they will draw off excess energy and if they manipulate it in other ways they will put in additional energy.

In moxibustion therapy a ball of moxa the size of a small pea is placed on the appropriate pressure point and ignited with a burning stick of incense. The aim is to avoid scarring if possible, and when it becomes very hot the moxa is removed before it actually burns the skin. Moxa is used less frequently than acupuncture, but it is sometimes found to be highly effective in controlling generalized chronic conditions such as, for example, lupus erythematosus. It can be used interchangeably with acupuncture in the treatment of mild, nonspecific problems. Moxa is also used in this clinic against warts and some localized fungal infections, and for bursitis and rhinitis, among other things.

Psychological and Social Aspects of Therapy

The doctors stress that they are dealing mostly with patients with diseases that have a strong psychosomatic component. They believe that obtaining the patient's cooperation in the healing process is vital and that this is more true for East Asian therapy than for the cosmopolitan style of therapy, where, they state, the drugs are so strong that some biochemical effect will take place whatever the patient's attitude. The *kanpō* doctors firmly believe that the functionings of man's mind and body are inseparable and that man's biochemical and physiological processes, which in turn depend on climatic changes, diet, and hereditary constitution as well as his social milieu, are constantly modifying his emotional and subjective state. The reverse is of course also true. It is a perfect example of Needham's "correlative thinking" (1962, p. 281), and it poses a dilemma. Since no one factor is considered primarily causal in precipitating ill health, what aspect, therefore, should one manipulate in order to start the therapeutic process? In actual practice, the problem is treated as though the physiological and biochemical aspects are most important. Therapy focuses on diet, herbal medicine, acupuncture, and massage with the ultimate objective of bringing about a physiological change within the body, leading to tension reduction and incidentally to a calmer emotional state. It does not emphasize reduction of stress in the social milieu or a psychotherapeutic approach.

This attitude has apparently been prevalent from early times, because there is little mention in the classics of verbal psychotherapy of any kind. On the contrary, the emphasis was on a quiet and calm meeting, often lasting several hours, between doctor and patient. This could lead to insights on the part of the patient and potentially to an acceptance of social conditions as given and unchanging and to a reaffirmation of the social order and of Confucian values.

Although the *kanpō* doctors take note of the patient's social situation, they use this knowledge only as a means of assessing the kinds of problems they are up against, as an aid in diagnosis. They never give advice on how to change the social situation or how to relieve stress at the social level unless the patient specifically demands this kind of information, which is rarely done. It is assumed that, though the social milieu, hereditary factors, the climate, and so on cannot be modified to any great degree, the correct emotional attitude will allow one to accept certain things as given and unchangeable. By inducing biochemical change, which helps restore balance to the emotional state, the vicious circle, *akujunkan,* as it is called, is thus broken.

There is also a belief that personality is a relatively fixed entity, that people are born with and socialized to certain personality types and actually label themselves as such. But, because emotional states are affected by the dynamic interplay between man and his environment, changes in emotion are viewed as natural and as having a transient effect on the basic personality. Emotions can therefore be changed therapeutically, but one's basic personality cannot be. These ideas are probably derived from early Japanese culture and show a combination of Confucian, Buddhist, and East Asian medical elements. According to Confucian tenets, social roles are ascribed rather than achieved, and the needs of the individual have always been subordinated to that of the group. One succeeded in life as part of a group, and group affiliation was a lifelong commitment—there was little room for social mobility. The individual, therefore, in order to succeed, has to be compliant and flexible toward the group. In contrast, possibly owing to

Buddhist ideas of *karma* and to East Asian medical theories, underneath the flexibility is a personality core which is seen as given and unchanging. Both doctors and patients believe, therefore, that tackling medical problems at the physiological end is the best method. Attempting to change the social structure or the family situation or trying to alter personality in any radical way is too disruptive and is considered to be virtually impossible. On the other hand, if the body chemistry is altered and the patient is brought back into physiological balance, he or she will then automatically have better emotional attitudes and thus be able to act in the best way at the social level. The ultimate aim is not "perfect health" nor the elimination of disease; it is adjustment to the environment.

Patients are never rejected from the *kanpō* clinic with the diagnosis that nothing is wrong with them. Using the East Asian pulse diagnosis, the doctors believe that they can always detect small deviations from normal. Moreover, they do not consider these small deviations to be trivial problems, because there is a belief that they act as signals and that if they are ignored, worse problems are likely to develop. No patient, therefore, is ever given to feel that he is making a fuss about nothing, and his ability to comment in detail on the state of his body is welcomed when a traditional diagnosis is made. Moreover, there is no sharp dichotomy visualized between states of health and sickness; they are seen as one continuum. Sickness is thought of as a normal response to the pressures of daily life.

The question then arises: Are the doctors providing a holistic treatment consistent with their philosophy and beliefs about the human body and the cause of disease? I believe that they feel that it is not their job to provide the "complete cure." In fact, they see their role as rather modest: they simply furnish the catalyst that sets the reaction in motion. This point will be developed more fully later when the concept of holism is discussed.

Life History Material on Two *Kanpō* Doctors

Without exception, all of the doctors at the clinic chose to specialize in *kanpō* because either they or a member of their family was cured of some chronic problem through the use of herbal medicine.

Dr. Nishimura was born in a small seaside town and is the son of a dentist.[2] His mother practices *shiatsu*. He says he has no special religious affiliation and is middle-of-the-road in politics. His father was ill for five years when Dr. Nishimura was a teenager, but after prolonged use of moxibustion he finally recovered. He recommended that his son try to study some East Asian medicine along with his regular studies in medical school. While a third-year medical student at Kyoto University, Dr. Nishimura started to come to the *kanpō* clinic to study in his spare time. He was asked to practice full time in the *kanpō* clinic upon graduation, and he cemented the situation by marrying the daughter of the director of the clinic. Dr. Nishimura says that when practicing medicine he thinks predominantly like a cosmopolitan doctor because the bulk of his education was in scientific and deductive thinking. He has also read many of the Chinese classics and believes that there can and should be a synthesis between the two approaches to man. In his private life, Dr. Nishimura lives out this synthesis to a remarkable degree. He lives in a modern apartment in Kyoto; one of the main rooms is completely Japanese in style and is used strictly in the traditional way. The other main room is furnished with extremely modern furniture, which exhibits the unusual quality in Japan of a deep appreciation for modern Western taste. Dr. Nishimura practiced *sumo* (Japanese wrestling) as a child and then took up judo, and is now a fourth degree black belt. He has also practiced the tea ceremony for six years and believes that much of his philosophical development is derived from this art. He is at present learning to play golf.

As a child he was given herbal medicine almost exclusively, and now, in his adult life, he and his family use only East Asian medicine and take great care to try to eat a balanced, traditional diet with as few artificial foods as possible. Like all East Asian doctors, Dr. Nishimura believes strongly that if his own health is not good, not only does this set a bad example but he cannot feel the pulses or practice acupuncture effectively.

He states that, in a way, the patient is the doctor. Each patient should be treated as an individual, and since the purpose of diagnosis is not to categorize a disease but to map a pattern of symptoms, the doctor must learn to make judgments principally from the patient's subjective assessment of his or her own state and not to rely solely on knowledge drawn from books or

2 Fictitious names are used throughout the book for all medical practitioners.

on laboratory tests. Dr. Nishimura considers that objective measurements do not always allow for fine enough distinctions to be made.

Dr. Nishimura says that on the whole it is easier to treat patients who are of middle age and upward, and this he attributed to the fact that they are more sensitive to nature's cyclical changes and to traditional values. He believes that they tend to look after themselves better because they are aware of the vulnerability of their body and health.

While the theory and practice of medicine have a fairly coherent philosophy in the West, based on the scientific principles of the use of experimentation and logical deduction, with the ultimate aim of objectivity, Dr. Nishimura believes that any medical system that leaves out a humanistic approach will never be satisfying. He is emphatic that the whole of *kanpō* cannot be subsumed under a scientific rubric as we know it today; that there must always be an intuitive, creative element in medicine. Further, he believes that the value system that is applied in medicine should never be derived from a scientific framework.

With regard to the classical Chinese system, Dr. Nishimura believes that philosophy played too great a part traditionally and that, as a result, the theory of medicine became highly elaborate and separated from reality, leading to the delivery of poor medical practice.

Dr. Nishimura attends medical conferences and conducts scientific research on *kanpō* because he believes that it is vital to establish rules in medicine wherever possible, because he feels that the classical theories must be tested thoroughly, and because he believes that the only way to promote the practice of East Asian medicine in modern Japan (and incidentally to gain financial support) is to impress medical administrators and cosmopolitan doctors by using their methods.

Dr. Yamada was born in Hiroshima into a doctor's family. His father had always had an interest in East Asian medicine and combined the use of a little acupuncture with his regular medical practice. When Dr. Yamada's father developed a kidney stone, he treated himself, using only moxibustion. Dr. Yamada became involved with the *kanpō* clinic during his student days, and then, as an intern, he was placed on a ward for nephrosis patients. He was very depressed with their lack of progress and was particularly concerned because he felt that, again and again, while the hormone treatment could often help the functioning of the kidneys, the depression and other side effects that occurred were so debilitating that gradually the patient's psychological cooperation was lost, and the medical problem was compounded. When allowed to try out herbal medicine in the university hospital with interested patients, Dr. Yamada felt so elated with the results that he asked to join the *kanpō* clinic permanently. Dr. Yamada states that he is basically a Buddhist, although he performs no rituals, and has read a lot on the subject. He believes that some form of religious belief is vital to the recovery of health. Like Dr. Nishimura, in his personal life he has always used East Asian medicine predominantly and tries to eat natural foods in season. He is a second degree black belt in *kendō* (fencing), and he too studies the tea ceremony. Because he and Dr. Nishimura are the same age and have trained in the same *kanpō* clinic, their beliefs are very similar. Dr. Yamada, however, is not one of the family, and one day he will have to leave the clinic. He says he cannot possibly afford to set up a *kanpō* clinic in Hiroshima and so he will probably take over his father's practice, where he will emphasize the use of acupuncture and moxibustion.

Conclusions

The *kanpō* doctors are M.D.'s who are trying to integrate the use of East Asian and cosmopolitan medical systems. They believe that both systems have shortcomings, which can be reduced by the use of the two systems in conjunction with each other. Their aims are to find environmental, social, psychological, and hereditary causes for why the patients have become ill, to establish in detail the patterns of symptoms they present and how these change with time, and then to apply suitable therapy. They use basically cosmopolitan notions of specific, cellular level, disease causation, cosmopolitan and East Asian diagnostic techniques, and a totally East Asian system of therapy. The function of therapy is to bring about biophysiological changes in the patient and to raise his ability and interest in being more responsible for his own body. While psychosocial dimensions of therapy are acknowledged, these are not considered within the realm of the doctor to deal with. The ultimate aim is not the restoration of "perfect health" (which they view as nonexistent), it is to bring the patient's body back into dynamic balance and harmony with his environment. Since they feel realistically that this state can never be maintained, they view the entire process of restoration of health as one of successful adjustment and compromise rather than a "total cure."

The value systems of doctors and patients in the clinic seem very close, and this certainly accounts for a large part of the patients' feelings of satisfaction. Both doctors and patients believe in combining science with the East Asian medical tradition; sickness is viewed as a natural state and is the result of a combination of precipitating factors; personal responsibility for the occurrence and alleviation of sickness is considered important; and finally, the avoidance of excesses and "unnatural" things such as synthesized food and medicine is valued.

Before comparing the *kanpō* clinic with other types of East Asian clinics, we shall turn briefly to herbal pharmacies and their role in the panorama of traditional medicine.

9

Herbal Pharmacies

In addition to the medical clinics that prescribe herbs as part of their therapeutic system, scattered all over Kyoto there are pharmacies that specialize in the sale of herbal medicine.

To practice pharmacy it is necessary to graduate from a four-year university program and to obtain a license by passing a national examination. While attending one of the major universities, it is often possible to specialize for one year in *shōyaku,* the study of natural materials as medicine. Many younger *kanpō* pharmacists have done this. The formal study and teaching of *shōyaku* on a large scale has been implemented only since World War II. Prior to this, it was usual for herbal pharmacists to attend high school and then to become an apprentice, usually in their father's business. When the licensing system was established those pharmacists who had five or more years of practical experience were automatically given a license.

Today there is a department of pharmaceutical standards in the government, which regulates the importation, quality, and sale, not only of synthesized medicine, but also of all herbal medicine. Restrictions on *kanpō* are mostly limited to the use of heavy metals. In Japanese folk medicine *(minkanyaku),* the use of animal material such as bear's gall, rhinoceros horn, monkey skulls, deer antlers, and snakes is common, and there are no legal restrictions on the sale of this type of material.

Kyoto was formerly divided into districts based on professional and occupational differences. The traditional area for pharmacists was on Nijō Street between Kawabata Street and Oike Street, and several of the oldest

PLATE 12. A pharmacist of the Edo period chopping up plant material, which he will later grind up into smaller particles using the pestle and mortar beside him.

kanpō shops in Kyoto can still be found in this area. One such shop belongs to Mr. Eguchi, who is the seventh generation in his family to run the business. The building is more than 250 years old, a beautiful reminder of the craftsmanship involved in the construction of upper-middle-class houses in Edo Japan. The shop, which used to be open-fronted, is now separated from the continuous noise of passing traffic by sliding doors and a display window full of dead snakes, squirrels, monkey skulls, giant salamanders, and other eye-catching items. Mr. Eguchi's ancestors were doctors, and the building was originally used as a doctor's office. Shortly after the Meiji

145

Restoration, Mr. Eguchi's grandfather decided to change his practice into a pharmacy rather than comply with the new edicts requiring that he learn cosmopolitan medical techniques.

Mr. Eguchi himself, upon graduation from middle-school, was apprenticed to his father, and now, at age fifty-five, he is a disappointed man because none of his three children wants to take on the business. His wife has been helping with the business for thirty-five years. They are practicing Buddhists and also attend many Shintō festivals. They describe themselves as old-fashioned Kyoto people, and Mr. Eguchi's hobby is growing *bonsai*.

Historically, in both China and Japan, experimentation with herbal mixtures was carried out inside the doctors' families and the knowledge thus obtained was kept highly secret, for the doctors believed that their continued success depended in large part on their developing a mixture more effective than those of their rivals. This naturally led to factionalism and intense competition. The general term for small family businesses where techniques are passed on secretly from father to son is *kaden*, and the herbal pharmacy business is one area where this tradition is still strong. Mr. Eguchi's pharmacy is just such a business; he still has the family records of the prescriptions passed on to him, and he uses them regularly. He says he has never read the classics, that they are too vague and idealistic, and that the inherited, "tried and true" recipes of his family are all that he needs. As with other aspects of the classical system, the pharmacopoeia give a theoretical presentation of ideal medical practice. The vast majority of patients received, and are still receiving, local variations of classical formulae, as is the case with Mr. Eguchi's customers.

Mr. Eguchi sells both herbal and folk medicine, and like all the pharmacists, he makes a clear distinction between the two, based on the definitions in Chapter 1. Although he believes that *kanpōyaku* (herbal medicine) is far superior to folk medicine, he supplies folk medicine to customers who come and ask him specifically for it. *Kanpō* materials are imported from mainland China, Korea, South East Asia, India, and Africa by wholesale companies, and Mr. Eguchi buys his supplies from the wholesale dealers.

The prescriptions Mr. Eguchi uses were originally based on the *gosei* and *gomi* systems of classification, but Mr. Eguchi never thinks in these terms. He simply remembers, for example, that for a cold with a headache and fever he should mix certain herbs, and that for a cold with nasal discharge, shoulder stiffness, and no fever other herbs are more appropriate. In his family records he has endless variations of patterns of symptoms with the appropriate herbs listed underneath.

The folk medical supplies are delivered directly to Mr. Eguchi's shop by hunters and collectors of herbs who drive in once a month from the mountains. Mr. Eguchi buys supplies from them only when they have been collected in the correct season. A bear's gall is not effective as a medicine unless the bear was killed in the fall or early winter, and then it is worth forty dollars. The leaves of plants are best if harvested in midsummer, but seeds should be collected in the fall, and roots in winter.

No attempt has been made to modernize Mr. Eguchi's building inside. All transactions take place with the participants sitting on *tatami* (straw mats). The main room is rather dark and full of stored medicine, mostly contained in very old and valuable medicine chests. Larger batches of dried materials and various parts of animals are strung from the ceiling. Several old tools for grinding, chopping, and sieving herbs lie on the floor and are still used regularly. The kettle is constantly boiling on the charcoal brazier, and customers are frequently offered a cup of tea. Mr. Eguchi and his wife both use the Kyoto dialect, and their approach to customers is one of polite but friendly service.

The customers are mostly neighborhood people, but because this shop has a well-established reputation some people travel for many miles to stock up with preventive medicines. The customers range from lower-middle-class (like Mr. Eguchi himself) to middle- and upper-class people who are not usually from the nieghborhood. Local customers are normally sold ten days' supply of medicine, which comes, on the average, to between seven and nine dollars. Mr. Eguchi says the number of customers has been increasing lately and that he also supplies medicine to several cosmopolitan doctors who suffer from chronic ailments. Approximately 70 percent of his customers have chronic problems, such as allergies, asthma, mild nervous problems, and tiredness; 30 percent have mild acute problems, including colds, headaches, sore throats, stomach complaints, and so forth. He sees some cancer patients for whom he prescribes pain-relieving mixtures. People with serious acute problems very rarely come to the shop, nor do people with skeletal, muscular, or joint problems.

When a customer enters the shop he or she is usually asked to sit down,

147

and Mr. Eguchi or his wife enters into an informal conversation, which gradually focuses on the customer's sickness. By law a pharmacist is not allowed to touch a customer, and so, in order to make a diagnosis, although Mr. Eguchi believes in the classical diagnostic system, he can only use the techniques of observation and questioning. This he does fully, and he keeps records on all his regular customers. He says he makes particular note of skin condition, the state of the nails, the sound of the voice, and the way the customer sits. Many customers who have already visited their family doctor often present Mr. Eguchi with a detailed diagnosis of their problems, but he finds that in order to prescribe according to his East Asian medical theories he must utilize his own knowledge of patterns of symptoms. Mr. Eguchi says that, in addition to questioning and observation, he uses his "sixth sense" (*dairokkukan*), and that this is where experience is vital. He states that "experience is knowledge." He gives advice on diet, based on classical theories, and he explains to the customer what he thinks the problem is, but he says he never uses classical terminology, because "customers these days think that is simply superstition, and they want a more scientific explanation." He believes that the primary cause of all diseases is an upset of the balance of *ki* owing to psychological stress and that his medicine will only relieve symptoms temporarily unless the customer can change his way of life.

Mr. Eguchi thinks that synthetic medicines should be used for all "serious acute" problems. He occasionally sends customers to acupuncture clinics, particularly if they have muscular problems. Mr. Eguchi says he has poor relationships with ordinary pharmacists, particularly those who have recently started to stock prepackaged herbal medicine—a new item on the market. These pharmacists, he says, are only interested in profit, and since herbal medicine has become so popular, they sell it, but they have no knowledge of its application.

Mr. Eguchi belongs to a local union with other *kanpō* pharmacists, which gives him some security as an independent businessman. He does not attend any conferences or read much about recent advances in *kanpō*. He says he enjoys his life, which is unhurried, and he appreciates the freedom and independence a company employee does not enjoy.

Not all herbal pharmacies have a long historical tradition; in the heart of downtown Kyoto, Mr. Watanabe owns a *kanpō* pharmacy, which has been in existence for only fifty years. Started by Mr. Watanabe's father, it is a tiny but tidy shop jammed full of *kanpō* and folk medicine. There are a table and two chairs in front of the counter, and customers sit comfortably and chat with Mr. Watanabe and each other. Mr. Watanabe, now forty-eight, graduated from Kyoto University with a degree in pharmacy. He reads profusely and talks freely about his philosophical attitudes and his way of life with no trace of his native Kyoto dialect. He has no formal religious beliefs. His son is at present studying pharmacy, but Mr. Watanabe says that knowledge learned at school regarding herbal medicine is very limited and research oriented and that his son will really start his training in the shop.

The customers are mostly middle and upper middle class; some are from the neighborhood, but many drop in after a morning's shopping in the downtown department stores. Several of the customers are doctors. Mr. Watanabe says all of them have chronic problems, with the exception of a few with coughs, colds, and stomach aches. He keeps records on all of his customers and writes the diagnosis out in patterns of symptoms according to the East Asian style. Careful note is taken of changes in symptoms as the disease progresses, and the prescription is changed accordingly. Mr. Watanabe makes his diagnosis primarily by questioning and observation in a traditional manner and states that he is aiming for a "scientific" approach to the classical theories. By this he means that, although he accepts most of the traditional theories, he would like to have the techniques and efficacy of herbal medicine tested rigorously on scientific principles. He sends his customers to cosmopolitan doctors if he has any doubts about his diagnosis, but he never sends them to acupuncture clinics. He believes that the training of acupuncturists is inadequate. He states that no one in his family has been to a doctor of any kind since his son was a baby.

Mr. Watanabe has read modern editions of the classics, and his shop window displays open copies of some of them along with tall jars of beautifully prepared herbs. He uses about thirty basic preparations for all his customers and has supplies of a further two hundred herbs, which he can add to the basic recipe as he sees fit. Folk medicine is sold only when requested by a customer.

He gives clear explanations to customers in scientific terms, and he frequently lectures them on their shortcomings with regard to diet and the overuse of synthetic medicine. "Poor diet is the most fundamental cause in all sickness," states Mr. Watanabe. He believes that overdependency on medicine is a big problem in modern Japan: "People have to learn once again how to be responsible for their own bodies"—a sentiment that echoes the classical tradition.

Several of the major pharmaceutical companies have recently produced mixtures of herbs packaged in boxes in an easy-to-take form. Many customers like this because, since it is mass produced, it is cheaper than individually prepared mixtures, and because it does not have to be prepared in the home before it can be taken. A ten days' supply costs about six dollars. In order to keep his business prosperous, Mr. Watanabe feels he must stock these popular brands, but he agrees that prepackaged medicine violates the classical principles and cannot be adjusted to the customer's individual needs.

Mr. Watanabe belongs to the *kanpō* pharmacy union and attends pharmaceutical conferences related to *kanpō*. He feels secure, enjoys his independence, and believes he is doing an important and responsible job in his community. His calm, friendly confidence is most impressive.

Mr. Sakura is a licensed pharmacist who, until his retirement, worked in a large pharmaceutical company producing drugs. Three or four years before his retirement he became interested in *kanpō* because of his concern about the side effects of modern medicine. Upon retiring at sixty, he bought an elegant, traditional shop in the Katsura region of Kyoto and transformed it into a *kanpō* shop. He taught himself how to mix medicines by reading modern translations of many of the classics and by studying at seminars given by *kanpō* doctors. He says that the prescriptions inherited through the years and used in most traditional herbal pharmacies are little better than folk medicine, which he does not believe to be very effective. Mr. Sakura states that his medicine is mixed according to the classics and is true *kanpō*. He is well acquainted with the *gosei* and *gomi* systems of classification.

The clientele at the shop, which is now two years old, is gradually increasing, and his customers average ten a day—a number that Mr. Sakura considers just right. He can make a living, has time to chat with the customers, mix the medicine, and relax as well. His five brothers are all doctors, and when he has any doubts about his diagnosis he confers with them, and they in turn refer patients to him. Mr. Sakura believes that diseases arise through lack of balance in the body and stresses multi-causality rather than uni-causal origins for the lack of balance. He uses classical methods of diagnosis and even takes the pulse if he sees fit. He is not concerned about legal restrictions on touching his customers, since he feels he knows them all as friends.

Mr. Sakura believes that *kanpō* is superior for all types of chronic diseases. He stocks no cosmopolitan or boxed, herbal medicine and does not refer patients to acupuncture clinics. The calm assurance of Mr. Sakura leads to a ready trust, and he, in turn, is happy with the knowledge that he is making the best of his retirement.

Today there are many cosmopolitan pharmacies in Kyoto in which the owner has decided to stock prepackaged herbal medicine. The usual reason given for selling it is that "these days customers constantly ask for it because they are frightened of strong drugs." The financial aspect of selling *kanpō* is often mentioned, too: ordinary pharmacists believe that good herbalists are making large profits because of the recent increased interest in *kanpō*. Very few of these pharmacists have learned about the prescription of herbs in college, but since each box is labeled with details as to which disease it is suitable for, this does not present a problem, and it is handled as though it were synthetic medicine.

In summary, the customers who come to the herbal pharmacies are of three basic kinds. The majority have a family doctor whom they consult for all types of acute problems and also for major chronic problems. But for minor ailments, particularly those associated with pain, such as headaches, stomach aches, menstrual cramps, mild neuralgia, and so forth, they make use of an herbal pharmacy, just as their parents did before them. They choose the local herbal pharmacy where common bonds of community involvement enhance feelings of trust.

The second type of customer comes from families that have always tried to avoid the use of doctors or of synthetic medicine. These customers are frequently from upper- or middle-class traditional Kyoto families, or from the families of priests, or are part of a religious organization. Historically, the urban upper classes and priests had the most ready access to *kanpō* (see Chapter 4). Many have continued to follow the East Asian belief system through the years, and they resort to a cosmopolitan doctor only when beset by a really acute problem. Much of the herbal material they buy is used for prevention rather than for therapy. This second group of customers tends to

151

choose a pharmacist because of his long family tradition as an herbalist, and they often travel considerable distances to buy their medicine.

The third type of customer is part of the recent "*kanpō* boom," as it is known in Japan—people who are concerned about the side effects of synthetic medicine and are causing a rush of business for the herbalists. Included in this group are cosmopolitan doctors, people with long-standing chronic complaints, and many mothers of small children. Along with increased patronage there is a broadening of the categories of illness that are considered suitable for the pharmacist to handle. After first receiving the diagnosis from their family doctor, many patients take not only mild problems but internal complaints of all kinds to the herbalist, including mild ulcers, mild heart problems, liver problems, and so on.

Although some people in Japan go to the family doctor with almost all of their medical problems, many others prefer to consult with a licensed pharmacist for advice on diagnosis and prescription. A trained pharmacist can prescribe the use of a wide range of drugs, including many antibiotics. Herbal pharmacists generally provide even more advice and friendly service than is the case in ordinary drug stores in Japan, and the fact that they keep detailed records on their customers indicates that they think of them more as patients than as customers and as taking part in a series of treatment sessions. The fact that medicine is usually prescribed by the pharmacist for each customer individually after a long exchange of information encourages feelings of responsibility and closeness between customer and pharmacist.

It is still usual to prescribe mixtures of up to ten or more herbs. The raw materials vary from coarsely chopped plant material to finely ground bone. There is no need for accurate measurements, and the pharmacist often estimates the quantity by eye or makes use of the calibrated boxes traditionally used for measurement in Japan. The process is much more reminiscent of preparations in a kitchen than of those at a modern prescription counter, particularly since the customer, on receiving the medicine, will take it home, boil it up, and strain it. In Japanese, people describe the ingestion of medicine as "drinking," demonstrating once again the close association between medicine and nutrition in general and that the taking of medicine is considered natural and part of everyday life.

From the descriptions given above it can be seen that herbalists hold several systems of belief and that their methods of training are varied.

Paradoxically, in the more traditional, well-established shops the herbalist often upholds the classical tradition the least. In these cases, keeping a pharmacy is a job inherited from one's father—it is simply a business. These men do not take part in the *kanpō* world and have little contact with other East Asian medical practitioners. They are careful to preserve the traditional appearance of their shops in order to attract customers, but they try to couch their language in scientific terms because this is what they believe their customers best understand. They are older people, often not well educated and with little knowledge of the classical books. They have learned their techniques on the job and are looked down upon by younger and better-educated pharmacists. Custom is on the increase in these shops but not nearly as rapidly as in the shops of more recently established, up-to-date herbalists.

Newly established or young herbalists tend to be university educated and genuinely concerned about the ultimate objectives of cosmopolitan medicine; they have consciously opted to adhere to the traditional system of beliefs as closely as possible. For this reason they are often opposed to acupuncturists, whom they judge on the basis of the education that they receive in East Asian medical schools—which they feel to be of low quality and designed to eventually subsume traditional theories totally under a scientific rubric. Good education in the minds of these herbalists combines both scientific and traditional knowledge with experience.

In order to promote East Asian medicine these herbalists attend conferences and support research projects because they believe that when biochemistry is better refined, much of East Asian medical theory will be explained on the basis of scientific theories. But they are also convinced that science as we know it has its limitations. Mr. Watanabe states: "People are not completely rational machines; they are intuitive too, and intuition is based on synthesis, not deduction. Man's body is such that it can never be totally explained by deduction, nor can it ever be cured by attacking one weak spot with heavy doses of synthetic medicine."

Mr. Watanabe, Mr. Sakura, and herbalists like them, are trying to reeducate their customers to return to the old Japanese attitudes of being in harmony with nature by living a life without excesses and by modifying behavior on the basis of subtle signals, both emotional and physiological, emitted by their bodies. They remind their customers of how strong the human body is, that it naturally tends to return to equilibrium, and that nonpurified forms of organic materials, whether food or medicine, are what our bodies are best able to metabolize. They are opposed to many ordinary pharmacists, who, they believe, are too willing to sell great quantities of synthetic medicine.

Their shops are clean and efficient, elegantly decorated with traditional wood and textiles, and with some technological aids incorporated. They represent what many Japanese seem to be searching for today: the ability to master and use scientific techniques without applying the philosophical premises of science to every aspect of life.

PART FOUR

The East Asian Medical System
in Urban Japan: Acupuncture,
Moxibustion, and Massage

10

Acupuncture and Moxibustion Clinics: The Setting and the Patients

Do not seek to follow in the footsteps of the
men of old; seek what they sought.
Matsuo Bashō
(1644–1694),
The Rustic Gate

On a sidewalk in downtown Kyoto, a large billboard advertises the complete range of East Asian medicine available at the top of a nearby flight of dark and narrow stairs. The clinic is known as a "pain clinic" and is open six days a week from 9 A.M. until 5 P.M.

Dr. Nagai, a forty-two-year-old M.D. who specializes in anaesthesiology, established the clinic in 1968. His father was an artist who had always used East Asian medicine when he was ill, and Dr. Nagai first became interested in the system through his father. After practicing and teaching cosmopolitan medicine for seven years, Dr. Nagai decided that his chief interest was in pain and that in order to study it he would open his own clinic and practice East Asian medicine with a minimum of influence from cosmopolitan medicine. Dr. Nagai maintains ties with several major universities as a teacher and researcher and frequently travels abroad to lecture.

The four assistants employed by Dr. Nagai are licensed acupuncturists, and since he is often absent, it is the assistants, directed by the fifty-two-year-old senior member of their group, who actually do most of the work. Dr.

157

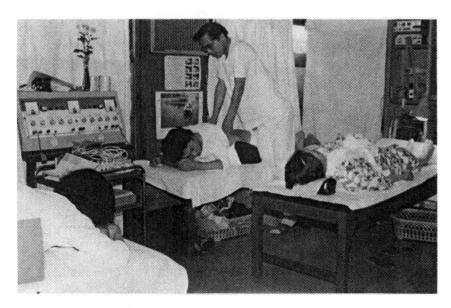

PLATE 13. A busy downtown acupuncture and massage clinic.

Nagai's wife and one female assistant manage the financial accounts, keep patients' records, fill prescriptions, make lunch and cups of tea, and generally deal very efficiently with all organizational matters.

The clinic consists of two treatment rooms, a tiny waiting room, and a small office. The sexes are separated; in the men's treatment room there are five examination tables, and in the women's room there are eight tables. Both rooms are small, crowded, and warm, with an inviting aroma of burning moxa. The walls are covered with classical diagrams of the East Asian medical system of beliefs, and with photographs of Dr. Nagai and his colleagues performing acupuncture. There is also a vast array of impressive electrical instruments in the rooms; some are in use regularly, others are stored high up on shelves and covered with dust.

Patients climb the stairs, change into slippers, and take a seat in the waiting room, where they can help themselves to a cup of tea, read, and chat. As in all the clinics, there is no appointment system, but the waiting time is rarely more than thirty minutes. Dr. Nagai's wife greets patients politely, but on the whole the language used in this clinic is informal Kyoto dialect with no special concern shown for the delicate nuance of polite Japanese language.

In both treatment rooms there is a ceaseless flow of chatter, not only in relation to examination and diagnosis, as most patients join in the gossip and friendly banter that is very much a part of the hour-long treatment session. The therapists sometimes smoke while treating patients. Several of them, including Dr. Nagai, have long hair and are occasionally unshaven. Dr. Nagai's dog is frequently seen lying in the office. Of all the clinics visited, the therapists here were the most informal. They work in close and friendly association with each other and spend much of their free time together, including their annual summer vacation, when the clinic is closed for two weeks and the entire staff, including the dog, goes on a trip together.

Mrs. Otani, one of the regular and more vociferous patients, likes the friendly atmosphere in this clinic and enjoys her visits, which she views as a time to relax from her busy life. She is sixty-one years old and was born in the countryside in Tottori prefecture. She moved to Kyoto with her family when she was eight years old, later married a low-ranking civil servant, and now lives with her two children, her daughter-in-law, and her grandchild. She is a member of the Jōdoshin sect of Buddhism. Four years ago, Mrs. Otani developed lumbago, which did not give her constant pain but nevertheless caused her great discomfort. The origin of the problem was overwork, according to Mrs. Otani. At the cosmopolitan hospital, where she first went, she was given injections and a corset to wear, but she experienced no relief. She then tried a local acupuncture clinic for three years and received only sporadic relief from the pain; this was her first experience with East Asian medicine. At the suggestion of a friend, Mrs. Otani transferred to Dr. Nagai's clinic, and she states that after four months of treatment she felt much better and claims that she is now coming to the clinic twice a month solely as a preventive measure.

Mr. Hirai was born in Kyoto, has been married for four years, and is a Christian. He is thirty-three years of age and was graduated in law from Kyoto University. As a highly educated person he is in the minority in this clinic and does not join in the general chatter and banter. When his eyes started to hurt four years ago, Mr. Hirai went to an eye specialist and was told that there was nothing wrong with him. The doctor prescribed tranquilizers and told him that he was too nervous (*shinkeishitsushō*). Mr. Hirai agreed with the diagnosis of nervousness and says he is constantly under stress at work; but he was worried about his eyes and felt he had been rejected by the specialist. Mr. Hirai had been given acupuncture and moxibustion as a child and decided to try the clinic when he saw an advertisement for it in a newspaper. Several of his relatives who are doctors teased him about his visits to the acupuncture clinic, but Mr. Hirai continued to come, and after two months he felt very relaxed, and his eyes did not hurt anymore. Although Mr. Hirai finds it difficult to pay the fees, he says he will bring all his medical problems except surgical ones to the clinic in the future. Because of their concerns about industrial pollution and the bad side effects of synthetic medicine, both he and his wife are very happy for him to receive a type of therapy which they view as "natural." Although they think the problem will probably return at particularly stressful times, they feel at ease now that they know what to do about it.

Mrs. Otani and Mr. Hirai each underwent the usual examination and diagnosis, which takes about twenty minutes. Patients sit and answer detailed questions about their life history, social circumstances, and experiences in other medical systems. A diagnosis chart is prepared according to the four classical methods of diagnosis (see Chapter 3). Under diagnosis by observation are included details on weight, posture, face color, skin color, and texture. The second group, diagnosis by listening, includes the state of the voice, state of breathing, type of cough, and types of intestinal noises. Diagnosis by questioning includes details on appetite, vomiting, smoking and drinking habits, favorite foods, dryness of the mouth, sleep habits, sweating, eye fatigue, urine and stools, pain, menstruation, and details on cold, heavy, or numb sensations. The blood pressure is taken when it is necessary. This is followed by abdominal palpation in the East Asian style, palpation of various acupuncture points for pain sensations, and pulse diagnosis in the East Asian style. The patient's body is marked with a ballpoint pen at the spots that are painful.

With the exception of Dr. Nagai, the therapists in this clinic have not been trained to use the stethoscope. Other diagnostic checks characteristic of cosmopolitan medicine, such as examination of the tonsils, adenoids, and lymph glands, are not made. There are no laboratory or X-ray facilities in the clinic; patients are sometimes asked to bring with them the results of laboratory tests performed at other clinics or are sent to cosmopolitan hospitals to receive tests.

Unlike the doctors at the *kanpō* clinic, the therapists' stated aim is to adhere to the classical system of diagnosis as closely as possible. Nevertheless, the therapist records his diagnosis in both cosmopolitan and East Asian medical terms; the chief complaint is recorded in scientific language, and a pattern of less obvious systems is also noted. A further purpose of the diagnosis is to ascertain whether the patient is in a general yin or yang state, which is equated with hyper- or hypoactivity of the body in the cosmopolitan system.

Every patient receives either acupuncture or moxibustion treatments and sometimes massage as well. Acupuncture is always performed with the needle hooked up to an electrical device so that the patient receives a mild flow of electricity along with acupuncture treatments. Virtually no advice is given during examination and treatment, either on preventive medicine or possible changes in daily habits.

Because Dr. Nagai is an M.D. he can prescribe herbal medicine, and many patients leave the clinic with a ready-to-take supply. The variety of herbs used is much more limited than in the *kanpō* clinic, and prescriptions are not adjusted carefully as the patient's symptoms change, although strict adherence to classical theory requires this.

Patients at Acupuncture Clinics: General

Mrs. Otani and Mr. Hirai are typical of many patients at this clinic in that they do not live in the neighborhood. Many patients travel up to one hour to come for treatment. Forty-five percent of them live in a rural environment. Neither the educational level nor the income level is high. Of twenty-five patients interviewed, those who live in rural areas are from farming families, and urban residents come mostly from lower income brackets. Religious belief and practice is typical for modern Japan (Japan, Ministry of Education, 1971).

The average cost of treatment at the clinic is about eight dollars, including the price of herbal medicine. The actual expense is therefore about the same as at the *kanpō* clinic. Expense, however, is not the primary basis on which decisions are made about the choice of a clinic. The correct atmosphere (*funiki*) is considered most important; by this is meant the appearance of the clinic, the appearance and language of the staff, and the education and economic backgrounds of the other patients. This downtown center, with its crowded setting and informal atmosphere, is viewed by its patients as appro-

161

priate for them. Most patients in the clinic speak only the Kyoto dialect and would feel uncomfortable if the doctor addressed them in formal Japanese. (The therapists adapt their language noticeably when dealing with clients from a professional background.)

The majority of the urban sample felt that paying the bills was difficult, though the patients from farming families did not find it so; this probably reflects the comfortable financial position of many rural families today owing to government subsidies. Many patients combine their visit to the clinic with a downtown shopping expedition or a visit to an inexpensive restaurant or both. Therapy becomes incorporated into a period of relaxation and pleasure.

Dr. Nagai believes that his patients are of two kinds. There are those who have always been in contact with the East Asian medical system and have consistently used it along with cosmopolitan medicine all their lives—these are people from lower-middle-class urban, and rural environments. The other type of patient is from a middle- or upper-middle-class professional or business family and until recently has mostly used the cosmopolitan medical system. This second type of patient has frequently become interested in the East Asian system through recent publicity in the mass media and, on experiencing a chronic disease, has decided to look for an East Asian style of clinic. Such patients are at present in a minority, but Dr. Nagai believes that they represent a vanguard of rising interest in traditional medicine which will soon spread to the urban middle class in general. Some of these patients are doctors who practice cosmopolitan style of medicine.

The use of moxibustion in the home, massage, and folk medicine is more prevalent among rural patients than urban ones. Urban patients, on the other hand, are more inclined to buy herbal medicine from a pharmacist. Rural patients stated that they do not need exercise; city dwellers felt that they did not have time for it, although it was necessary. General questions about preventive medicine often produced the response that one *should* take time to look after one's health but that family obligations and the work situation are such that it is impossible. Care with diet and with preventive medicine in general is practiced meticulously by most mothers in regard to their children, but adult patients, both male and female, stated repeatedly that social and work obligations did not allow them enough time to look after their health satisfactorily.

Medical Problems and Experiences

Between four hundred and five hundred patients are seen at this clinic each week. The medical problems handled during one month are presented in Table 14. The majority of the twenty-five patients interviewed had either muscular, joint, or skeletal problems. Three of them had neuralgia, and four suffered with mild nervous disorders or tiredness. There was one case of asthma, one of stomach ulcers, and one of addiction to tobacco. The patients classified themselves as having chronic problems and used cosmopolitan medical terminology to describe their symptoms.

As with the *kanpō* patients, the duration of the sickness was extended: eight patients had been in ill health for more than four years, nine had been ill for between one and three years, and only eight had been ill for less than one year. Unlike the patients at the *kanpō* clinic, these patients had not been attending the clinic for many years. Only four had been coming for more than one year.

Of the twenty-five patients sampled, twelve had first consulted a cosmopolitan doctor (many of the patients had visited several doctors) and had then come to the acupuncture clinic after having rejected cosmopolitan medicine. Though none of those interviewed had been to the *kanpō* clinic, some patients had tried other acupuncture clinics, others had been to clinics specializing in massage, and still others had consulted bone manipulators. The majority of the rural patients had used folk medicine or massage or

TABLE 14
Principal Conditions Treated at the Acupuncture Clinic in One Month (June)

CONDITIONS	PERCENTAGE
Lumbago	23.0
Neck and shoulder stiffness	21.0
Arthritis	7.3
Sciatica	6.0
Headache	4.6
Brachialgia	4.5
Whiplash	3.1
Intestinal problems	3.1
Rheumatism	1.5
Other	25.9

Note: Figures from unofficial clinic records. Categories are those used by the clinic.

moxa in their homes for many months before coming to the doctor. Unlike the *kanpō* patients, these people had "shopped around" considerably before arriving at this clinic, and not one of them had been referred by their family doctor.

Should a future illness arise, the majority of the sample, like the patients in the *kanpō* clinic, will choose between the East Asian and cosmopolitan medical systems on the basis of self-diagnosis. If they classify their problem as acute, they will visit their family doctor; if chronic, they will go to the East Asian doctor. Further questioning made it clear that these patients' understanding of "acute" (*kyūsei*) and "chronic" (*mansei*) does not correspond to that of the *kanpō* patients. The *kanpō* patients use the term "chronic" to mean a recurrent disease or one of long duration. The patients in the acupuncture clinic use the term to convey the idea of muscular, joint, or nervous problems, as opposed to "acute" diseases, by which are meant all infections, all problems of the internal organs, including asthma or ulcers, and all skin diseases. Furthermore, although herbal medicine is prescribed at this clinic, it is not considered a major part of therapy as it is in the *kanpō* clinic. Acupuncture and moxibustion are viewed as crucial by both doctors and patients. Every patient receives acupuncture or moxibustion or both, whereas many *kanpō* clinic patients receive only a supply of herbal medicine. Although Dr. Nagai advertises that he offers the complete range of East Asian medicine, and despite the fact that he is an M.D., the patients think of his clinic as less prestigious than the *kanpō* clinic and as being on the same level as other clinics offering only acupuncture and moxibustion and run by licensed practitioners. The setting of the clinic and the appearance and language of the practitioners reinforce this impression.

To summarize the attitudes of patients toward East Asian medicine: many patients, even those who use East Asian medicine regularly, are aware of herbal pharmacies but not of the existence of *kanpō* clinics, even though there are three in Kyoto. They think of clinical East Asian medicine as comprising the use of acupuncture, moxibustion, and massage as the principal forms of therapy. Their beliefs about the usefulness of this kind of therapy is limited to a small range of illnesses, including muscular, joint, or nervous problems, or for complaints of general debility. Their conception of the usefulness of East Asian medicine is therefore much narrower than that implied by the classical texts. Once introduced to *kanpō*, patients usually extend their idea of what East Asian medicine is suitable for to include chronic problems of all kinds, because herbal medicine is thought to be especially suitable for chronic internal complaints, respiratory problems, and skin diseases.

Patients' satisfaction with the acupuncture clinic is less marked than at the *kanpō* clinic but is still frequently expressed. There are more patients in this clinic who drift from one acupuncture doctor to another, and I heard some grumbling about lack of progress and painful insertion of needles. However, since lower-class people in Japan are generally more vocally expressive than upper-class people, and since receiving treatment is usually a social rather than an individual affair, in the acupuncture clinic there is more freedom to banter and to express complaints. Many of the patients who had tried other acupuncture clinics felt that this one was particularly good, and they were willing to travel great distances to receive treatment even though a local practitioner was available to all of them. Among acupuncture clinics, Dr. Nagai's is thought by the patients to be a cut above the others. Although Dr. Nagai himself does little of the treatment, the patients stated that his presence gives them extra confidence, and they are also clearly impressed by his foreign visitors and the attention that the local press has given him. Dr. Nagai does not have close relationships with cosmopolitan doctors in Kyoto and very few patients are referred to him from the cosmopolitan system.

Of the patients interviewed, sixteen said that they had made good progress and would soon stop coming. Five others stated that, though they experienced total relief from pain, when they stopped treatment the pain returned. Four patients (two of whom had received treatment over several months) felt they were making little progress so far. Like the *kanpō* patients, these people emphasized social, psychological, climatic, and hereditary factors as being the precipitating causes of their problems rather than physiological or mechanical changes in their body's functioning. Relatively few patients expressed concern about the side effects of synthetic medicine, unlike those at the *kanpō* clinic.

Other Acupuncture Clinics

While some clinics in Kyoto try to provide the full range of traditional East Asian therapy, most advertise as offering only acupuncture and massage or acupuncture and chiropractic. Clinics are usually filled with an impressive array of machinery, which can help to locate the pressure points, determine the electrical resistance of the skin, or cauterize the skin without actually burning moxa, for example. But in most clinics the therapists have reverted to techniques that involve actual physical contact with the patients, and the machines lie collecting dust on high shelves.

The most typical kind of acupuncture clinics are run by licensed practitioners in a converted room of their own home. The majority of patients who come to these clinics live in the immediate neighborhood. Although they have a family, cosmopolitan style of doctor for most of their medical problems, they automatically select the local acupuncturist to visit when they have muscular or skeletal problems or minor ailments such as general malaise (*karada ga darui*). Some patients consult their family doctor at the same time, but most do not, trusting the acupuncturist to deal with this limited range of medical problems. Patients are predominantly of lower- or lower-middle-class families, and incomes are derived from laboring, artisan, shopkeeping, or clerical work. Through community activities the practitioners are well known to the patients before they come to the clinic, and patients therefore know the kind of personality and the approach the practitioner is likely to take before they visit him.

In these clinics the process of diagnosis is often very brief and limited to questioning the patient about painful sensations, numbness, cramps, and so on. The patient usually presents the doctor with a self-diagnosis in cosmopolitan medical terms, and treatment of the painful spot may commence without further ado. A considerable number of therapists have incorporated into their practice the use of the chiropractic diagnostic technique of checking for tension around the spinal column, and in these cases diagnosis is more thorough. Very few practitioners check the pulse or keep charts on their patients.

A few practitioners maintain close relationships with the neighborhood M.D. and have patients referred to them, but most do not have this advantage and survive completely independently, having only occasional interaction with other East Asian medical practitioners.

One such practitioner who uses both acupuncture and chiropractic is Mr. Taguchi, who is forty-eight years old, belongs to the Zen sect of Buddhism, and holds the sixth rank black belt in judo. He also has rank in *kendō* (fencing). He stands about 6' 1" tall and is a powerfully built man who wears his judo clothes while he practices medicine in his own house, which serves as his clinic. He has one assistant, and his wife handles the administrative side of the business. Although Mr. Taguchi's father was also an acupuncturist, "he just applied what he'd learned in school—he wasn't treating the whole man," says Mr. Taguchi, who prides himself on his holistic and philosophical approach to his patients. Mr. Taguchi, always an urban dweller, was a schoolteacher for several years. To attain high rank in *kendō* he had to study Buddhist and Confucian philosophy and write scholarly papers related to his studies. He also had to pass an examination in traditional bonesetting and certain manipulatory techniques before he was qualified to help any student of the martial arts who should become injured while training. After completing these studies, Mr. Taguchi decided to become an acupuncturist and enrolled in a school of East Asian medicine. Upon graduation he spent a further year of training in chiropractic and osteopathy.

Set in a quiet back street, the small clinic, which uses half the entire house, is filled with equipment. Besides two ordinary examination tables, there is a special new couch for chiropractic, imported at great expense from the United States, and another couch that automatically massages the entire body at the flick of a switch. Both couches are usually occupied, and other patients lie on Japanese mattresses on the floor. There is no segregation of the sexes. Mr. Taguchi treats several patients at the same time, and as he moves between them he alternates friendly conversation with short moral lectures. "Without a patient's trust it is impossible to perform a proper treatment," states Mr. Taguchi. The room is never quiet, for patients listen to and converse freely about each other's problems. The walls of the clinic are covered with calligraphy the meaning of which has a heavy Confucian flavor and relates to the maintenance of status and role in human relationships. The god-shelf (*kamidana*) on the wall above the prone patients is filled with talismans and souvenirs of journeys to many Shintō shrines.

Mr. Taguchi describes himself as a "lone wolf." He is the only practitioner interviewed who chooses not to belong to some form of union or medical association. He says he prefers to spend his free time exercising, keeping himself fit, and playing with his two children rather than sitting in boring meetings. Like all East Asian practitioners, Mr. Taguchi works a long six-day week, from 8 A.M. to 6 or 7 P.M. each day, with only thirty minutes for lunch.

Compared with Mr. Taguchi, Mr. Ando is a mild, unassuming man. He lives in a section of Kyoto close to the Nishijin textile factories and occupied mostly by *burakumin* (the outcast group) and Koreans. He is a licensed acupuncturist, fifty years of age, married, and has three children. Mr. Ando has no formal affiliation with any religious organization. Born in the Nishijin area, the son of a worker in the textile industry, Mr. Ando has always lived in the same part of Kyoto. When he was six, a typhoon ripped through the city one night, destroying his parents' home and others around it and leaving Mr. Ando with a crippled right leg. He spent the next eight years of his childhood mostly in bed, read voluminously, and was finally able to graduate from high school. Since the family was poor and the country was recovering from the war, Mr. Ando could not fulfill his wish to go to medical school; besides, medical schools rarely accept students who are handicapped. He decided, therefore, to make East Asian medicine his profession and was accepted as a student at the Higashi Honganji school in Kyoto. Upon graduation, Mr. Ando was apprenticed to an East Asian doctor, with whom he worked for twelve years. At the age of thirty-seven he decided he was financially secure enough to set up his own practice in his new, small house located a few blocks from the place of his birth. He continues to live in this house and holds his clinic in one small room, which has a private entrance and a waiting hallway. The patients are seen one at a time in the peaceful, tiny room, which opens onto a small garden.

Unlike most East Asian practitioners, all of Mr. Ando's patients are referred to him by cosmopolitan doctors with whom he maintains good relations, because patients use their health insurance coverage when they come to see him. He is therefore reimbursed by the government for treatment sessions according to the points systems (see Chapter 1) and is one of ninety such acupuncturists in Kyoto. The first visit to the doctor is worth 90 points ($2.75), and subsequent visits are 52 points, or $1.56. Mr. Ando can accumulate further points only by performing acupuncture, moxibustion, or massage. He is not refunded for any diagnostic procedures or for other forms of therapy, and patients bring copies of their medical charts showing the diagnosis already determined by their family doctor. One treatment of acupuncture is worth 40 points ($1.16) as is a single treatment of moxa, but if the two are performed together, they are worth only 60 points ($1.78). Massage is assessed at 50 points ($1.50) for the whole body and at 10 points (30¢) for a single limb or for the torso. Patients are allowed fifteen treatments the first month and ten treatments the second month. If they wish to continue, they must pay for their treatments themselves. Mr. Ando spends each morning in the clinic; afternoons are set aside for house calls, and evenings are again spent in the clinic. From 9:30 P.M. onward he works for up to two hours filling out all the forms required by the health insurance bureaucracy. He likes to see about twenty patients a day—if he sees more he feels that he is rushing his work—and spends between twenty and thirty minutes with each patient. If the patient is a new one, Mr. Ando will earn a maximum of $5.85 for the treatment session; if the patient is not new, his return will be $4.88 or less.[1] Mr. Ando chats informally with patients during treatment. He finds it difficult to establish good rapport with some of his patients and attributes this to the constraining nature of the health insurance system and to the fact that the majority of his patients are *burakumin* or Koreans. He is politically active in a movement to improve the rights of *burakumin*, though few of his patients are aware of this fact.

There are some acupuncture clinics that specialize in dealing with a certain kind of clientele or in dealing with one or two specific medical problems. For example, the wealthy ladies of Kyoto visit their favorite acupuncturist on the second floor of his small home with such regularity that he will have to expand his business or start refusing clients. He is a blind man who started out in medical school and, on losing his sight when halfway through his training, took up acupuncture instead. He is reputed to be the best acupuncturist in Kyoto.

Some doctors specialize in acupuncture for children, and one such man, following his family custom, practices in the front room of his tiny, traditional house. He uses 22-carat gold needles, which he draws over the body surface to provide a mild stimulus rather than actually inserting them through the skin. He handles children up to seven years of age and deals with problems of *kan no mushi* (childhood irritability), asthma, night crying, bed-wetting, and even mental retardation. For this last problem he inserts needles directly into the brain; he states that this has a good effect on *some* children

1 Based on 1974 rates of exchange.

who are slow in both motor and verbal development. For problems of enuresis he provides a stimulus to the hips and up and down the backbone where the bladder meridian runs. With difficult cases he inserts the needles at the *chōkyo* point on the bladder meridian.

In central Kyoto a pharmacist who specialized in the study of herbal medicine in college spent an extra three years obtaining his acupuncture, moxibustion, and massage licenses. Although not an M.D., he can now practice the complete East Asian medical system and keeps an immaculate, modern clinic and herbal pharmacy. He has lectured in Europe and offers free seminars once a week in his house for students of East Asian medicine. He supplements their formal college education with an introduction to classical theory, which he believes is essential to a good practice.

Just outside Kyoto lies the headquarters of Ōmoto, one of the new religions of Japan. Medical facilities are provided in the main building, and in these clinics doctors of both cosmopolitan and East Asian medicine work side by side. Patients can choose which type of doctor they want, and they are also advised which system would probably be best for their particular problem.

Finally, there are probably one or two East Asian medical clinics in Kyoto that specialize in performing abortions. I could not obtain an introduction to them, but several informants pointed out their existence. Stimulation of lower points on the bladder meridian are said to terminate pregnancy.

Moxibustion Clinics

A clinic in the eastern section of Kyoto advertises itself as offering internal medicine and moxibustion. On the first floor of this clinic, two M.D.'s practice cosmopolitan medicine; on the second floor the father of one of the doctors, himself an M.D., has retired from the practice of internal medicine and now uses only moxibustion. The second-floor clinic is in one large, old-fashioned, dark room filled with the pungent smell of burning moxa. It has six examination tables and a row of chairs usually occupied by waiting patients chatting noisily. Two licensed assistants actually administer the moxibustion while Dr. Ishino, the M.D., sits to one side and observes the proceedings. There is no separation of the sexes, and when a patient is called, he or she partially undresses in front of everyone and then lies down on an examination table.

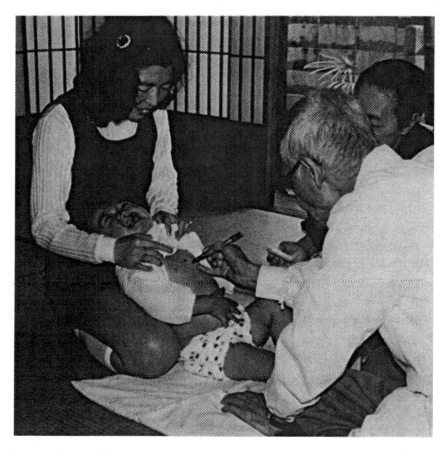

PLATE 14. An M.D. administers moxa mixed with oil at a baby clinic held in a Kyoto temple.

The diagnoses and treatments are recorded carefully on charts. The diagnosis, cosmopolitan in style, is usually made on the first floor or in another cosmopolitan clinic before the patient arrives in the moxibustion clinic. Dr. Ishino uses neither herbal medicine nor acupuncture, since he considers these to be very inferior to moxibustion. His family, doctors for five generations, have always used moxa to supplement their cosmopolitan medical practice because they believe it is often highly effective in the treatment of chronic problems, not only of the joints, muscles, and nerves, but also of the internal organs. According to Dr. Ishino, moxa is effective against some, but not all, bacterial and fungal infections, including some types of tuberculus bacillus, streptococci and staphylococci, and ringworm.

171

However, most patients prefer to receive antibiotics for bacterial infections, although moxa is acceptable for fungal problems.

Moxa, classified as yang in type, is usually preferred by women, who for the most part are classified as yin. Dr. Ishino does not accept the yin/yang classification system, but he does agree that moxa apparently acts as a kind of "warming agent," increasing general body metabolism and reducing nervous tension.

The policy at this clinic is to use cosmopolitan medicine first, and if and when that fails, to apply moxa to the patient. No dietary advice or guidance of any kind is given during therapy, and conversation between therapist and patient is limited to the bare essentials. Dr. Ishino is rather brusque, does not use polite forms of language, and often spends his time during treatment sessions reading the newspaper. The assistants are, on the whole, silent and reserved. But the success of the treatments at this clinic are well known, and patients come from as far as fifty miles away to receive them.

Mrs. Kato is fifty-eight and married to a certified public accountant. She has been coming to the clinic as a patient for six months and has been suffering from asthma for ten years. Two years ago the condition became very bad and was compounded by a heart problem. The medicine received from the family doctor did little to help, according to Mrs. Kato. It was her twenty-eight-year-old daughter-in-law who suggested that she try the moxa clinic. Mrs. Kato had been coming for six months when she was interviewed, and for four months she had not suffered from a single asthma attack. She had, of her own accord, started to use herbal medicine to build up her general strength, but she continues to visit her family doctor regularly and to receive the medicine he prescribes because she feels embarrassed about stopping her visits to him. Mrs. Kato throws the medicine away when she returns home, but she says the family doctor believes her improvement is due to his therapy.

She does not find the trips to the moxibustion clinic particularly relaxing, nor does she feel that she receives any help or guidance apart from the actual moxibustion treatment. But she is delighted to be able to carry on her life without discomfort and is prepared to come to the clinic on a permanent basis if necessary.

Because the clinic specializes in moxibustion, one expects to find more female than male patients and this is indeed the case. Seventy-five percent of

PLATE 15. Waiting in line for treatment at the baby clinic.

all the patients are female. Young children are rarely brought here as patients, and the youngest person interviewed was thirty-two years old.

Occupations and educational levels vary considerably. Patients who are referred to the clinic by other doctors receive treatment under the health insurance sytem, while those who come on the recommendation of friends must pay. The fee, however, is minimal: one dollar per treatment. Patients from the first-floor clinic are referred to the second floor within a month or two of becoming ill if no improvement occurs with cosmopolitan therapy.

Virtually all the illnesses treated are diagnosed either as neuralgia, joint problems, migraine headache, asthma, or lumbago. Half the patients have had previous experience with East Asian therapy. Many patients believe that acupuncture had not helped them at all, whereas they find moxa to be highly effective. It was emphasized by all patients that moxa is good for the whole body, but they felt that acupuncture has a much more local effect.

Three times a month a downtown Kyoto temple is turned into a temporary clinic to which babies are brought by their mothers and grandmothers to receive a special type of moxa treatment. It is administered by an eighty-two-year-old M.D., now blind in one eye and almost totally deaf. Dr. Kinoshita grew up in the countryside about fifty miles outside Kyoto in Shiga prefecture. He was born into a wealthy family with a long tradition of medical practice going back nearly four hundred years. His ancestors developed a technique in which moxa, mixed with a little oil, was dotted onto certain pressure points and left in place, rather than being ignited and burned. This technique became well known as especially suitable in the treatment of babies. The details about the proportions of moxa and oil and the specific pressure points at which to apply the mixture were handed down secretly from generation to generation in a closed family tradition (*kaden*) until Dr. Kinoshita finally received them. Dr. Kinoshita's father took his license in cosmopolitan medicine soon after the Meiji Restoration, and Dr. Kinoshita himself was graduated from Kyoto University, where he spent many years doing research in physiology, especially in relation to the East Asian pressure points. When his father died, Dr. Kinoshita returned to Shiga prefecture to take on the family practice.

The clinic is predominantly cosmopolitan in style, but patients who request East Asian therapy can receive it—there is a good supply of herbal medicine, and the special moxa technique is available for babies. For the past fifteen years, Dr. Kinoshita has traveled to Kyoto to make his technique available to city dwellers. He is given free space to work inside two of Kyoto's temples, and he has his wife and one nurse to assist him. On treatment days a large billboard is posted outside the temple, and from 9 A.M. until 2 P.M. Dr. Kinoshita sits in a simple matted room and attends to a steady stream of babies whose mothers hold them while they receive the treatment. The waiting time may take up to twenty minutes, treatment time takes two or three minutes, and the cost is one dollar. Dr. Kinoshita talks to the mothers only if they ask him direct questions, and he wastes no time in playing with or calming the babies. He makes no diagnoses, but simply repeats exactly the same treatment on all the children. The moxa is dotted onto well-known acupuncture points: at the navel, the chest, on the side of the neck, the central forehead, the temples, the center of the back, and the calves. He assumes that all babies are receiving regular examinations by pediatricians and that they have no acute or major functional problems. The treatment is designed to alleviate mild symptoms such as colds or constipation, but it is used above all to combat the problems of excessive night crying and of babies who exhibit what can best be described as hyper-irritability (*kan no mushi;* see Chapter 6). This problem usually manifests itself physically as excessive fussiness and an inability to relax easily. Sometimes there is frequent, mild vomiting and hot flushes.

In general the syndrome is regarded with mixed feelings: a baby with *kan no mushi* is likely to grow up into a sensitive, intellectual adult, and many parents want to encourage this; on the other hand, it means that the child is very hard to handle—something that most mothers do not welcome.

Occasionally, Dr. Kinoshita sees babies who suffer from convulsions. In these cases, he applies moxa to the soles of the feet at the *yosen* point.

Dr. Kinoshita views himself as a scientist. His physiological experiments have convinced him that acupuncture and moxibustion techniques do stimulate the nervous system. He is not completely convinced that his own family techniques of mixing the moxa with oil has any effect on the body, but he continues to practice it because, he says, "the mothers want it and I hate to see an old tradition die out." Like other practitioners, Dr. Kinoshita believes that the stimulus of acupuncture is immediate and of short duration (*shunkanteki*), while that of moxa lasts over a longer period of time (*jizo-kuteki*). When properly applied, moxa, Dr. Kinoshita believes, can keep the level of natural resistance in the body extremely high—that is, it encourages antibody production—and even if a person becomes sick, his recovery will be unusually fast.

Mrs. Honda is a regular visitor to the temple clinic. She is thirty and lives in an Osaka suburb with her husband, their ten-month-old baby, and her mother-in-law. Her friends describe her life situation as old-fashioned and somewhat of a trial for her. Her mother-in-law is a retired teacher of *ikebana* (flower-arrangement), and she supervises Mrs. Honda's life and work very closely. Mrs. Honda does all the housework, but she is not allowed to make any choices about the selection of meals or the selection of furnishings for the house, which belongs to her mother-in-law. Mrs. Honda's husband leaves for work in an insurance company at 7:30 A.M. each day and arrives home each night to be tended to by the women of the house. His mother is most concerned that he should get a good night's sleep each night to cope with his long day at the office, and she complains bitterly if the baby cries in the night and wakes his father up. As a result, the moment the baby stirs Mrs. Honda starts to feed him, and the baby has settled readily into the habit of waking up regularly five or six times each night to nurse. Mrs. Honda is tense and exhausted, and the baby has been diagnosed by his family as *kan no mushi*. Mrs. Honda gives the baby patent medicine powders regularly but also takes the baby to the temple, thirty miles away in Kyoto, for regular treatments from Dr. Kinoshita, whom a friend told her about. She enjoys the expeditions enormously, for they give her a chance to have half a day out of the house, and she says that both she and her baby are relaxed for a few days after each treatment. Mrs. Honda is well aware that the problem is basically one of social relationships and feels that her mother-in-law's attitude is really to blame. She does not believe that there is anything really wrong with her baby and does not think of him as ill. But she cannot even voice these ideas except with one close female friend of her own age and cannot see any alternative way of handling the problem.

Eighty percent of the children at the clinic are boys, which tends to confirm the widespread belief that boys are much more susceptible to *kan no mushi* than are girls. This is believed to be due to the nature of the relationship between mothers and their male babies, especially the eldest boy.

Families of all social classes use the clinic and most families do not inform their pediatrician of visits to the clinic—they state that they would be embarrassed to do so. It is most usually grandmother who advises the mother of the existence of the clinic and recommends that use be made of it.

Close by in a beautiful building that is part of a large complex of Buddhist temples, it is possible for adults to receive moxibustion treatments three times a week. The service is supplied by a sixty-year-old man who is a licensed practitioner. Mr. Adachi's family has been practicing East Asian medicine for more than one hundred years. The practice is designed principally to furnish preventive medicine. The clients are considered customers, not patients, and they come regularly to have moxa burned on the *saninko* point on the inside of the shin—this is the only pressure point that Mr. Adachi uses. No diagnosis is made, no advice is given, and no other type of treatment is offered.

Mr. Adachi lives beside the temple, and his customers are neighborhood people. The regular customers are all women, and most of them are over forty, although there are occasionally a few younger ones. The neighborhood is predominantly lower middle class. Most of the women are not involved with the temple for anything other than their treatments; they make a small donation in exchange for Mr. Adachi's work, and he is then paid by the temple.

All the customers have family doctors, and five of the ten customers interviewed had considerable experience with other types of East Asian medicine, principally for muscle and joint problems. They stated that by receiving moxa regularly, usually once a week, they avoided catching colds and other forms of infections; that their appetite was increased; that they slept well; and that their recovery from joint and muscle problems was fast and complete—something which they assured me was not true for their neighbors who did not burn moxa regularly. These comments are all reinforced by Mr. Adachi, and he added that the moxa was also very good for the psychological state (*kimochi*) of his customers. Mr. Adachi believes, like all the doctors interviewed, that women in Japan are more susceptible than men to illness. This is believed to be due to the fact that until recently women were subordinate to men all their lives, and to the belief that the expression of emotions in women, particularly anger, should be suppressed. It is therefore especially important for women to practice preventive medicine, and yang-type moxa is considered very suitable for yin type of people; that is, for most women.

Also, like most other practitioners, Mr. Adachi believes that the effect of moxa lasts longer than that of acupuncture. He usually places a thin slice of ginger on the pressure point and then burns the moxa on top of the ginger to avoid too much scarring. He believes that by using the *saninko* pressure point he can furnish a good stimulation to the entire body.

The examples cited above demonstrate the huge variety in the practice of East Asian medicine that can be found in Kyoto today. Almost all of the practitioners are in private business, and the creativeness and ingenuity characteristic of Japanese in an entrepreneurial or competitive role is readily apparent. Each East Asian medical clinic has developed a unique atmosphere designed to appeal to a specific segment of the population, and no one in Kyoto has far to look to find a clinic that will fill their needs. The result is that people from every type of social and educational background can be found in the clinics, although people of one kind of social class tend to congregate at the same clinics. The degree of formality in social relations maintained at the clinic depends on its location, the education of the doctors, and the kind of clientele it serves.

We shall turn briefly to clinics that specialize in massage before making a detailed summary of the data presented in this part.

11

Massage: *Shiatsu* and *Amma*

There are said to be more than two hundred and sixty different schools of massage in Japan and, because each school trys to develop its own technique, more than two hundred and sixty styles of massage. Most of these schools were established by the end of the Edo period (mid-nineteenth century), and all were classified under the title of *amma,* which is the general term for massage.

The schools were divided into two basic types: those designed to provide therapy and those used simply for relaxation and pleasure. The therapeutic schools generally performed a wider variety of techniques, going beyond what is usually thought of as massage. They were heavily influenced by the samurai tradition and the martial arts in which men studied techniques of bone manipulation and emergency repairs to be performed on oneself following injury in combat. This therapeutic type of school for massage became formalized in the Meiji era (1868–1912) when the first theoretical book was published, and later, in the Taishō era, it took on the general title of *shiatsu,* which means literally "finger pressure." Massage practiced for the purpose of relaxation retained the general title of *amma* and is the style practiced at hot-spring resorts.

Although the schools specialize in particular styles of massage, the techniques are nevertheless similar enough to be classified into eight basic types:

1. Thrusting: the ball of the thumb is pressed hard on the body with one continuous movement.

2. Grasping: skin and muscles are grasped by the hand and then manipulated vigorously.

179

3. Pressing: pressure is applied with the palm of the hand or the fingertips; the force is less than thrusting and not necessarily continuous.

4. Rubbing: a quick forward and backward motion with the fingers or palm of the hand.

5. Rolling with the back of the hand: gentle pressure exerted with the back of the clenched fist.

6. Pinching: muscle components are pinched between thumb and forefinger, released, and pinched again.

7. Rubbing between the palms of the hands: used for the limbs and the lumbar region.

8. Tapping: performed with one or more fingers or with the side or back of the hand.

Each style is considered particularly suitable for one or more parts of the body—for example, lateral thrusting is recommended for head and neck massage, and pressing with the palm of the hand is recommended for the abdominal region. The *shiatsu* schools emphasize the thrusting and pressing styles of massage, and the *amma* schools prefer the rubbing techniques; all of the schools use the complete range of styles to a greater or lesser extent.

Traditionally, when using massage for therapeutic purposes, a masseur paid particular attention to manipulation at the principal East Asian pressure points. As with acupuncture and moxibustion, it was believed that pressure on specific points at the surface of the body could affect the internal organs. For patients with hyperactivity of a specific organ (*jisshō*), pressure could be applied to reduce activity; for hypoactive problems (*kyoshō*), certain techniques could increase the metabolism.

From the beginning of the Meiji era (1867), both styles of massage were influenced by the West. Some of the *shiatsu* schools, particularly those in the Osaka and Kyoto regions, came into contact with chiropractic techniques. Under this influence, they chose to emphasize the spine and the related nervous system as central to therapy, to reject the meridian theories, and to pay no particular attention to traditional techniques.

Western styles of massage also became popular in Japan, and many practitioners of *amma* gradually gave up their traditional techniques and started to perform a general, rubbing style of massage with emphasis on muscle tissue rather than on pressure points. Recently, many of the practi-

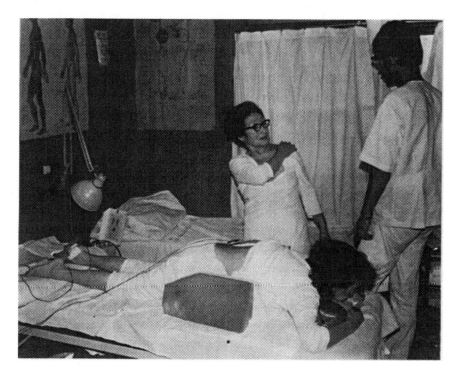

PLATE 16. Discussing shoulder tension before treatment.

tioners using the Western style have started to advertise their practice, using the work "massaji," adopted from English, and indicating more clearly to clients that the service is for relaxation and not for therapy.

The variety of beliefs and practices prevalent in the acupuncture and moxibustion world is also present in the massage world. Furthermore, some masseurs are opposed to acupuncture and moxibustion, while others believe strongly that treatment should include all types of classical East Asian therapy to provide a more holistic approach.

Two *shiatsu* specialists were interviewed. One, Mr. Katayama, is seventy-two and lives and works in an old house in southern Kyoto. He performs all his treatment on *tatami* (straw mats), and when a patient is called, he or she is ushered into one of several small, four-mat rooms. After changing into a cotton *kimono*, the patient lies down and is told to "calm down his feelings" (*kokoro o shizumeru*) and is left to lie by himself for fifteen minutes before

181

treatment is started. Mr. Katayama does not use chiropractic techniques, although he has learned them, but prefers to work mostly on the pressure points.

The other practitioner, a forty-five-year-old weight lifter and third rank judo expert, holds a busy clinic in his tiny, modern apartment. A quiet-spoken, gentle man, Mr. Sato ignores the traditional techniques and thinks in terms of the nervous system and its relationship to the internal organs while he massages.

Both practitioners believe that massage tones up the action of the muscles, improves circulation, appetite, and excretion, and also functions to stimulate antibody production. Cosmopolitan medicine, according to Mr. Sato and Mr. Katayama, is designed to deal with diseases after they are well established and clearly identifiable, and *shiatsu* is most effective in halting the development of mild symptoms into a severe problem.

Although acupuncture is capable of producing a strong stimulus, the practitioners say it "just takes away the principal symptoms of diseases—it does not tone up the whole body." They draw on Shintō values to further justify massage as opposed to moxibustion and acupuncture. According to Shintō beliefs, one should not damage the body in any way. "Moxa leaves scars on the body and damages the skin, and to do acupuncture it is necessary to make holes in the body, but massage," states Mr. Katayama, "is the oldest and most natural technique available to man." They claim that the actual touch of the doctor's hand in treatment is important psychologically, and they believe that massage is superior for this reason too. Both doctors like herbal medicine, though they feel that its action is rather slow.

The Patients

The proportion of men is slightly higher than that of women in the massage clinics. The practitioners believe this is because many men are frightened of acupuncture and moxibustion and feel happy about receiving massage. Certainly many patients expressed their dislike of both acupuncture and moxibustion, including Mr. Mizoguchi, who is a thirty-six-year-old company employee. He had contracted Beçhet's syndrome three years previously and was told at the university hospital that he could only be given

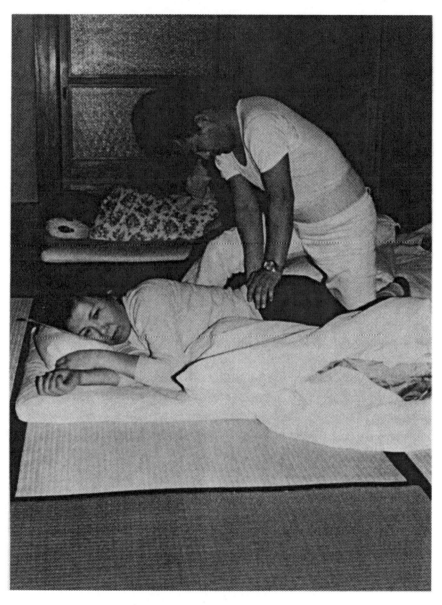

PLATE 17. A blind practitioner performing *amma*.

temporary relief through medication and that his condition would probably gradually deteriorate. The disease caused encephalitis and orogenital lesions, and affected the optic nerve so that his vision deteriorated within one year to the point that he was officially designated blind.

A friend of Mr. Mizoguchi's introduced him to an acupuncture clinic, and to everyone's surprise his body reacted very dramatically to the treatment. Red weals occurred where the needles were inserted, and marks remained on the skin for months after the treatment. He became dizzy and tired, and was unable to move his limbs freely during treatment and for several weeks afterwards. When the acupuncture therapists encouraged him to try massage, which they indicated used a much lighter stimulus, Mr. Mizoguchi came to Mr. Sato's clinic. When he was interviewed, he had been receiving *shiatsu* six days a week every week for two years. His symptoms had completely disappeared and his vision had improved enormously. Mr. Mizoguchi had also taken herbal medicine regularly throughout his illness. Mr. Sato informed him that there is often spontaneous, though temporary, remission with this problem, something Mr. Mizoguchi had not been told at the hospital, and Mr. Sato also stated freely that he had no idea if the *shiatsu* was really responsible for his patient's improvement. Mr. Mizoguchi states that his company has been very kind throughout his illness. He was off from work totally for six months with no reduction in salary and has only very gradually taken on a full work load again since that time. At home, Mr. Mizoguchi's family has been supportive, and he is full of praise for the patience of his wife. He says they now have a very close relationship, "unusual for us Japanese." Mr. Mizoguchi is a well-educated man and now understands that his medical problem is enormously complex and not well understood, and he does not describe himself as "cured." But he believes (despite Mr. Sato's expressed doubts) that the *shiatsu* treatments have helped produce a remission and that it is a pleasant form of treatment with no bad side effects. Although he worries at times about a recurrence of the disease, he intends to continue biweekly *shiatsu* treatments. He also intends to confine himself to the use of herbal medicine and a traditional Japanese diet as far as possible. He doesn't regard himself as under stress either at home or at work and hopes to preserve that situation, which he thinks is vital to good health.

Mr. Shiraishi is also a patient of Mr. Sato's. He is forty-two, a company employee working for the petroleum industry, and had been to the clinic only four times when he was interviewed. He was feeling tired and run down. Though he has a family doctor, he stated that "this is not a problem for my regular doctor—he would only give me a painful injection."

Mr. Shiraishi is also acquainted with both acupuncture and moxibustion and dislikes them both. Several years ago he was diagnosed at a large hospital as having a stomach ulcer, and because he is concerned about the side effects of synthetic medicine, he went to a herbal pharmacist who gave him medicine that totally removed the symptoms to the satisfaction of his family doctor. Since that time he has taken herbal medicine regularly as a preventive measure. Mr. Shiraishi says that he cannot change his stressful working conditions and expects to continue relying on East Asian therapy to combat this.

The price of the hour-long treatment is adjusted in both clinics according to the patient's income and varies from three to five dollars. Like patients at other East Asian clinics, people at massage clinics are from all economic levels and choose a practitioner where the atmosphere feels good to them and also where patients are mostly from their own social class.

Fifty percent of the patients with muscle, joint, or nervous conditions do not go to their family doctor but come directly for massage. Of the remaining 50 percent, the majority give up the services of their family doctor for problems like these once they have started coming for *shiatsu*. Patients with internal problems use both their family doctor and the masseur at the same time. In general, the therapeutic effect of *shiatsu* is thought by the patients to be ineffective against specific internal organs, although the doctors do not agree with this opinion. People suffering from postoperative stiffness also frequently attend these clinics. There is no referral system from cosmopolitan doctors, and patients come when they are introduced by friends and former patients.

Amma: The Massage Parlor

Among the bars, restaurants, and pachinko parlors of the Kyoto entertainment area traditional houses of massage are dotted. In addition, every major area of Kyoto has several smaller massage centers designed principally for relaxation and not for therapy. People who visit these houses are called not patients but customers.

One of the oldest massage centers is set in a tiny alley just off the busy Kawaramachi and Shijō street intersection—the heart of downtown Kyoto. The building is two stories high. The owners live on the first floor, and the second floor is devoted solely to the practice of massage. The main room is large, twenty *tatami* (straw mats) in size, and up to twenty customers can be handled at one time, one to each mat. Customers take off their shoes in the entrance way, pay five dollars to the manager, and climb the stairs. At the top of the stairs, a masseur, often blind, greets the customer and leads him to a vacant mat. The customer removes only outer garments and lies down with a small, hard pillow as support for the head during the hour-long treatment.

The building is open from 11 A.M. until 2 A.M. seven days a week, and the manager employs forty masseurs, who work one of two shifts. All the practitioners are licensed and half of them are blind. A masseur can also be called to one's home by telephone, and the cost is then eight dollars.

Every customer receives a complete body massage in which stimulation of the muscles is central. If a customer so desires, he or she can also have acupuncture. The customer usually directs the masseur to his tense spots and asks for special treatment at these places. The practitioners are familiar with the meridian system and the pressure points but do not make use of them in their technique. Unlike the *shiatsu* practitioners, the *amma* specialists massage through a towel; they explain that this is to absorb sweat and to avoid putting too much pressure on the customer. Since the customer is fully dressed, the towel seems redundant, but its use is more readily understood when it is recalled that massage frequently takes place at hot-spring resorts or after a bath. Whatever the practical purpose of the towel, it symbolizes a distance between customer and masseur, which is not necessary in a relationship between medical practitioner and patient and which indicates that this is not primarily a therapeutic session. The masseurs all state, however, that their techniques are beneficial both as a preventive measure and as actual therapy.

Customers

During the day customers at the massage parlor are mostly elderly people and local businessmen. In the evening the type of clientele gradually changes, and by midnight the building is full of *geisha* and women of the entertainment world. Occasionally a group of gangsters (*yakuza*) may appear, in which case everyone else hastily departs.

Some customers chat with their masseur, but most lie quietly and relax. All the customers that were interviewed claimed that a massage and a hot bath is the best method of relaxation that they know of. Most customers had been coming to this clinic for several years, and two customers in their eighties had been coming regularly for twenty and thirty years respectively. People of all economic levels are represented. Compared with patients at East Asian medical clinics, this group of people appears to be tradition-oriented. Of twenty people interviewed almost everyone had personal acquaintance with acupuncture and used moxibustion in the home. They expressed a strong preference for herbal medicine over synthetic medicine. Every informant carries out regular practice of religious ritual both in the home and at public places of worship.

None of the customers regarded themselves as ill, although several were suffering from shoulder stiffness or lumbago. Every customer was using *amma* as a preventive technique and a means of relaxation. Should they become ill, they would visit their family doctor, and possibly an East Asian practitioner at the same time—this would depend on the illness in question.

The function of *shiatsu* and *amma* clinics is different. *Shiatsu* is used both preventively and therapeutically. People go to *shiatsu* clinics in the role of a patient expecting to receive treatment for muscle, joint, or nervous problems and for conditions of general debility. They also use *shiatsu* in conjunction with cosmopolitan medicine when they are suffering from internal problems. Many patients resort to *shiatsu* only when they feel that cosmopolitan medicine has failed them. Others have previous experience with the East Asian system and, on becoming ill, will go to their family doctor if they believe they have an acute problem; alternatively, they will select a *shiatsu* clinic if they consider themselves to have a chronic or mildly incapacitating problem.

Shiatsu practitioners and patients are in agreement that the treatment is milder than acupuncture; they believe it is more "natural" and less painful. They also assert that it is better than acupuncture in that the whole body receives treatment regardless of the medical problem, whereas acupuncture, they believe, acts only on certain parts of the body. *Shiatsu* is therefore regarded by its practitioners and adherents as more holistic (*zentaiteki*) than acupuncture. Patients frequently select massage clinics because they dislike acupuncture or moxibustion or both, and they make greater use of herbal medicine bought at pharmacies than do patients in the acupuncture clinics.

This may be because patients who give preference to massage treatments over acupuncture or moxibustion are frequently people who avoid all forms of what they describe as "artificial" treatments or medications. Along a spectrum of things defined as "natural," good food, herbs, baths, and massage are all indigenous forms of medical treatment; acupuncture and moxibustion are not, and can be faulted as agents of defilement in strict Shintō terms. Moreover, food, herbs, baths, and massage are all associated with early socialization and with a warm relationship with the family and in particular with one's mother.

Patients at *shiatsu* clinics are not especially religious or conservative as one might have expected from the attitudes noted above. All types of income and educational levels are represented. Some of the patients seem to reflect a swing back to traditional ideas by members of the middle and upper middle classes.

People go to receive *amma* not in the role of a patient but as a customer receiving a service. The masseur is not called *sensei* (doctor), and the customer frequently guides the session by indicating to the masseur what he or she wants. Though the majority of the customers feel simply in need of relaxation when they come for treatment, *amma* is nevertheless considered both a preventive measure and a treatment for mild problems. The masseur is simply a technician who aids in what amounts to self-medication.

Clientele come from all types of educational and economic backgrounds, though they represent the traditional, conservative segment of each social class. Their high rate of formal involvement in religion attests to this. Moreover, they describe themselves as traditional people who take an active part in many of the classical art forms of Japan. They have had wide experience with East Asian medicine and take herbal medicine in preference to synthetic medicine whenever possible—not because they are suffering from long-term chronic complaints but because they and their families have always felt that "natural" herbal medicine is better.

The *amma* parlor is always busy, but there has not been a recent increase in the number of customers as there has been in the other types of clinics investigated. Although *amma* was an integral part of the East Asian medical system, and although it has been credited with great therapeutic value through the years, it seems that the Japanese who are now rediscovering East Asian medicine do not turn to *amma* but choose instead to go to other types of clinics. The *shiatsu* therapists and acupuncturists enjoy higher prestige and regard themselves, and are regarded, as more knowledgeable and scientific than their counterparts who perform *amma*.

The fact that the *shiatsu* clinics are not associated with the entertainment world or even with hot-springs resort areas adds to the medical image, whereas the idea of *amma* can never be separated in the minds of most people from pleasure and relaxation. But there is, of course, no hard and fast distinction between therapy and relaxation—it is, as always in Japan, a matter of degree.

Summary of Attitudes and Experiences of Patients in the East Asian Medical System

Patients of all economic and educational levels come to East Asian medical clinics for treatment. With the exception of people who want *amma* and who are usually tradition-oriented, patients at the clinics cannot be distinguished from the general population except insofar as they are suffering from some kind of chronic or debilitating problem. The clinics are usually crowded, and it is claimed that the numbers of patients are increasing rapidly. About half the people interviewed were trying East Asian medicine for the first time, while the others were already familiar with it. It is usually people from upper-class and lower-class families who are most used to the traditional system; in these families people resort regularly to both cosmopolitan and traditional practitioners, depending on their medical problem. It is in these families that most use is made of traditional medicine inside the home. New patients come mostly from the middle classes; people from this social class do not usually try East Asian medicine, which they regard as old-fashioned, until they are driven to it out of desperation when they believe that cosmopolitan medicine has failed them. Many of these patients are unwilling to inform their family doctor of their visits to East Asian clinics; they think that their family doctor would be opposed to it, and they are embarrassed to admit that they feel that they have been let down in the cosmopolitan system. On the other hand, they have often read very positive reports about traditional medicine in newspapers or magazines or have seen programs on television about it, and they soon find when they actually arrive at the clinic that many people of their educational level and interests are there too. Patients are usually introduced to the clinics by friends and relatives, hence one kind of social class tends to congregate at one clinic. About 20 percent of patients are introduced by their family doctor, who has good relationships with a traditional therapist (this excludes those using the health insurance system, who must all be referred by their cosmopolitan doctor).

The cost ranges between $1 and $15 per visit, but all clinics use a sliding scale to accommodate poorer people. The price need never present an economic burden to a patient, who can find a cheap clinic if one is required.

Patients at acupuncture, moxibustion, and massage clinics believe that these kinds of therapy are most suitable for muscle and joint problems or painful conditions related to the nervous system, such as neuralgia. They also use the clinics when they are suffering from migraine or mild complaints not readily diagnosed in the cosmopolitan system. A few patients with complaints that are widely recognized as psychosomatic, such as asthma or ulcers, also try acupuncture clinics, but usually on referral from their cosmopolitan doctor. It is only patients at the *kanpō* clinic who present a full range of medical problems, but even there acute cases are seen only rarely. A few patients at the *kanpō* clinic give up their family doctor and put themselves entirely into the hands of the M.D.'s at the traditional clinic. All the other patients continue to make regular use of cosmopolitan medicine.

Most patients agree that moxibustion has a longer-lasting and more profound effect on the entire body than does acupuncture, and it is thought to be especially suitable in the treatment of women. *Shiatsu*, believed to affect the whole body, is regarded as a light kind of stimulus and more "natural," although paradoxically it is also distinguished as habit forming. Herbal medicine, despite the fact that it often tastes disagreeable, is thought of as like a food and is believed to bring about the most profound change of all if taken over a long period of time.

Both doctors and patients agree that acupuncture is extremely effective in the treatment of psychological problems such as phobias, tobacco addiction, obesity, bed-wetting, and *kan no mushi*. This gives further credence to the belief that East Asian medical techniques can help change psychological attitudes and actual behavior.

The clinics themselves are pluralistic in their approach and provide an enormous variety in attitudes toward health care. Some try to combine cosmopolitan practice equally with traditional concepts and practice, others lean toward preserving the traditional approach as closely as possible, and still others apply traditional therapeutic techniques while limiting themselves to cosmopolitan concepts. There are both M.D.'s and licensed practitioners who believe in each of these approaches. The settings of the clinics are equally varied. Some, usually those using cosmopolitan concepts, are modern, clean, and replete with instruments and machinery. Others are in more traditional settings where no use is made of instrumentation. But there are also modern, sterile clinics where practitioners wear white coats and use contemporary examination tables while adhering to a completely traditional therapeutic approach. Several clinics specialize in dealing with particular problems or techniques, and patients may travel for more than an hour to come to the clinic of their choice.

The level of formality at the clinics also varies, depending on the education of the doctor, the location of the clinic, and the clientele. Clinics for wealthier patients make use of polite, formal language and allow the patients some privacy. In neighborhood clinics language becomes much more informal, and receiving therapy is a public event. Patients at these clinics stress the feelings of communality that they experience and how they are able to relax and express themselves verbally and rather freely. These informal therapy sessions are often compared to a visit to the public baths, which is known to be a time for relaxation.

Historically, in daily life, the Japanese affirmed their hierarchical social structure by making class distinctions in modes of dress, language, and nonverbal behavior. Today these distinctions can still be made to a large extent. The public bath, or the hot-springs resort, provides an interval of escape from the restrictions of society—one enters what is known as *hadaka no kankei* (nude relationships). The sexual element is completely muted under these conditions, and nudity gives one a chance to relax completely by shedding, along with one's clothes, social responsibility, class distinctions, and the burden of maintaining face with the world. It is the most traditional method used to restore balance to the body, and East Asian medical clinics can apparently assume a very similar function. Under these circumstances the therapeutic setting itself can lead to a reduction in stress.

Similarly, where massage, moxa, or herbal medicine are made use of in the clinic, these techniques will act as reminders of the supportive family unit and of all the powerful symbolism it is associated with in Japan (Dore 1967, p. 136). Moxa is particularly significant in this respect. When burned, the aromatic oils produce a highly evocative aroma that cannot fail to remind anyone who had childhood contact with it of their early experiences. For these people therapy commences the moment they set foot inside the door of the clinic.

In contrast, in clinics such as that of Mr. Katayama and in the *kanpō* clinic, where the patient is allowed to lie quietly and in privacy during therapy, there is encouragement of introspection. The use of meditation techniques and introspection is considered an essential aid to self-discipline and spiritual growth in the Zen tradition. This tradition has influenced the martial arts and other situations in which a performance is called for and where it is usual to practice introspection just prior to physical action in order to coordinate one's physical and mental energies to the best advantage. Similarly, the concept of health includes the idea of being in a controlled, balanced state, and introspection can be used to great advantage, for through self-reflection a sense of individuality, intact and temporarily freed of social burdens, is attained.

Techniques of diagnosis vary from clinic to clinic. Some clinics, such as that of Dr. Nagai, strive to maintain a very traditional system, supplemented with cosmopolitan techniques only if they are really in doubt as to what to do. At the *kanpō* clinic doctors try to combine both cosmopolitan and traditional methods to the fullest extent. In most small clinics, however, treatment proceeds after points of tension are ascertained and on the basis of the patient's self-diagnosis.

When the doctor or therapist discusses medical matters with the patient, the language used is inevitably that of cosmopolitan medicine. Most therapists stated explicitly that if they did not use scientific terminology, it would be hard to maintain a patient's faith. This is true even in clinics where the practitioners are trying to preserve tradition.

Patients are never rushed in the treatment session, which lasts on average forty-five minutes, and they are encouraged to return more frequently and for a much longer duration of time than would be usual in the United States. Ultimately, the patient himself, and not the doctor, makes decisions about return visits and termination of the treatment sessions. The doctor sometimes suggests what would be an appropriate interval between visits, but there is no appointment system, and responsibility rests with patients to come when they feel the need. Doctors do not tell patients when they are better and when they should stop treatment—patients take the initiative in reaching this decision. This attitude on the part of the doctors promotes the involvement of the patients and their responsibility in the treatment process.

There is an acknowledgment on the part of all the doctors and the majority of patients of the social and psychological dimensions of disease, which are viewed not as subsidiary to therapy but as an integral part of the entire healing process. In most clinics, however, patients receive therapy that is reductionistic in approach and designed solely to provide relief from physical symptoms. With the exception of people at the *kanpō* clinic, patients do not expect to make any major changes in their way of life as part of their treatment. These points will be dealt with in greater detail in Chapter 14.

The question of efficacy is of course important but enormously difficult to assess. Science is showing that traditional East Asian therapy can produce profound effects on the physiology of the body, (Pomeranz et al. 1976; Risse 1973; Sakaguchi 1963; Sjolund et al. 1976) and it is quite possible that the techniques used produce a direct impact on the course of the disease. But, if we are to understand more completely how these therapeutic techniques work, not only in curing disease but in healing illness (Kleinman 1973b, p. 161), we must understand their place in the entire medical system and acknowledge the beliefs, values, and expectations that patients bring to the healing process. It is also important to recognize that the objectives and needs of doctors and patients vary within any given medical system, making the task of analysis extremely complex. At the moment discussion will be limited to the patient's subjective judgment of the issue.

Patients who have discharged themselves do not usually use the word for cured (*naotta*) when they discuss their medical problems; they prefer the term "have become better" (*yoku naru*). Almost all the patients interviewed were very sensitive to the possibility of a recurrence of their problem, which they tended to view as a natural response to the general stress of life. They expect that their symptoms will be largely alleviated and that they will be generally free from pain, but they do not assume that the problem is necessarily solved for more than a temporary period of time. There is no great dichotomy acknowledged between a state of health and one of ill health: one's body has certain weaknesses, and these will manifest themselves from time to time.

Many patients in all types of clinics stated that they experienced relief of symptoms, often rather dramatically. This was particularly noticeable with problems of acute muscle spasm, whether of the back, the respiratory tract, or elsewhere in the body. But most patients find that in order to sustain relief of symptoms they must come for regular treatments over a period of many weeks, and it is during this time that some patients try other types of medicine both traditional and cosmopolitan. A few patients experience no relief at all; for example, while some patients with rheumatism and rheumatoid arthritis are helped, others seem to be totally unaffected. Many of these patients give up traditional therapy and return to their cosmopolitan doctor. Some patients suffering from, for example, whiplash, osteoarthritis, or lumbago are helped, but others find that they must continue treatment on a permanent basis to maintain relief of symptoms.

There are cases of malpractice in this medical system as in all others. Practitioners cite instances of colleagues reputed to be generally negligent, who have taken on patients with advanced medical problems that should have been dealt with by surgery. I saw one patient and viewed slides of four others who had received moxibustion repeatedly over a large portion of their bodies and had the scars to prove it. These patients were suffering from a variety of chronic problems and had eventually transferred themselves to alternative East Asian clinics. Slides had been taken for presentation at a conference on traditional medicine, in which malpractice would be openly censured by the practitioners themselves.

The most frequent comment for patients who are helped in the clinics is that they are delighted to find a type of therapy that produces very minor side reactions, if any at all, and one that they can continue to receive, and rather cheaply, on a long-term basis if necessary, without any fear of un-wanted consequences. Patients also tend to emphasize that they may not be totally cured but that they have been restored to a state in which they can resume their major role in life, whether it be as a professional, a housewife, or a blue-collar worker. This is the point to which they wanted therapy to bring them and thus they are satisfied. This theme will also be expanded in Chapter 14, once the philosophy and objectives of traditional practitioners have been developed in more detail.

12

East Asian Medical Schools

In the Kyoto-Osaka region there are eight schools with a total of more than 3,000 enrolled students in training to take licenses to practice acupuncture, moxibustion, massage, bonesetting techniques, or combinations of these. Four of the schools in Osaka are private and among them they have an enrollment of more than 2,300 students. The fees average about $360 per year, and two of the schools offer both day and night programs. The other four schools are supported by local government or by large Buddhist organizations. The students who attend them are all blind or physically handicapped in some way or are from families with very low incomes; their training is free.

The largest school in Osaka was founded in 1925; it closed during the war and reopened in 1959. The present director of the school states that the education offered today is basically in anatomy and physiology, with East Asian medical theory superimposed in the final year and a half of study. He says that the strength of East Asian medicine lies in therapeutic techniques, but adds that general attitudes and theories of diagnosis and disease causation should come from scientific sources. The director said that, for example, although acupuncture is particularly good for relieving pain, no satisfactory explanation for the occurrence of pain will ever be forthcoming except in a scientific framework, and he limits his own explanation to neurophysiological dimensions.

"It is essential that future East Asian practitioners should be able to use scientific language and thought in their work in order to communicate both with cosmopolitan doctors and with their patients," states the director. He feels that the classical, experiential (*taikenteki*) base of East Asian medicine is not satisfactory and that East Asian medical schools will not attain the status of universities until they have proved themselves to be scientifically sound. At least half the resources of the school are therefore devoted to research. Students spend a lot of time learning the mechanism and use of instruments designed, for example, to help find the pressure points or to cauterize the skin exactly as moxa does. The school emphasizes the importance of classifying data obtained from patients in an effort to rationalize and speed up diagnostic techniques and therapeutic procedures. The director also believes that the caliber of the students will increase as the status of the school improves through the implementation of a scientific orientation.

At present, students are required to be high school graduates upon entry. About half of them are women. Recently, many students have been older people, often retired company employees or housewives with older children. Several students are priests, since some smaller temples are taking advantage of the increased interest in East Asian medicine and are setting up medical clinics on their premises to augment their financial resources.

In Kyoto there is a public school for the blind, which was founded in 1888. Students attend from kindergarten onward and can eventually graduate either as musicians or as East Asian medical practitioners. One of the oldest teachers in the school, a blind man, said that blind practitioners of East Asian medicine endure much adverse prejudice from nonhandicapped practitioners. He states that with the push to make East Asian medicine scientific, and the desire to obtain university status in the schools, people feel that having large numbers of blind people in their profession is disadvantageous. Partially to counteract this tendency, and in the hope that their graduates can compete successfully in the outside world, the school for the blind stresses, even more than other schools do, highly scientific explanations. The classical theory of meridians is totally rejected, and the students are taught instead only the locations of the main pressure points and the scientific theories for their special properties. The transmission of stimulus through acupuncture and massage is explained entirely in terms of the nervous system. The school has a large library of medical books in Braille, both East Asian and cosmopolitan, which all students are required to read. After graduation, most students from the school work in massage parlors, where little medical knowledge is required, although a few of the very best East Asian clinics in Kyoto employ blind practitioners.

The most traditional of the East Asian medical schools is attached to Higashi Honganji temple of the Jōdo Shin sect of Buddhism, in central Kyoto. This school was founded in 1925 specifically to give training to disabled or very poor students. Its director, a Buddhist, believes strongly that if East Asian medicine tries to become totally rational (*riseiteki*) and scientific, it will fail. He states that there will always be a psychological and emotional aspect to illness, which cannot be helped by science but which the East Asian medical system is designed to deal with. "A good doctor," states the director, "will always have to be able to consider the patient as a whole person and not as an object carrying a disease." Anatomy and physiology are taught in this school, but in close conjunction with traditional East Asian medical theory. Courses in the classics in modern translation are also required.

The faculty at all of the schools are graduates who, while in the early years of their private clinical practice, have chosen to cultivate their ties to the senior faculty at the school. As the need arises, some of these people are then asked back as teaching staff without further formal training. Most teaching positions are part time and supplement clinical work; in research-oriented schools teaching and research appointments are usually combined.

The majority of students, therefore, study at schools where the approach is as scientific, that is, as rational and objective, as possible. The art of acupuncture and moxibustion is taught as a therapeutic technique to be used in conjunction with an objective approach to the body. The textbooks used in the schools reflect these attitudes. Those of the Osaka school, for example, are concise, well-organized volumes devoted largely to the application of acupuncture and moxibustion, and emphasis is placed on anatomy, physiology, and the nervous system. The history of East Asian medicine receives ten pages; traditional theories of explanation, including the yin/yang and five-phase theories, the concepts of *ki*, meridians, and pressure points, and the theory of the progression of diseases with time, receive twenty pages; nutrition, the relationship of man to the environment, exercise, preventive medicine, hygiene, and doctor-patient relationships are not dealt with at all. Knowledge about the meridians and pressure points is expanded in a book that deals with their interrelationship with the nervous system.

One volume is devoted entirely to diseases, their origin, their characteristic symptoms, and the recommended treatment. Explanations of origin and symptoms are given in cosmopolitan medical terminology. For example, the origin of stomach ulcers is listed under four separate points, which can be summarized as follows: an obstacle that blocks blood circulation in the stomach lining; high acidity of the gastric juice; damage to the mucus membrane of the stomach; and "emotional excitement" (*seishin kandō*). A long list of somatic symptoms is then cited. Under treatment the recommended pressure points at which to apply acupuncture and moxa are listed. All diseases are dealt with in a similar fashion—that is, the origin of illness is described mostly in terms of change in function at the cellular level, and if psychological origins are cited, they are referred to in an extremely peripheral way; symptoms are described totally in terms of somatic change, and emotional states are not referred to. Finally, treatment is limited solely to the application of mechanical therapeutic techniques.

Actual techniques of diagnosis are dealt with in some detail, however, and the classical categories used in diagnosis are maintained and explained carefully (see Chapter 3). In this instance a more holistic approach to the body is preserved. Several pages are devoted to the clusters of symptoms that are associated with certain body types (Association of National Training Institutes 1973, p. 112). A yang person is described thus: "Many are red faced, they have very firm muscles, are strong willed and with a bright, lively personality. They have plenty of determination. On the whole they do not get ill easily, but once sick their symptoms are violent and readily manifest, but they recover relatively quickly." Yin people have "soft muscles and hence bad blood color and weak stomach and intestinal function. They get sick easily, and once sick it rapidly becomes chronic. Symptoms are often not distinct or clearly indicated." People with hyperactivity of the kidneys are described in the following way: "They have a dusky or swarthy face color and adequate muscle development. Outwardly they seem difficult to deal with, but they have a mild personality, form close friendships, and are sociable people. From early times this type of person has been thought of as having a vigorous sexual desire." People with hypoactivity of the lungs are characterized as follows: "Their face color is pale, they are on the thin side and so their digestive function is weak. They have cold dispositions but a firm will and hence show perseverance. They contract ailments of the digestive and respiratory organs very easily."

In summary, while most of the teaching is reductionistic in approach, certain aspects focus on the patient as a whole person and the interaction of emotional states or disposition with the physical state. But, even where this is considered, it is not in terms of the individual's life experiences, as would be the case in psychotherapy in cosmopolitan medicine, but in terms of standard personality types, as was the case in the classical East Asian texts and also reminiscent of Hippocratic doctrine. Virtually none of the information given to students deals with the interrelationships of the patient with the natural environment or social milieu; in this respect, modern texts diverge most radically from classical teaching.

Naturally, the materials taught in school reflect the orientation of the national licensing examinations, which concentrate almost exclusively on anatomy and physiology, with emphasis on the nervous system. Questions are also devoted to the position of the meridians and points and to the point that should be used in order to deal with named diseases given in cosmopolitan terminology. There have recently been very few examination questions devoted to etiology or actual diagnosis of problems, nor are students usually held responsible for information related to classical theories, to the history of East Asian medicine, to the relationship of the occurrence of disease to the patient's way of life, or to environmental conditions.

Both the teaching techniques and the examination system encourage a drive toward the modernization of East Asian medicine in terms of concepts that are scientifically acceptable. Meridians and pressure points are not satisfactorily established as scientific facts; they are concepts that appear to have the potential of being explained this way when more is known about the autonomic nervous system and electrochemical activity at the cellular level. Similarly, precise observation and classification of symptoms—an essential part of the traditional system—is an acceptable, scientific task. Since graduates of East Asian medical schools will not have access to laboratories, X-ray machines, or the use of the stethoscope, they must be trained in other techniques of diagnosis. The classical system is therefore largely retained but is rarely brought up in examination, and students complain that they spend almost no time at all in school in practicing actual diagnostics.

Traditional theoretical explanations that are least readily subsumed under a scientific rubric are reduced to a minimum. Even theories on the effects of climate, nutrition, and one's social milieu on health are virtually abandoned because these topics are not fashionable in mainstream cosmopolitan medicine.

Upon graduation it is usual for a student to become apprenticed to an experienced practicing doctor. Many East Asian practitioners who were interviewed agreed that only during actual clinical practice had they begun to really understand traditional medicine, and that this knowledge bore very little relationship to materials taught in school, which were too abstract. This situation is partially the result of some basic assumptions that are shared by teachers and licensing boards alike. It is assumed that the formal school education is simply a preliminary training period in which one absorbs a certain body of knowledge in order to meet the minimum requirements for obtaining a license. A young graduate is expected, not to go out and set himself or herself up independently in clinical practice at this juncture, but rather to become apprenticed to a senior practitioner. The assumption is made that the *sensei-deshi* (master-apprentice) system, in which training for all professions and trades formerly took place, is still active. This is in fact the case. The whole, formal school training has therefore been tacked rather awkwardly onto the more informal clinical learning situation. In busy clinics with a large number of patients suffering from a variety of problems, recent graduates feel particularly inadequate as far as diagnosis is concerned. Others, who are apprenticed to tradition-oriented therapists, must be entirely retrained, with modern editions of classical texts as guidelines.

Other practitioners, usually in small neighborhood clinics, pointed out that because they see only patients with a limited number of medical problems, mostly skeletal and muscular, they actually apply a very small segment of the theoretical knowledge that they learned in school; that they are really technicians and not doctors in that all they do is administer therapy in a rather mechanical fashion.

In the *kanpō* world today, there is little conflict; but in acupuncture and massage circles, tension is rife. Everyone involved agrees that acupuncture should have greater status, but people are divided as to how that status should be improved. The factions are based initially on loyalty to one's school, and since the majority of the schools believe that research and the scientific method will bring both status and financial rewards, most recent graduates feel this way too. However, quite a few students will become apprenticed to practitioners who are striving to preserve a more traditional approach to East Asian medicine, and because of the very strong nature of the bonds between teacher and apprentice in Japan, students will eventually adopt the views of their later teachers.

As Nakane (1970, p. 48) has shown, factions are characteristic of Japanese society in general and are the product of the hierarchical and vertical organization that is typical in group situations. Subordinates are expected to remain loyal to their superiors, whether teacher or employer, throughout their lifetimes, and the only way to achieve innovation and independence on the part of a subordinate is to splinter off from the parent group with a few followers. In the East Asian medical world in Japan (not including *kanpō* doctors), there are three separate licensing organizations and several workers' unions. Apart from these divisions, there are numerous subdivisions based initially on the teaching schools. But, over the years, graduates have struck out independently and set up separate factions. Factions distinguish themselves by allegiance to the group leader and by the stress they put on certain aspects of theory or special techniques that the leader has developed. Some of the distinguishing features are, for example, the use of only a few special pressure points; the use of a new piece of machinery; emphasis on chiropractic diagnostic techniques; treatment of only one type of medical problem; emphasis on scientific research, and so on. This, naturally, leads to a considerable variety in actual medical practice and to great divergence from original theoretical sources. It was pointed out earlier (see Chapter 4) that there is a long historical precedent for this kind of organization in Japan, which encourages pluralism, competition, and innovation within all types of systems.

In contemporary Japan some graduates will become apprenticed to M.D.'s who, because they have no loyalty to teachers in traditional East Asian medical schools, can be particularly innovative. Many M.D.'s who enter East Asian medicine strive to retain a strongly traditional approach; they have for the most part taught themselves traditional medicine after graduation from ordinary medical school and are better able to compartmentalize the two approaches, and they are also very secure about their status as professionals. They, and a minority of the licensed acupuncturists, believe that the status of East Asian medicine would be best improved by preserving its unique qualities: its holistic and individualistic approach to man; its respect for the ability of the body to heal itself; and its reliance on "natural" therapeutic agents, among other things.

Practitioners who believe that traditional medicine will flourish best under a scientific rubric are antagonistic to therapists, including M.D.'s, who strive

201

to retain traditional elements viewed as nonrational and old-fashioned. Moreover, most practitioners are ambivalent about the presence of blind people in the profession in large numbers, and the practice of *amma* is regarded as a lowly occupation. Some therapists regard moxa as being either useless or dangerous; others believe that all types of massage are virtually useless as therapy. Hostilities are rife, and because of poor relationships it is almost impossible to obtain an introduction from one type of practitioner to another. There is, therefore, no concerted effort on the part of traditional medical practitioners as an organized group to influence governmental policy directly. Some of the major schools hope that if they can demonstrate an ability to do quality research, they will be granted the status of a university, and traditional medicine will be put on a much firmer footing. Other, smaller factions are content to work hard at an occupation which they believe is rewarding, without striving for improved status at the regional or the national level.

13

Philosophy and Attitudes of Acupuncture, Moxibustion, and Massage Specialists

Beliefs Regarding Traditional Concepts

Since there are many factions present in East Asian medical circles, it is not surprising that practitioners hold a wide variety of attitudes toward medical practice. This situation is reinforced because conferences and journals tend to be regionally organized and do not cut across the boundaries of loosely knit aggregates of several factions. Furthermore, M.D.'s who practice East Asian medicine usually attend their own conferences and do not contribute to those of licensed therapists.

Dr. Nagai, whose clinic was described previously, is an M.D. who represents the school of thought that strives for as close an adherence to the classics as is feasible. In his seminars on classical theory given for his assistants, Dr. Nagai refers most frequently to the *Huang-ti Nei Ching* (the Yellow Emperor's Classic of Internal Medicine) and not to the *Shōkanron*, which is so often quoted in the *kanpō* clinic. This is because the *Nei Ching* is particularly useful for students interested in general philosophical theories, whereas the *Shōkanron* emphasizes prescriptions and herbal lore.

Dr. Nagai accepts the traditional philosophic explanations in their entirety with the exception of the divinatory beliefs. He states: "If the five evolutory phases and the correspondence system, for example, are ignored, then the philosophical basis of East Asian medicine is destroyed and the system is of little use." He stresses the implicit unity in the yin/yang system and describes it as "dualism within monism." Dr. Nagai also points out that there are no "normals" in East Asian medicine and no fixed standards. Everyone either is relatively healthy or is not, based on the state of one's relationship with the environment—something that is in constant flux.

Like that of the *kanpō* doctors, Dr. Nagai's approach is a highly ecological one. For example, he says, "To set out to eradicate a bacterial infection with heavy doses of strong medicine will upset the balance of the body radically and the result will probably be the production of some other chemicals in excess inside the body. Preventive medicine is a much better approach than allopathic medicine. But, if prevention should fail, then only bacteria which are extremely toxic should be controlled, and even then, by using as mild a dose of herbal medicine as is feasibly possible."

Again: "In wintertime it is winter inside your body too—metabolism changes with the seasons. This is why eating foods that are in season is important; they have the correct nutrients, which are in harmony with the season and therefore with the body needs. People get sick by living in overheated houses and by eating watermelons in winter."

Dr. Nagai visualizes *ki* as electromagnetic and thermal energy. He teaches that the human body is constantly interacting with the environment through the flow of *ki,* and he is at present conducting experiments on the flow of *ki* in soybeans in an attempt to demonstrate his point scientifically. Kirlian photography, Dr. Nagai feels, may help to explain *ki* better.

"All diseases can be thought of as energy problems," states Dr. Nagai; "they can be detected through pulse diagnosis long before changes are visible microscopically." He adds that by the time a disease has developed to a secondary, visible state, it is sometimes already too late to stop it. If a potential disease is caught very early, then precise analysis is not necessary: although the form of the future disease is not yet manifest, it is possible at very early stages, when there is simply an imbalance of electrochemical changes in the body, to diagnose and apply East Asian therapy without specific details. Treatment can begin at once and at little expense. Many of Dr. Nagai's patients seem to share his belief, since large numbers of them come to him each week simply on a preventive basis.

"This is an extreme statement," Dr. Nagai says, "but I feel that people don't really need cosmopolitan doctors much, except for a few major operations and injuries from car accidents. This sounds cruel, but I think we

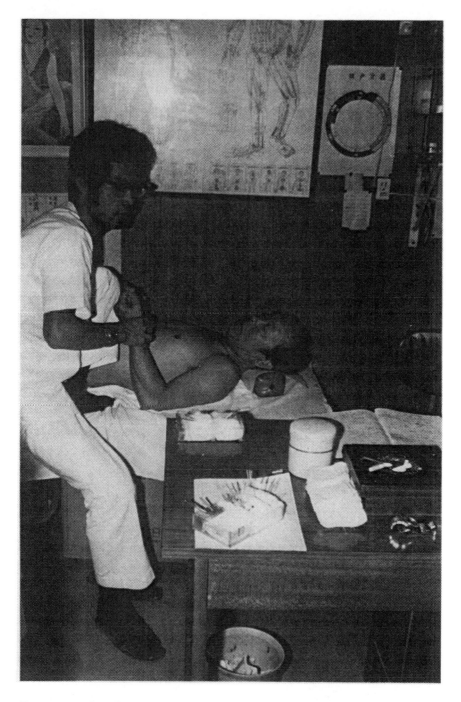

PLATE 18. Pulse-taking in an acupuncture and moxibustion clinic.

shouldn't put all our energy into saving people who are beyond a certain point. Cosmopolitan medical people like to make headlines with new techniques performed on crocks (*ikiru shitabane*), but this is not medicine."

In contrast to Dr. Nagai, Mr. Taguchi (see Chapter 10) believes that using a combination of cosmopolitan, "rational" medicine and what he calls "intuitive" East Asian medicine is essential for good results. While he believes that the origins of all diseases lie in one's attitude of mind (*kokoro*), he acknowledges that diet, hereditary constitution, climate, and so on have a great effect too. However, he believes that dietary and herbal therapy by themselves, for example, will be only temporarily effective unless the patient learns and changes his attitudes as a result of his sickness.

Mr. Taguchi uses the yin/yang distinction in diagnosis. He believes that yin people must receive treatment that will improve their appetite, speed up their metabolism, and make them more extroverted, and that the reverse is often true of yang people. He also takes note of complexion, posture, and points of tension. These are the only specific details from traditional theory that he consciously makes use of in his practice. He states that practice of the martial arts reinforces his belief in *ki,* but he is content to explain it as a "kind of energy." In a separate building near his house, Mr. Taguchi has access to a small laboratory where he experiments with East Asian medical techniques. He believes that the meridian system will ultimately be explained in scientific terms—as part of the nervous system—but he is quick to add that even if East Asian medical theories about body structure are eventually subsumed under scientific explanations, the need for a traditional, holistic approach to the body will not be reduced, but should, on the contrary, be reinforced.

Mr. Ando holds beliefs that are rather similar to those of Mr. Taguchi, but he works within the health insurance system, hence the actual application of his beliefs is quite different from that of Mr. Taguchi. According to Mr. Ando, diseases arise as a result of being out of balance with nature. He thinks that an individual's diet and psychological states must be carefully controlled to maintain the balance, and although he does not believe in formal religion, he states that "the strength of Man unified with Nature is a spiritual force (*shizen to ningen o tsunagu chikara wa hitotsu no kami da*). Culture and specialization have separated us all from this strength."

Mr. Ando believes in the yin/yang classification system of diseases, medicine, and food, and he also uses the correspondence system for general reference. He thinks of the internal organs in a traditional, functional way, but he never uses traditional terms to explain things to patients. He says that patients would lose faith in a doctor who said, for example, that their kidney meridian was off balance when they had come to see him about an asthma problem. The traditional concept of meridians is not acceptable to Mr. Ando, who thinks that the effect of stimulation of pressure points on internal organs (which he does not deny) is best understood in terms of the nervous system. He states: "Accepting everything in the Chinese medical classics is like believing every word of the Bible. I can give good treatment without accepting the meridian or pulse theories, but I do believe in *ki*—there are definitely energy exchanges between man and his environment."

Experience in the practice of moxibustion has led Dr. Ishino to conclusions radically different from those described above. He uses a belief system drawn entirely from cosmopolitan medical theories, and he is convinced that ultimately East Asian medicine will be totally explained by, and subsumed under, the cosmopolitan style of medical practice—he uses moxa simply as a tool to enhance cosmopolitan therapeutic techniques.

Dr. Kinoshita describes himself as first and foremost a scientist and expresses doubts about his own traditional clinic for babies (see Chapter 10) because it is not based on scientific premises. He believes that there may be many useful general concepts in the classics, but he will not accept the theory of meridians or the concept of *ki*, for example, until they have been proved scientifically. He states: "What East Asian medicine needs today is a Renaissance, then perhaps it will have something to offer Western medicine." He believes that recent medical developments in China are very significant, and that the Japanese should learn from the Chinese attempts to modernize East Asian medicine. "Without science, the practice of acupuncture is purely a shamanistic tradition," states Dr. Kinoshita, but he hastens to add that "scientific knowledge must be supplemented with experience—only with experience can a doctor interpret groups of symptoms accurately."

The practitioners of *shiatsu* stress the importance of tiredness and overwork (*karō*) in the origin of disease, but they also acknowledge that other social factors, such as diet and general stress, are important. They are unacquainted with most classical theories and make no use of them, though both of them believe in the concept of *ki*. One practitioner accepts the idea of meridians and points, whereas the other believes only in pressure points.

The variety of attitudes apparent regarding traditional theory is also evident during diagnosis and therapy.

Diagnosis and Treatment

Dr. Nagai believes that he can detect virtually all problems through East Asian diagnostic techniques, but he likes to have his ideas confirmed by X-rays and laboratory tests on certain occasions. He says he tries to think holistically all the time in dealing with patients. Even with something like a carbuncle, the right question to ask, he says, is not "What bacteria caused this?" but rather, "Why did the carbuncle arise on this particular spot in the body and not another?" And, "What meridian, or part of the nervous or venous system, is close to the carbuncle, and therefore what other parts of the body might be affected by or are affecting this particular spot?"

The aim of treatment is to restore balance, and to achieve this Dr. Nagai believes that all types of therapy should be integrated; in actual practice, however, emphasis is placed on acupuncture and moxibustion treatments. In this clinic, as in others, there has recently been a reduction in the stimulus given to patients because experiments in physiology have shown that even a mild stimulus, either from a needle or through burning moxa, brings about marked electrochemical changes in the body. When practicing acupuncture Dr. Nagai uses classical techniques for the insertion and withdrawal of the needles. By manipulating the needles in a certain way, he attempts either to draw off excess energy or to supply energy when it is deficient. Very few practitioners in other clinics apply these techniques so rigidly today.

Despite his close adherence to the classical tradition, Dr. Nagai is not opposed to supplementing the system with technology. Most patients receive electrical acupuncture, and Dr. Nagai believes that the mild, constant stimulus supplied by wiring the needle to an electrical source is superior to a hand-held needle. When the needle is held by hand, it is the rotation of the needle once it is inserted into the body which acts as the source for electrochemical changes in the surrounding cell tissue. When electrical acupuncture is applied, rotation of the needle is, of course, not necessary. All acupuncturists state that when a needle is properly inserted, a certain point is reached when the flesh seems to grip at the needle and a mild vibrating sensation can be felt in the fingertip placed on the head of the needle. This condition is known as *tokki*. The patient is also aware when *tokki* is achieved—a variety of sensations occur, such as mild throbbing, tingling, or an aching. In electrical acupuncture, once this condition is established, the needle is connected to the electrical input and left in place for between ten and twenty minutes. After the initial sensations, the patient rarely experiences any discomfort. Electrical acupuncture acts as a labor-saving device, since once the patients are wired to the machine, they can be left unattended. In many clinics, such as the *kanpō* clinic, electrical acupuncture is considered too strong a stimulus and is never used.

Like the *kanpō* doctors, Dr. Nagai treats patients for problems of vitiated blood (*oketsu*). The *kanpō* clinic doctors use only herbs to improve circulation and to dissolve small blood clots. Dr. Nagai uses rubber suction bulbs attached to a glass cup, which is placed on the patient's body so as to produce a vacuum into which capillary blood is drawn. The belief is that sometimes small clots of blood, accumulated during the menstrual period or through bruising, for example, become trapped in the small capillaries at the body extremities and cannot return to the liver with the venous blood. This results in a variety of discomforts, such as dizziness, headaches, and heightened irritability.

Despite his orientation in tradition, scientific experimentation is considered important by Dr. Nagai; he believes that research will confirm many aspects of the classical system. He considers the present training of therapists to be inadequate and modified into a pseudoscience that does an injustice to both science and East Asian medicine. He believes that training should start with a thorough grounding in the classics and carries out this belief in his seminars. Dr. Nagai also feels that some sort of religious beliefs about the nature of man, his relationship to the cosmos, and his ability to transcend his daily state are essential in both a good therapist and the patient, but he states that formal Buddhism in Japan has lost its power to evoke feelings of this kind.

Although Mr. Taguchi takes the pulse in traditional style, the system that he relies on most in diagnosis is a chiropractic technique in which he assesses the state of the internal organs by feeling for points of tension along the spine. Patients' charts are kept in the clinic but are rarely referred to after the initial examination. Mr. Taguchi uses acupuncture, moxibustion, massage, and chiropractic in therapy and recommends the use of natural food and herbal medicine, although he is not allowed to prescribe it. Patients are sometimes sent to get laboratory tests in order to confirm a diagnosis, and they are also occasionally referred to cosmopolitan doctors.

Mr. Taguchi has developed a speciality of treating glaucoma and cataracts by administering acupuncture on the bladder meridian. If the disease is not too far advanced, he claims he can effect a cure, and patients with the problem come to his clinic from all over Kyoto.

Unlike all the other practitioners interviewed, Mr. Taguchi believes that part of his job is to actively encourage psychological and social change in patients. "I am like god's messenger (*kamisama no otsukai*)," says Mr. Taguchi. "I intervene to bring people back to their natural state. First I work on the body, and then, while I'm working, I talk, and the patient talks, and we try to change their emotional state (*kokoro o ochitsukeru*)." Because of the advent of the nuclear family, the development of large apartment complexes, and similar trends, Mr. Taguchi believes that the family no longer fulfills its proper function as a place where sickness is shared. His traditional attitudes are highlighted in statements such as the following: "If any child under the age of fifteen becomes ill, it is the fault of the mother. She has been too selfish (*wagamama*) and the child could not *amaeru* ("presume upon her love") sufficiently. After fifteen, the child has come of age (*genpushiki*) and is then responsible for his own health." On further questioning, it became clear that in this context Mr. Taguchi was thinking primarily of chronic and recurrent diseases such as asthma, eczema, nephrosis, frequent colds, stomach troubles, and bed-wetting. He does not hold the mother responsible for measles, mumps, chicken pox, or other common diseases of childhood.

Mr. Ando, Dr. Ishino, and Dr. Kinoshita do not make any diagnosis in their clinics. When they are in doubt about treatment procedure, all of them resort to cosmopolitan diagnostic techniques, either directly or, in the case of Mr. Ando, indirectly. Dr. Kinoshita states firmly that he does not believe in the traditional pulse diagnostic system—he considers that it is impossible to tell the state of the internal organs without laboratory tests, but he also thinks that blood pressure measurements can be equated with traditional ideas of increased and reduced body functioning (*kyoshō* and *jisshō*). Neither do the *shiatsu* practitioners use standard diagnostic techniques in their practice. When using *shiatsu*, they say, it is not important to make a diagnosis, because massage is at once both a diagnostic and a therapeutic technique (*shokushin sono mama chiryō ni naru*). During a treatment, the entire body must be massaged, and areas of tension are noted and given special attention. All of the practitioners are agreed, with the exception of Dr. Kinoshita, who has doubts about his own therapeutic system, that they are providing therapy that will have an effect on the body's entire system, and they state that removal of the major symptoms is not their sole purpose in therapy. There is also general agreement with Mr. Ando's statement about using mild therapy wherever possible: "If you start with a big stimulus, the patient will experience side effects of dizziness, tiredness, or even fainting. If the body is repeatedly overstimulated, it will gradually stop responding to treatment unless a stronger and stronger stimulus is given. A light stimulus is all that is needed—just enough to reverse whatever reaction has gone to excess in the body—there should be no side effects at all." This attitude toward treatment sessions means that patients must be prepared to come for therapy frequently and over a long period of time.

With the exception of Dr. Nagai and occasionally of Mr. Taguchi, advice on diet, exercise, climate, and other types of preventive medicine is not offered in any of the clinics. Even in the case of Mr. Adachi, whose entire clinic is devoted to burning moxa as a preventive measure, no verbal advice is offered and virtually no social interaction takes place.

This enormous variety in beliefs and practice within what superficially appears to be one unified medical system illustrates some fundamental points about Japanese culture in general. It is characteristic of almost any type of learning situation, whether it be the early socialization process, students in school, or trainees for a job, that precise goals and methods of achieving the goals are laid out carefully in advance. As novices, people are required to learn without questioning authority and to thoroughly internalize, usually through repetitive action, a given body of knowledge or activities. Once graduation, licensing, or initiation is achieved and mastery is acknowledged, then individual initiative, responsibility, and creativity in application of the knowledge is expected. The philosophy of Zen Buddhism is greatly influential in this attitude toward training, and it was applied very widely throughout the Edo period. Its most obvious mode of application in modern Japan is in the arts, Kabuki, flower arrangement, the martial arts, and so on, but it is also evident in skilled labor, catering, advertising, and marketing of goods in general. People who enter into entrepreneurial, competitive situations often believe that by being innovative as well as efficient they can provide the best kind of service and attract customers.

East Asian doctors are mostly self-employed businessmen, often in direct competition with one another. Under these circumstances some individual specialization leading to a pluralistic system is necessary if the practitioner is to survive. While many of the schools are trying to rationalize and define the field of East Asian medicine precisely and clearly, most graduates, once they become practitioners, quietly oppose this and adapt the system to fit their own type of personality, the needs of their patients, and the social environment in which they find themselves. The results of this specialization can be seen in the great variety of traditional medical practice available in Kyoto today.

Dr. Kinoshita and Dr. Ishino provide the most reductionistic treatment, and they assume that only the parts of traditional medicine that can potentially be explained by science will continue to be useful. Both of these doctors have very little interaction with their patients, and they do not actually touch the patients at all. Both men have spent a large proportion of their lives devoted to research, and Dr. Kinoshita readily admits that the greatest challenge for him is in the laboratory. Both men are over seventy years of age and from upper-class families. In their lifetimes Japan has been transformed from a recently feudalistic society into one of the leading industrial nations. As young doctors they stood by helpless, as did doctors in the West, while patients died of cholera, typhoid, tuberculosis, and pneumonia. They have few misgivings about the advantages of science, but because their families were for many generations deeply involved with traditional medicine, they have decided to continue the family interest. In Dr. Ishino's case, it is modified drastically by cosmopolitan medical ideas, and in Dr. Kinoshita's case, it is a sideline and a form of community service. Treatment of patients in both their clinics appears rather abrupt, but the clinics are extremely popular, nevertheless. Both men have the advantage of advanced age and of experience on their side—something which many Japanese patients respect.

The *kanpō* doctors and Dr. Nagai approach traditional medicine in a different way. They have a thorough grounding and experience in science but have reached a point where they are consciously adopting traditional medicine in an attempt to counteract some of the problems they have experienced in using cosmopolitan medicine. Dr. Nagai has actively rejected much of cosmopolitan medicine, hence he is not taken very seriously by other M.D.'s. He grew up in a rural area, his father was not a doctor, and he did not go to Kyoto University medical school—these factors make him unusual, and his rather emphatic opposition to establishment medicine may well be related to his personal experiences with his colleagues. The *kanpō* doctors, on the other hand, are highly respected members of the medical community, both cosmopolitan and traditional. They actively cultivate both approaches to patient care and have a well-developed philosophy regarding the strong and weak points of both systems.

Although the licensed practitioners hold a variety of beliefs, in actual practice almost all of them provide therapy that is little more than a mechanical application of traditional techniques. Therapy is unhurried, often up to one hour's treatment, and the atmosphere is pleasant and relaxing; but advice on diet, climate, social matters, and psychological counseling are virtually nonexistent. Most therapists do not consider that it is their role to supply total care. Patients come to them with specific complaints, and therapists assume that the cosmopolitan family doctor is the principal medical adviser. They have no wish to encroach upon his role or status. They try to remove the complaints and incidentally improve the patient's general condition, and they assume the patient will continue to use the family doctor for most health care. Traditional therapists therefore come to view themselves as specialists in the removal of pain and in skeletal and muscle problems. Many of them are reluctant to give advice because they view their position as lower than that of the cosmopolitan doctor. What theory they learned in school gradually atrophies for lack of application, and in extreme cases the practitioner becomes known as a specialist in dealing with only one medical problem. Thus, he spends his days performing the same simple technique again and again. He makes no diagnosis or follow-up, keeps no records, and rarely develops rapport with patients.

Although the proffering of advice is not readily apparent, all the practitioners, with perhaps the exception of Dr. Ishino and Dr. Kinoshita, display an attibute that is greatly admired in Japan—that of empathy (*omoiyari*). Dr. Kinoshita and Dr. Ishino have nurses and technicians who substitute for them in this respect. Lebra (1976, p. 38) states that she is "tempted to call Japanese culture an '*omoiyari* culture.'" Sensitivity to the feelings of others, an ability to understand another's pain or pleasure, is valued highly. The therapists displayed the ability to be gentle in their touch and willing to listen to patients' troubles to a remarkable degree. When someone takes fifteen minutes to list his or her troubles, both social and physical (and this is by no means unusual), then all of the therapists make time to listen attentively and moreover to agree readily that life or work is hard and tough (*kurushii, kitsui*) or that the patient is suffering from overwork (*karō*). The patient does not expect the therapist to alter these facts of life, but he or she does expect that these sentiments will be shared and sympathized with. I have witnessed a *kanpō* doctor spend one hour on the phone after the clinic was closed, listening to a worried patient. He offered very little advice but showed understanding and no sign of impatience.

With the exception of the *kanpō* doctors, who are independently rather wealthy, all the other practitioners work extremely hard, long hours for relatively little profit. Patients can see that the house or clinic where they receive treatment is modest in style, and they do not have the feeling that the therapist is making a great profit at their expense, and not one person grumbled in this respect. Almost every practitioner is willing to make house calls and works a six-day week, including in the evenings—they are accessible whenever they are needed and give every evidence of putting good service before financial considerations.

In summary, the Japanese characterize themselves as a practical people and not given to philosophical speculation to the same degree as are the Chinese. When traditional East Asian medicine is put into practice in contemporary Japan, it is usually done so in a highly pragmatic way: a trend that was established in historical times (see Chapter 4). All the doctors believe that the therapeutic techniques produce changes at the cellular level in the body; they are not agreed on just how this occurs, but they are convinced of the results. They are also equally convinced that, with reasonable application of caution, the techniques do not cause harmful side effects. They therefore feel very positive about using the system and are convinced of its worth on these grounds alone.

The intricacies of the classical theoretical system are applied only in a very general way and sometimes not at all. Where they are applied they are used most frequently by therapists well versed in trends in the scientific world, who have equated traditional theory with ecological and cybernetic models. It is in the application of herbal medicine as therapy that the most traditional terminology and adherence to classical theory is retained. It is also in this area that reductionism is rejected most actively. The *kanpō* doctors are adamant in their belief that injections of a single purified active principle from crude herbal extracts are harmful and contrary to their basic principles of providing a little medical assistance to the healing powers of nature.

The classical texts stress the importance of preventive medicine, good diet and exercise, and the maintenance of a balanced emotional state and social relationships. Little effort is made to deal overtly with any of these issues in the contemporary clinical setting. Traditionally, it has been the function of the family and the educational system to foster this type of learning, and doctors could reasonably assume that patients were sensitive to these issues. In the *kanpō* clinic careful advice is given nowadays regarding diet, but this is done because the doctors are concerned about the impact of a Western diet on their patients, and as a direct response to loss of traditional dietary values. They have taken this function on because they believe that the family and the educational system are inadequately informed in this respect. They also offer occasional advice about care in certain types of weather and the importance of regular exercise—this is considered necessary information for young people living in nuclear families. In other cases it is regarded as not important or even presumptuous for a young doctor to tell an old person how to adjust to the forces of nature. Mr. Taguchi is the only practitioner interviewed who gives unsolicited advice on human relationships and social behavior. He was a schoolteacher for many years before he became a therapist, and he is still active and holds extremely high rank in the martial arts. He is therefore used to being in the role of a teacher and counsellor. In school and as a senior member of a martial arts center he is expected to teach good social decorum and good control over the expression of emotional states. Mr. Taguchi gives off an aura of great calm and self-confidence while at work in his clinic, without being oppressive. He is a good listener and also a great talker. The advice he gives, however, is almost never directed at a specific patient's social problems, but is for general consumption and is couched in Confucian ethics. Even in this clinic, social and psychological issues are not dealt with directly.

To some extent the mass media have taken on the role the extended family used to play. There are many television programs, magazine articles, and books that deal with nutrition, hygiene, and health in general, and as was pointed out earlier, many families are beginning to take an interest again in traditional approaches to health. I think it unlikely that East Asian practitioners will expand their role radically to incorporate more preventive medicine into their practice. I believe that they view this as intimately related to the family, work, and the educational system and not within their immediate realm of activity.

However, a good practitioner will always listen to complaints and show empathy. He will take even the most minor of subjective symptoms seriously and allow plenty of time even for patients who are outwardly not suffering to any obvious degree. We shall now turn to the complex issue of holism in medical practice and explore the implications of the above findings in more detail.

14

Holism and East Asian Therapy

The concept of holism has two meanings to an East Asian doctor: that of considering all the parts of the body to be interconnected and mutually affecting each other, and that of viewing the human body as being in constant interaction with, and affected by, the environment, both social and physical. The doctors in this study, without exception, all believe that they are using therapy that will do more than remove the principal complaints of the patient and that will have some effect on the entire body. This is true even where the practitioner provides exactly the same kind of treatment to all his patients. Some practitioners consider that they induce a series of electrochemical energy changes involving the nervous system. Others believe that they are dealing with *ki* and the meridian system. Both explanations incorporate the idea that treatment at one part of the body will be transmitted throughout the body. All the practitioners therefore believe that they are providing a holistic treatment in the first sense described above.

The *kanpō* doctors, Dr. Nagai and Mr. Taguchi, are the only practitioners who make any practical attempt to deal with the second concept. In these cases the doctors make use of social, psychological, and dietary information in addition to noting physical symptoms in an attempt to account for the origins of the disease and to aid in diagnosis. But, with the exception of Mr. Taguchi, actual recommendations to patients are limited largely to dietary matters and to the administration of medication; even Mr. Taguchi's advice on social relationships is very general and is not directed to any one specific patient and his or her individual problems. While a holistic approach is

217

acknowledged as necessary and is acted upon regarding etiology and diagnosis, the practitioners do not provide a holistic approach to therapy but restrict themselves almost exclusively to manipulating reactions inside the body.

The Role of the Family in Healing

In the East Asian medical system, the focal point of the healing process is thought of, not as the interaction between doctor and patient, but rather as the sick person at the center of an involved family. Sickness is regarded, not as the concern primarily of an individual, but as an event for which the entire family unit has a shared responsibility. Lebra (1976, p. 36) comments: "The suffering of a group member is vicariously experienced by the other members, arousing guilt feelings in the latter even when they are by no means responsible for the suffering." In the case of illness family members empathize with the sick person. The mother of a young child may feel deep guilt for the actual occurrence of the illness and believe that her failure to provide adequate nurturance has left the child vulnerable, a view that Mr. Taguchi and other practitioners confirmed. Even when family members do not feel personally responsible for the occurrence of the illness, they do feel that it is their responsibility to share the burden of being sick.

The healing process is viewed, therefore, as something to be collectively participated in by the family members, and people are willing to interrupt major undertakings, such as study abroad, to return to the family when someone becomes more than mildly ill. Illness is regarded by the entire family as a kind of liminal period, to use Turner's terminology (1969, p. 94). It is a time when one can legitimately withdraw from the everyday demands of society and devote one's attention to the family; it is a chance for potential growth in family understanding and unity, a goal that is fundamental in Japanese values. Not only does the sick person take time off from work without guilt, but so too do other family members if they are required to assume the role of a home nurse. There is no question of allowing sick persons to manage by themselves as best they can, as might be the case in America, or of having the neighbors pop in, as might happen in England. It is only when a young mother becomes ill (see Chapter 5), and when she returns to her own mother that her illness, rather than acting as a focus for family unification, can act as a disruptive and unwelcome element.

Not only do family members participate in the healing process, but there is an attempt to contain sickness within the immediate family as far as is possible, for other reasons related to the unwillingness of Japanese people to be dependent upon outsiders. Reliance upon others imposes obligations that one is morally obliged to repay. People therefore try not to burden others, and the result is a quiet insistence on self-help wherever possible. This kind of attitude encourages the prompt use of self-medication in an attempt to avoid getting ill, on the part of people who are not living with their immediate family. For example, the person in charge of a male residence unit at a university in Kyoto commented that he regularly clears out hundreds of half-used bottles of medicine after the thirty students have returned home at the end of each academic term.

Insistence on self-help also encourages acceptance of responsibility and active participation on the part of the patient in the healing process. Should the therapist take too active and domineering a role in this respect, the patient and his or her family would feel embarrassed, that the therapist had stepped outside his role, and that they were under an obligation to the therapist—which would make any future encounters rather unproductive.

Expressions of dependency needs are acceptable within the family. The sharing of responsibility within the family for suffering and recovery from illness takes a characteristic form, which enhances its effectiveness. Since the direct expression of emotion is considered disruptive to the maintenance of harmonious family relationships, it is not surprising that concern about illness is expressed largely through nonverbal interaction rather than by an exchange of dialogue related to feelings about and reactions to the situation. Patients can and do describe pain and other physical sensations in minute detail. They also state at times that they are frightened or worried. But neither they nor the family usually wish to discuss directly, for example, chronic tense interpersonal relationships, either within or outside the family, which could have precipitated or exacerbated the illness. This is so, despite the fact that interpersonal relationships are readily acknowledged as a source of stress leading to illness.

Emphasis on nonverbal communication is reinforced by the value placed on intuitive understanding (Morsbach 1973). Buddhism teaches that intuitive understanding leads to insight, and it is considered to be more refined and aesthetic than rational, deductive, and verbal communication. A mother prides herself on her intuitive understanding of her baby; a good mother anticipates the needs of the child by being receptive to nonverbal indications of discomfort before the baby actually starts to cry. Love, care, respect, and so on are demonstrated, at all stages of the life cycle both within and beyond the family, by actions more frequently than with words. Conversely, people learn to express their needs through their behavior, and illness is readily interpreted as a indirect appeal for care and attention. This is particularly true of non-life-threatening, mild, or chronic, recurrent problems. These kinds of problems are thought of, not as invasions of the body by unwanted forces, but rather as an unharmonious state due to lack of personal care. They are considered to be illnesses rather than diseases (Kleinman 1973, p. 160) and hence have broader implications than simple malfunctioning of the body, implications that are within the realm of the family and not the doctor.

The use of simple remedies in the home provides a very good opportunity for the kind of nonverbal communication that is enjoyed and prized within a family. Massage and bathing allow prolonged tactile contact. The preparation of infusions of medication from everyday plant material provides oral gratification (even though they are bitter tasting at times). All of these activities are associated especially with early childhood and the close attention and loving care that most Japanese children have received in abundance. They are symbols of solidarity of the primary group and of the fact that the family will help one of its members through a difficult time. Victor Turner (1967, p. 28) stated that ritual can demonstrate "polarization of meaning," that is, psychological needs are linked through the use of symbols and ritual to the social order and the shared values of a society. In the Japanese family, through the use of oral and tactile healing rituals, dependency needs are fulfilled and are associated positively with family unity.

Undisguised verbal complaints about family members, particularly those from members low in the hierarchical system, such as Mrs. Honda, directed toward higher ranked individuals, such as her mother-in-law, are strongly tabooed. However, patients' responses to the causes of mild and chronic diseases (see Chapter 7) indicate that they are highly sensitive to psychosomatic explanations for the occurrence of illness. Informants such as Mrs.

Honda believe that somatic complaints, in this case those of her baby, are the expression of social and psychological problems, and since the mutual interaction of mind and body has never been a topic of serious debate in East Asian thinking, it is natural that they should do so. By focusing on physical complaints, patients and their families are able to come to terms with and allude indirectly to the tabooed topic of stress in interpersonal relationships.

Somatization and the Response of East Asian Practitioners

All the practitioners interviewed believe without exception in the psychosomatic concept of disease causation, but like their patients they choose to focus on somatic complaints as the point of departure for therapeutic intervention. Dealing directly with psychological and social factors would destroy patient rapport and minimize cooperation.

East Asian practitioners feel particularly confident when dealing with minor somatic complaints. They solicit these details actively to aid in diagnosis; they believe strongly that all minor complaints should be dealt with seriously, otherwise more complicated problems are likely to arise; and they believe that their therapeutic techniques are able to relieve minor physical symptoms. Those therapists who use traditional diagnostic techniques feel confident that they can deal with patients' problems at a very early state of development, and they regard this as a positive attribute.

It is believed that minor physiological imbalances and somatic changes can be detected in all patients, even those diagnosed as, for example, cases of neurosis (Reynolds 1976, p. 15). Consequently, few patients ever leave a traditional medical clinic without receiving some form of treatment directed toward the production of somatic change.

Work carried out independently by Kleinman (1976), Marsella, Kinzie, and Gordon (1973), Tseng (1975), and others is of great interest in this connection. Their results show that both Chinese and Japanese patients tend to present somatic complaints rather than psychological complaints when suffering from mental illness (diagnosed by means of cosmopolitan medicine) with much greater frequency than patients from Western cultures. Kleinman (1976) says of a group of twenty-five patients with a depressive syndrome:

> Twenty-two of these cases (88%) initially complained only of somatic complaints (i.e., they did not complain of dysphoric affect or report it when queried). During their subsequent treatment in the psychiatric clinic, ten patients (40%) never admitted to experiencing dysphoric affect. Seven of these patients (28%) rejected the idea that they were depressed even after they had been successfully treated (i.e., had experienced complete symptom relief) with anti-depressant medication. (P. 3)

These patients looked upon their physical complaints as their "real" sickness. Leaving aside the important and unanswered problem to date—whether all labels devised out of the practice of medicine in the West can be applied cross-culturally—let it simply be said that this pattern of somatization is significantly different from findings in the West and is apparently reinforced by the traditional medical system and by cultural values, so that the experience and expression of disease, in this case depression, is manifested in a relatively culture-bound form.

The most characteristic type of neurosis in Japan, *shinkeishitsusho*, also takes a highly distinct form. It is thought to originate as a result of hereditary factors, overdiscipline and overprotection during childhood, and the institutionalized family structure and educational system. In Doi's experience, the problem seems to arise as a result of an inability to *amaeru*, thus giving rise to anxiety (1973, p. 130). *Shinkeishitsu* patients characteristically exhibit a strong desire to lead a full life, perfectionist tendencies, and an extreme self-consciousness, which inhibits their ability to fulfill their ambitions. They are thought by many to possess more than average intelligence and creative potential. Physical manifestations of the problem are, among others, fatigue, heavy head, headaches, insomnia, dizziness, and gastrointestinal complaints.

Reynolds (1976), in his attempt to relate the occurrence of *shinkeishitsu* neurosis to Japanese social structure, explores the social dimensions of early socialization. He points out that in order to survive successfully in a society that favors nonverbal communication and is opposed to the direct expression of feelings toward others, it is necessary to learn how to be able to influence the behavior of others indirectly. While this can lead to a sensitivity toward others, in some people who are "oversocialized" it leads to anxiety because they can never get direct feedback about other people's feelings toward themselves.

Someone who has little success in his subconscious endeavors to receive care from others through his nonverbal manipulations is likely to come to believe that the cues he is giving are not correct or are somehow inducing the wrong results. Under these conditions, a syndrome characteristic of *shinkeishitsu* neurosis develops, known as *taijin kyofuku* (anthrophobia). Patients with this problem exhibit phobias in which they are concerned about their body odor or have a fear of blushing, of appearing ugly or dirty, of stammering, of excess sweating, and so on. They are also overly concerned with contracting disease—this symptom was exhibited more than any other in a group of patients suffering from this obsessive-phobic syndrome studied by Reynolds. There are hospitals throughout Japan that specialize in the treatment of *shinkeishitsu* neurosis. Moreover, many of the patients of East Asian medical practitioners are people who exhibit this problem.

Therapists believe that babies exhibiting nervous complaints (*kan no mushi*) are likely to develop into adults with *shinkeishitsu* tendencies. They agree unanimously that *kan no mushi* is the result of overindulgent and overprotective mothering. Overnurturance limits the natural desire of the baby to explore its environment through manipulation and also slows its maturation somewhat. The baby with *kan no mushi* is already expressing through its body the need to be allowed more freedom and independence. At later stages of development, according to the practitioners, these same children frequently develop asthma, eczema, or other allergic problems.

The child who is constantly indulged never learns how to manipulate others in later life to obtain its needs—it has always had its needs met; thus those who have the chance to *amaeru* most as children, are the very people who in later life are the least successful at it. It is significant that men, who are indulged most as children, have a higher rate of occurrence of *shinkeishitsu* than women.

Although problems related to dependency needs are felt to a degree by all human beings, the particular patterning of the *shinkeishitsu* syndrome is largely culture-bound to Japan and, although enhanced by changes in family structure, is certainly not limited to modern times. It is not surprising, therefore, that people suffering from this problem use indigenous therapy, whether it be Morita therapy, described by Reynolds (1976), or the East Asian medical system.

Traditional therapists take positive delight in dealing with *shinkeishitsu* patients, who have frequently come from a cosmopolitan doctor who had either denied that their symptoms were "real" or told the patient that he was neurotic and given him an injection of a sedative. The East Asian practitioner agrees emphatically with the patient that all subjective complaints are "real," can provide a therapy that is successful in relieving mild symptoms, and uses a clinical setting and treatment techniques that are close to those used in a nurturant family situation.

East Asian medical practitioners in Japan appear, therefore, to be well adapted to helping patients who are manifesting problems that arise specifically as the result of socialization into Japanese culture. Given the long historical association of traditional East Asian medicine and Japanese culture, the two systems are bound to have influenced each other profoundly. Therefore, we can expect to find congruences between traditional medical beliefs, beliefs about early socialization practices, and the way in which the symptoms of illness are presented to a medical practitioner.

The Meaning of Therapeutic Efficacy

Just as the concept of holism reflects cultural values, so does the concept of therapeutic efficacy. Socialization in Japan encourages one to be actively dedicated to one's role, and this commitment should come before individual needs. An awareness and a need for a sense of belonging that is fostered in early childhood encourages commitment to one's role and group. Many observers of Japanese society have pointed out that social organization is extremely group-oriented, that a sense of identity is achieved through belonging to a group or groups (Lebra 1976, p. 22; Nakane 1970, p. 23; Rohlen 1974b), and that motivation for achievement is based on a desire for one's group rather than oneself to get ahead and be successful (DeVos 1973, p. 187).

Efficacy in healing is equated, therefore, not merely with removal of symptoms from the individual—in the minds of either the doctor, the patient, or the families—but more with psychosocial adjustment and recovery to participation in one's role. It is not by having oneself made whole again but by being able to make the group whole again that efficacy is measured. As Kiefer (1976, p. 281) puts it, "The Japanese tends to include within the boundaries of his concept of self much of the quality of the intimate social groups of which the individual is a member." Therefore, someone whose major physical symptoms have been removed but who still feels tired, anxious, or generally rundown does not regard himself as cured, for in this condition he cannot fulfill his role satisfactorily.

Both doctors and patients are prepared to spend a long time if necessary in continuing treatments well after the major symptoms have been removed, until the patients reach a point where they feel able to devote their full energy once again to their role. The length of in-patient residence in hospitals, standard times for recovery rates from medical procedures as defined by insurance companies, and sickness compensation from places of work all reflect very generous time off, as in Mr. Mizoguchi's case, to recover one's health. Patients really do not seem to resent traveling to the doctor, waiting for long periods before being examined, and devoting some of their free time to health-enhancing activities. Illness and recovery from illness can be accepted without guilt and can be viewed positively as time out from the otherwise inflexible demands of a tightly structured society. Going on group excursions or to a bar with one's colleagues fulfills a similar function—all these activities are used as opportunities to relieve tension, as a legitimate way to escape one's role periodically.

The sense of fatalism and resignation associated with Japanese culture (Lebra 1976, p. 165) also profoundly affects attitudes toward efficacy in healing. Buddhist concepts of karma and the doctrine of predestination, along with traditional medical beliefs, have imbued people with the idea that many illnesses cannot be totally overcome. Since an individual's karma (if one accepts this concept) or one's hereditary constitution and personality type play a profound role in the origin and course of a disease, the therapist is not usually considered the primary agent responsible for promoting the recovery of health. This is particularly true since patients are unwilling, for fear of being too indebted to the therapist, to make him take full responsibility. The therapist, on his part, sees himself in the limited role of stimulating the patient toward recovery. Both practitioner and patient are prepared to resign themselves to something less than complete recovery if necessary, particularly when psychological or social issues are heavily implicated in the

225

origin of the medical problem. Questions involving the possibility of major changes, such as finding a new place of work, changing one's marriage partner, or leaving one's parents, are simply not discussed. These things are accepted as one's given lot in life, and one should try to adjust to them even at the expense of one's health. Such radical social changes would be viewed as causing more harm than good because of the guilt involved in abandoning one's group and role. The practitioner, therefore, patches the patients up, as is often the case in other medical systems, and sends them, albeit after many hours of sympathetic treatment, back to a social environment that both he and the patients view as stressful and conducive to more ill health. Under these conditions patients do not expect to be cured. Patients such as Mr. Watanabe at the *kanpō* clinic are delighted to be free of their pain and other symptoms of illness, but they regard their recovery only as a remission until stress overtakes them once more. They also know that they can go back to the clinic at any time and receive sympathetic understanding even if they have failed to keep up the recommended preventive techniques. Should this happen, Mr. Watanabe has let down, not the doctor, but himself and his family. He is not a noncompliant patient so much as someone with a difficult life situation who is bound to need help at times. Because the therapist has not taken on full responsibility for the healing process, he does not have his own pride and reputation identified completely with the recovery of his patients. The practitioner does not experience a sense of failure when a patient returns in poor condition, and he can therefore maintain a sympathetic stance. This attitude is similar to that of Japanese parents. Lanham (1966, p. 324) and Vogel (1968, p. 244) have both noted a lack of ego involvement on the part of parents when children resist advice. Their authority is not threatened: they simply wait until the child is in a more cooperative mood to drive their point home.

In conclusion, the locus of responsibility for health and healing lies, in Japan, within the family, hence transactions in a clinical setting do not usually include, for example, psychological counseling or suggestions for changes in the social environment. East Asian medical practice, therefore, cannot be regarded as holistic in the meaning usually imparted to that word in modern Western usage—that is, that the social and cultural dimensions of illness are assigned importance at least equal to the naming and removal of a specific disease and that attempts are made in a therapeutic setting to change the patient's environment accordingly. It is only when the role of the family is taken into consideration as part of the total medical system that social and psychological dimensions of illness are brought into play in Japan. Even then the attitude taken toward the way in which these factors should be dealt with is characteristically different from that in the West. The Japanese widely accept traditional ideas of adjustment, rather than attempting to overcome and change all obstacles to individual advancement. Reynolds (1976) quotes a Morita therapist on this topic:

> Life energies are like a river, and symptoms are like boulders rising from the riverbed. If the river spends its force trying to destroy the boulders it flows no farther than the boulders. In the same way, if the river gives up and eddies around the obstruction it cannot flow on. But if the river flows on toward its ultimate objective, despite the rocks, it will eventually reach its goal, and in the process the rocks may be worn down. Even if they are not worn down, the goal is reached so it matters not at all that they continue to exist unchanged. (P. 168)

Lebra's comment (1976, p. 43) is also relevant in this respect: "Japanese individuality . . . rests not on the imposition of one's will on the social environment but on the refusal to impose oneself on it." By learning to adjust to and accept difficult social conditions, one can achieve the greatest sense of well-being. The guilt and doubts involved in undertaking radical social change to meet one's individual needs would be unlikely to induce feelings conducive to good health. This does not imply that Japanese people meekly succumb to all authority, as the opening of Narita airport and the reaction of certain environmental groups to pollution problems clearly demonstrates. What it indicates is that if an individual and his or her needs are at odds with what is considered best for group harmony and productivity, then the individual is likely to try to suppress his or her needs for the well-being of the group. Only thus can they feel at ease. Tseng (1975, p. 187) comes to very similar conclusions from working with Chinese patients in psychotherapy. He believes that guiding patients into an expression of antagonistic behavior toward parental authority, even where the authority is oppressive, may increase rather than resolve the patient's problems.

227

Similar attitudes prevail in Japan with regard to the physical environment. There is a tendency to adjust to nature wherever possible, rather than try to conquer it. Central heating is still unusual in Japanese houses, and people cope with winter by dressing warmly. Despite adequate refrigeration, there is sensitivity toward what food is actually in season, and choices are made accordingly. Technology can be used in interesting ways to enhance adaptation to the environment: one goes to see ghost movies in the summer months because it helps keep one cool.

It is, of course, in middle-class and upper-class families where people have the most freedom to visit the doctor frequently, where family members can indulge sick relatives, and where early socialization has been particularly close. In these families health care most nearly approaches the ideal of holism, although in practice the ideal is rarely attained. People from lower-class families make extensive use of the traditional medical system, but the treatment they receive, though it may last for an hour at a time and be physically relaxing, is ultimately reductionistic. The purpose is the removal of symptoms and little more, although both patient and therapist acknowledge that this is far from ideal.

We shall now turn finally to the practice of cosmopolitan medicine in Japan and to its interaction with the traditional medical system.

PART FIVE

The Cosmopolitan Medical System

15

Doctor and Patient Relationships in Cosmopolitan Medicine

He who complies with the ways of the world
may be impoverished thereby; he who does
not, appears deranged. Wherever one may live,
whatever work one may do, is it possible even
for a moment to find a haven for the body or
peace for the mind?

Kamo no Chomei,
An Account of My Hut, 1212

The phrase most associated with the practice of medicine in Japan used to be *i wa jin jitsu nari*, a phrase of Confucian origin and most frequently translated as "medicine is a benevolent art." Today, with encouragement from the mass media, this phrase has been adapted in the minds of many Japanese people to become *i wa kin jitsu nari*, with the meaning of "medicine is a money-making art." Cosmopolitan doctors blame this state of affairs almost exclusively on the organization of the national health insurance program, whose structure, they claim, forces them to relinquish autonomy in medical practice and turns their clinics into offices of petty bureaucracy.

The Japanese Medical Association is a highly organized, politically active group (see Steslicke 1973, for a full account of the political life of the JMA), and has been negotiating for reforms of the national health insurance program constantly since the end of World War II. One of the most important disputes, however, was related not to insurance but to the right of medical practitioners to sell medicine—something which they moved to affirm at their first meeting at the inception of the Greater Japan Medical Association in 1893. To the doctors of that time, most of whom had recently been practicing *kanpō,* the attempt to separate the sale of medicine from medical practice must have been seen not simply as an economic loss but as a threat to the efficacy of the therapeutic system. Since mixing medicine and changing the prescription daily according to the symptoms of each individual patient was central to the practice of *kanpō* (see Chapter 3), many doctors, still drawing on *kanpō* beliefs, would truly feel that they could not practice medicine to the best of their ability unless they had complete control over the prescription and sale of the drugs.

Between 1945 and 1960, this issue—*iyaku-bungyo,* the separation of medical treatment and the preparation and the sale of medicine—became a focal point once again in politics. One of the doctors interviewed reminded me of what General Crawford F. Sams, chief of SCAP (Supreme Command of the Allied Powers), Public Health and Welfare section, had to say on this topic. General Sams stated that there are two things in Japan that surprise most Americans: that doctors prepare and sell medicine and that dentists sell gold. He believed that if doctors continued to sell medicine they would be regarded as mere tradesmen and would lose respect.

A bill introduced in the Diet to separate the practice and sale of medicine actually passed, but before the date for its implementation in 1955, the JMA lobbied successfully for amendments permitting doctors to continue to sell medicine, which they do to this day; the sale of medicine is the major source of income for all doctors in private practice. Their income from the examination and treatment of patients is controlled by the administrators of the health insurance systems, and all patients must be seen under one of several authorized insurance programs. The JMA is not completely opposed to socialized medicine, but has organized to bring about major modifications in its implementation, which have been partially successful.

One major complaint of doctors is that they are underpaid. The value of their work is assessed according to the points system (see Chapter 1), and doctors who were interviewed stated that in order to maintain what they described as a middle-class income they must see about one hundred patients a day; this means, naturally, that they cannot spend much time with each patient. Most doctors would like to see both public and private medical care implemented. Another of their complaints is that they must spend hours each day filling out forms related to the points system and that this detracts from medical care. At the very least, they would like the several insurance systems merged into one so that the office work would be simplified.

A further complaint, echoed by all the doctors interviewed, was that people over seventy years of age receive all their treatment completely free under the health insurance system; many of these people, therefore, come to the doctor for an examination every day and take up valuable time, which could be better spent with patients who are more in need of care. The doctors pointed out that this situation is not simply a consequence of free medical care, but is also due to rapidly changing social and moral standards. Old people, formerly taken care of inside the family, are now frequently living on their own, lonely and bored. Upon retirement, their horizontal bonds in social relationships are few, because in the residential community family and vertical bonds are the most binding. Furthermore, informants claim that there are few established social meeting places for old people in modern Japan. Old people's homes are in short supply and often are not considered socially acceptable. Because of their need for comfort, many of the elderly have turned to the free medical system. Today's hospitals were described to me by doctors as being like old people's homes, and the office of the family doctor is frequently turned into a meeting place for the elderly with *go* boards and *shogi* (Japanese chess) available.

Certainly the life of the Japanese doctor is harder and less financially rewarding than that of most American doctors. Table 15 is adapted from *Nikkei Medical* (1973), and it should be noted that the cost of living in both the Tokyo and the Kyoto-Osaka region is higher than that in New York. It should also be noted that Japanese family-style doctors usually work six days a week and are also available for house calls. The doctors' claims—that they must see numerous patients and that they must sell medicine to maintain a reasonable standard of living—seem justified.

The results of a national survey of patients' attitudes toward treatment they had received in their doctor's office was also presented in the same edition of *Nikkei Medical* and appear in Table 16. These results corroborate many of the complaints made by patients who had transferred to the East Asian medical system. There is a general belief, reinforced daily by reports in

TABLE 15
Japanese and American Doctors Compared

BASIC DATA	JAPANESE	AMERICAN
Average number of patients seen each day	65	17
Average number of hours worked each day	9	8.3
Average annual salary	$14,000	$42,000
Number of days spent at conferences annually	9	23.6
Average number of vacation days taken annually	5	21

the mass media, that doctors sell medicine in great excess in order to make a profit and that this practice has led to numerous iatrogenic problems. Another major complaint about the cosmopolitan medical system is that the doctor sees too many patients. This leads to long waiting times, poor explanations, wrong diagnoses, and so on.

Doctors and patients blame each other for problems in the medical system, but one thing is clear—the almost unanimous agreement that there are many shortcomings. The structure and implementation of the health insurance system, as in other societies with socialized medicine, is undoubtedly the source of much dissatisfaction, but I believe that in the case of Japan there are further contributing factors. My hypothesis is that despite more than one hundred years of cosmopolitan medicine as the only official medical system, doctors, medical administrators, and the attitudes of patients are still considerably influenced by beliefs derived from the East Asian medical system. When these beliefs are applied to the receiving and administering of cosmopolitan medicine, conflicts are bound to arise. Many Japanese, like

TABLE 16
Complaints of Patients about Cosmopolitan Medical Treatment
(in percentage)

PATIENTS' COMPLAINTS	PERCENTAGE
Received more medicine than was necessary	48.7
Had to wait more than one hour	44.0
Inadequate explanations	36.2
Wrong diagnosis	32.7
Treatment was too expensive	21.0
Experienced ill side effects after the treatment	19.0
Was asked to return for further treatment unnecessarily	15.0

their counterparts in the West, initially felt that a medical system based on scientific values would, after more research, be able to provide answers to health problems that could transcend cultural limitations. But it is becoming abundantly clear in Japan, as it is in the West, that this premise has two major faults. First, as Freidson (1970, p. 206) and Kleinman (1973b, p. 159) have so adequately pointed out, there are invariably two aspects to all kinds of medical practice: the isolation and elimination of diseases, *and* the social and cultural aspect—that is, the system of ideas on which medical practice is based. Even "scientific" medicine is *not*, after all, "an unchanging biological reality that is as independent of man as the realities of physics and chemistry" (Freidson 1970, p. 206). Furthermore, when "scientific" medicine is newly adopted in a society, parts of the cultural tradition from the source society are also adopted. It is impossible to simply accept only those parts of medicine that are experimentally verified, because so much of medicine does not fall into this category. Thus, cosmopolitan medicine in Japan at first reflected a German approach, particularly in medical education, to such an extent that it was usual for diagnosis forms to be written in German. Today, medical practice shows American influence. Second, beneath these influences lies a system of ideas derived from traditional Japanese values. Medicine, like so many other things in Japan today, appears, on first glance, to be thoroughly Westernized, but a second look confirms that the more correct word to apply is modernized, and modernized in a uniquely Japanese way.

It is necessary for us to understand this phenomenon because it is central in helping to account for the recent resurgence in the popularity of traditional medical systems. With this end in mind, nine cosmopolitan doctors practicing in Kyoto were interviewed regarding their medical beliefs and practices.

Analysis of Some Beliefs and Practices of Nine Cosmopolitan Doctors

With two exceptions, all of these doctors frequently see ninety or more patients a day (see Table 17). Of the two exceptions, one, an internist, deliberately restricts the number of patients he sees because he wants to avoid a busy life. By seeing fifty patients a day, he makes a marginal profit, he says. The other is an obstetrician, therefore most of his practice does not

TABLE 17
Data on Cosmopolitan Doctors

Owns his own clinic	+	+	+	+	+	+	+	+	+
Length of time in practice in years	37	15	20	17	11	29	6	16	25
Specialty*	Int	Ob	Int	Int	Orth	ENT	Ped	Int	Int
Member of the JMA	+	+	+	+	+	+	+	+	+
Number of patients seen each day	50–100	50–60	110–115	100	70–90	200	60–90	50	100–120
Makes house calls	+	−	+	+	−	−	+	+	+
Time spent with each patient in minutes First visit	10	15	5	5	10	3	5	10	5
Subsequent visits	3	5	3	3	3	3	3	5	3
Sells medicine	+	+	+	+	+	+	+	+	+
Time with paperwork each day in hours	2	1	2	2	1	2	2	1	2
Number of in-patients	−	14	20	−	1	1	1	−	−
Number of nursing assistants	−	8	6	1	1	1	1	−	1
Assistance from wife	+	+	+	+	+	+	+	+	+

*Int = Internal Medicine; Ob = Obstetrics and Gynecology; Orth = Orthopedics; ENT = Ear, Nose, and Throat; Ped = Pediatrics.

come under the jurisdiction of the health insurance scheme. Examination during pregnancy and the delivery of babies must be paid for privately, and this is his major source of income. He sees fifty patients a day and is the only doctor of those interviewed who does not sell medicine.

Apart from these two, all the doctors spend less than ten minutes with each patient and state that at second and subsequent visits the time spent is about three minutes per person. The doctors feel pressured under these conditions. When the necessary office work and house calls are included, it is clear that there is very little free time. Without their wives, who do most of the paperwork and reordering of supplies, few doctors could survive. Even so, many practitioners often do not finish their day's work until ten o'clock in the evening. Despite this pressure, patients are asked to come back for frequent checkups. When antibiotics are prescribed, for example, it is usual to sell the patient a three-days' supply and to ask them to come back then for a checkup. A further three-days' supply is often issued, and after yet another visit to the doctor the patient receives a final batch of medicine. Many patients feel better after three days and do not return to the doctor. The infection sometimes flares up again in a form resistant to the antibiotic, leading to a chronic problem and dissatisfaction for both doctor and patient.

Doctors also believe that patients with comparatively mild symptoms, such as a common cold, a cough, or a mild stomach ache, *should* come to the doctor.

The structure of the points system clearly encourages these attitudes. The more patients a doctor sees and the more shots and medicine he can prescribe, the more money he makes. But I think these attitudes are not related solely to the profit motive. Reconsideration of some of the basic characteristics of East Asian medicine indicates that the situation may be attributed partly to other influences. First, as Porkert (1976, p. 67) points out, one of the claims made for East Asian Medicine, and stressed by Japanese practitioners, is that it is possible to diagnose and treat diseases which are manifest only as minor functional changes and which would not be detectable through the use of standard laboratory techniques. In order to practice his art well, the doctor wants to see the patient as soon as the patient feels a little off balance. In the East Asian tradition, if diseases are left untreated until an advanced stage, the doctor's chances of success are considerably lowered because the therapeutic techniques are not designed to deal with problems of this kind. Furthermore, if diseases are not caught in this early stage, it is believed, these nonspecific symptoms, rather than just going away, are likely to be the origin of serious diseases. In other words, all diseases, apart from sudden accidents, originate as minor states of imbalance, which gradually become chronic and more severe and may leave the patient susceptible to infection.

Second, in order to practice *kanpō* well, a practitioner must watch very carefully for any change in symptoms and adjust the prescription accordingly. Ideally, one should check on a patient several times a day.

Several of the doctors interviewed emphasized that one of the advantages of the health insurance system is that patients, now that they need not worry about the financial aspect, come early to the doctor. Two of the doctors added the Japanese adage *kaze wa man byo no moto* ("ten thousand diseases arise from the common cold"). The cosmopolitan doctors' belief that it is important to see patients with mild symptoms and to check a patient's progress frequently may be partially atributed, therefore, to East Asian medical influences, which of course are not taught formally in medical school, but to which every Japanese is still socialized.

Attitudes toward medication also reflect traditional beliefs. First, the doses of medicine tend to be milder than in the United States, and the patient is often directed to take the medicine four or even five times a day. In *kanpō* and in East Asian medicine in general, frequent mild treatments are thought to be less harmful to the body, to stimulate the body to heal itself, and to eventually bring about a more long-lasting effect than do strong treatments carried out less frequently. Second, family-style doctors in Japan do indeed prescribe a lot of medicine compared with the amount prescribed in the United States, but they feel it is necessary because they are concerned about the side effects of the medicine on other parts of the body. Compared with American doctors, Japanese doctors apparently think much more holistically. One doctor informed me that for all cases of bronchitis, for example, he would give an antibiotic, and he would also prescribe a stomach settler and a diuretic because both the stomach and the kidneys would be affected by the antibiotic. He would also recommend vitamins to build up the body in general and give aspirin to induce perspiration. Another doctor regularly prescribes two types of medicine for anemia and, in addition, stomach settlers, a diuretic, and vitamin pills. All the doctors and many of the patients interviewed said that it was not at all unusual for patients to leave the doctor's office with up to eight types of medicine, and I have observed this personally. Moreover, many doctors and patients prefer injections to oral medicine. The stated reasons are that shots work faster, that they cause no side effects in the stomach, and that they can work on the whole body.

Large sales of medicine mean a profit, but the doctor is also thinking in a traditional, holistic fashion about the welfare of the patient, though in an inappropriate context. If he were prescribing herbal medicine he would mix up to twenty types of herbs to affect the whole body and to help remove very mild symptoms. When this belief system is applied in cosmopolitan medicine, and when eight types of purified medicines are ingested five times a day for a period of months or even years, the result can be disastrous. Japanese doctors and the public are becoming very sensitive to this issue, particularly since the thalidomide problem, and both sides tend to heap the blame very readily onto the structure and bureaucratic nature of the health insurance system.

Reports in the newspapers add to the mounting anxiety of the Japanese public with respect to medical care. From the *Japan Times*, July 15, 1974, comes this article:

> According to statistics, the total amount of fees paid to doctors for treatment of illness and injuries during the fiscal year amounted to a colossal 3,399,400 million yen ($1.1 billion), an increase of 24.7 percent over the previous year. The ministry also revealed that drug and injection fees doctors charged constituted 40.8 percent of the whole medicare cost.
>
> This ratio, which was somewhat less than the previous year's 43.7 percent, was still far in excess of the 20–30 percent level prevalent among Europeans countries and America.

Comments on the overuse, ineffectiveness, and side effects of medicine appear almost daily:

> Reports submitted by the Osaka University hospital showed that out of 394 disorders reported, 248 came from the

239

harmful side effects of drugs. The researchers discovered that
antibiotics, especially those used in treating tuberculosis, were
responsible for 35 disorders, including loss of hearing.
(*Mainichi Daily News*, April, 30, 1974)

The Central Pharmaceutical Affairs Council, in its report to
Health and Welfare Minister Kunichi Saito, said Monday that
about 10 percent of 943 medicines examined were
"ineffective." (*Mainichi Daily News*, August 13, 1974)

Sixty-three families with thalidomide-deformed children
signed documents on Sunday with the government and the
Dainippon Pharmaceutical Company at the climax of eleven
long years of negotiations for damages and relief measures
for the victims. The signing ceremony produced no cheers.
Both the parents of the deformed children and the president
of the pharmaceutical company sobbed openly. (*Mainichi
Daily News*, October 14, 1974)

The inset photograph with the last article shows the president of the pharmaceutical company shaking hands with the deformed children in a gesture
of apology.

Pollution problems are also reported regularly:

Forty-four more persons in Kumamoto prefecture are
officially designated as victims of Minamata disease, a kind of
organic mercury poisoning. This increased the total number
of officially listed victims of Minamata disease patients in
Kumamoto to 670, and that in the western part of Kyushu to
746. Ninety of the 746 victims are already dead. (*Asahi
Evening News*, July 17, 1974)

Three *tōfu* [soybean curd] manufacturers in Tochigi prefecture
plan to sue Ueno Seiyaku Pharmaceutical Company in Osaka
to seek compensation for damage to their health and the
death of a relative, allegedly caused by AF2, a germicidal
additive for foods such as *tōfu*, ham, and sausage. (*Japan
Times*, May 2, 1974)

Under these circumstances, what is surprising is the claim of the doctors that patients only come to see them for medicine and feel cheated if they leave the doctor's office without any. Several doctors stated that if they do not sell the patient some form of medicine, even a placebo, the patient will probably go to another doctor: "Patients prefer medicine to good food." The doctors also complain that patients overdose themselves with medicine obtained from the drugstore. Two doctors stated that they believed much of the dependency on medicine is caused by the doctors themselves, who issue so much medicine. Another said that because medicine is so cheap for the first time in Japanese history, people rush to buy it. Two other doctors pointed out that wartime shortages had left the Japanese overly concerned about health, vitamins, and so on.

The fifty families questioned about attitudes toward East Asian medicine were also asked about experiences with their family doctor. An examination of their attitudes will help to explain the situation more clearly.

Patients' Expectations and Attitudes toward the Family Doctor

One of the best ways to assess how doctor-patient relationships have changed is to look at the patterns of gift-giving between them. It is customary in Japan to give presents at the end of the year (*o seibo*) and in July (*o chūgen*) to people to whom one feels indebted. Usually the presents are given to social superiors, or to equals, particularly to business colleagues, teachers, and other professionals. People make a point of giving presents to others who have gone beyond the defined bounds of their duty and have also expressed kindness and benevolence and have shown great responsibility. Until World War II most doctors could expect to receive such gifts. Among the informants only eleven practice this custom today, and all of these eleven people have been going to the same family doctor for at least nine years. The other informants still practice the custom of gift-giving in other situations, but they said it was no longer necessary to keep it up with their doctor. The transaction in a doctor's office is simply one of services rendered, for which the doctor is paid indirectly. Today many doctors receive presents only when they extend themselves in an emergency or if they make repeated house calls.

Some patients pointed out that gift-giving is a double-edged sword. Not only does it express thanks, but it also is a way of requesting special attention for the future. The informants stated that because of the national health insurance system, equal treatment is more or less assured for all in the doctor's office, and thus presents are not needed.

This change in custom indicates changes not only in patients' attitudes but also in expectations. Most patients appear to want a largely objective and scientific approach on the part of the doctor and do not feel the need of being in a formally established relationship reinforced by the act of regular gift-giving. That the doctor does not know the entire family situation is not considered a handicap to his treatment sessions. The exceptions to this are the families who have a long-established relationship over many years with their doctor, who is invariably over fifty years of age.

Nearly every informant stated that the ideal doctor is a man between forty and fifty years of age—that is, a man who, they hope, combines sound scientific training with maturity and experience. Prior to the Meiji Restoration, the ideal age would have been above fifty—in the East Asian medical system knowledge is obtained through experience.

Despite the changed attitudes and expectations, the family doctor is generally trusted, and because there is a stable population, half the informants and their entire families continued with the same doctor for many years. Nevertheless, the majority of informants feel that too much medicine is prescribed, and great quantities are thrown away unused (see Table 18). But overprescription does not necessarily inspire a lack of trust—there is an acknowledgment that the doctor has to make a living and therefore he must sell medicine. It is considered rude to tell the doctor that he is overprescribing, and the easiest way to maintain a good relationship is to buy the medicine and throw away any excess. However, informants who had changed doctors had all done so because they thought their doctor gave too many injections, which they disliked, or because they were concerned about possible iatrogenic effects of drugs.

The doctors were viewed by more than 50 percent of the informants as too busy; nevertheless, approximately 55 percent said that the doctor had time to listen to their complaints. Five minutes with the doctor is generally considered adequate. Satisfied informants made comments like the following: "I don't expect close relationships with the doctor these days." "It's simply a money-based relationship." "He's too busy, but I must trust him anyway." "I'm never really sick so I don't have much to say to him." "With

TABLE 18

Attitudes of Fifty Families toward the Family Doctor

	LOWER MIDDLE CLASS	UPPER MIDDLE CLASS	TOTAL PERCENTAGE
Trust in the doctor	18	14	64
Lack or have little trust in doctor	7	11	36
Over ten years with the same doctor	14	11	50
Changed doctor because of dissatisfaction	3	5	16
Avoid all doctors if possible	2	0	2
Doctor prescribes too much medicine	17	19	72
Throw out a lot of medicine	13	15	56
Doctor gives too many shots	11	6	34
Doctor listens well to complaints	14	14	56
Doctor is too busy to listen well to complaints	11	11	44
Doctor makes house calls	25	25	100

modern medicine the doctor doesn't need to know all the family informa-tion."

When trust, or the lack of it, in the family doctor is correlated with other variables in the patients' situations, some interesting results emerge (see Table 19). Of those informants who trust the doctor, the majority come from families with no experience with serious illness or who view themselves as generally healthy. Those in the second largest group who trust their family doctor have chronic illnesses in their family for which they take some form of East Asian medicine, but they maintain a trust in the family doctor for acute ailments both major and minor. Only 10 percent of the informants who have chronic illnesses and consult only their family doctor maintain their trust in him.

Among the informants with little or no trust in their family doctor, the largest group had experienced chronic illness in their family and were posi-tive about East Asian medicine. The smallest group, only 4 percent, had no serious illnesses and disliked all doctors and medicine. The final group, the 16 percent of the informants who are not sick and have little trust in their family doctor, are of two types: some of these people fall into traditional, rather conservatively aligned families, such as families of some priests who have never been fully won over to cosmopolitan medicine; the second and larger part of this group is composed of people who have recently become

TABLE 19
*Attitudes of Patients toward Their Family Doctor; Experiences with Illness;
Experiences with East Asian Medicine*

GROUPS		NUMBER OF PATIENTS	PERCENTAGE OF PATIENTS
(1)	Trust in family doctor No serious illness No East Asian medicine	16	32
(2)	Trust in family doctor Chronic illness Use East Asian medicine	9	18
(3)	Trust in family doctor Chronic illness No East Asian medicine	5	10
(4)	No trust in family doctor Chronic illness Use East Asian medicine	10	20
(5)	No trust in family doctor No serious illness Use East Asian or folk medicine	8	16
(6)	No trust in family doctor No serious illness Avoid all doctors	2	4

interested in East Asian medicine through the mass media but who have no personal illness that precipitated their interest. Despite the lack of trust, none of these patients actually give up their family doctor.

Categories 2, 4, and 5 of Table 19 (54% of the sample) represent the types of patients who were interviewed in the East Asian medical clinics. People who fall into categories 2, 3, 4, and 5 are those who complain most vehemently about the overprescription of medicine.

In summary, the most important reasons for a lack of trust in cosmopolitan doctors and an increased interest in East Asian medicine is an encounter in the family unit with a chronic disease. Under these conditions, concern about large doses of synthetic medicine becomes marked. In the case of acute ailments the patients do not expect or need much attention from the doctor. They want the disease objectified, that is, they want it labeled with a scientific term, and they want to receive medicine that is specific to the disease, so that the problem will be eradicated. Injections are considered especially effective as treatment. On recovery from an illness, patients simply throw out excess medicine. Expectations about chronic diseases are different, however, and it is under these conditions that complaints arise most frequently about poor explanations, wrong diagnoses, overprescription, too many shots, and lack of concern on the part of the doctor.

. Like the doctors, patients are influenced by traditional East Asian beliefs. For them, it is important to go to the doctor when they catch a cold or have a cough. Many patients come with nonspecific complaints such as a "heavy head" (*atama ga omoi*), or complaints of feeling "languid" (*karada ga darui*). All these patients leave the doctor's office with an injection or oral medicine or both, and they feel most satisfied if they can return to the doctor to have him check changes in symptoms.

Japanese are socialized to be sensitive to mild functional changes in their bodies (see Chapter 5), and the traditional medical belief system and socialization practices have reinforced each other in this respect through the years. Prior to World War II, such minor ailments would have been dealt with inside the family, with the grandmother as the source of advice on the best method of treatment, or if the symptoms persisted, by the East Asian style of doctor. Today, many people go to the family doctor with these minor complaints, which the East Asian doctor could handle so adeptly but for which the cosmopolitan doctor has little effective therapy to offer and for which he therefore gives placebos.

The inexpensiveness and the ease of a visit to the family doctor are two reasons for the choice of the cosmopolitan medical system. Another is that after the postwar years and until recently it was generally believed that cosmopolitan medicine could handle all medical problems better than other types of medical systems could. Furthermore, in a nuclear family, popular medical techniques are no longer effectively passed on. Finally, knowledge about preventive medicine was also transmitted to most people as part of the oral tradition, and although young Japanese people, especially new mothers, read avidly about protein levels in bean curd, vitamin C in oranges, and so on, they feel inadequately informed in this area. There is general agreement on the part of the informants, which was confirmed by both cosmopolitan and East Asian doctors, that older people know from experience how to maintain a balanced diet and how to adjust their clothing and heating systems correctly to seasonal changes. Younger people, it is agreed, are in a transition phase; they eat a mixture of Western and traditional foods, mix

245

their styles of clothing, and mix their styles of heating and cooling of buildings. It is therefore easy to make mistakes. Mothers of small children feel especially vulnerable if their own mother or mother-in-law is not on hand to advise about preventive medicine in child care; the alternative is to make frequent visits to the family doctor.

However, preventive medicine is not usually taught to patients by the doctors, because they are not financially rewarded on the points system for verbal advice, and there is a tendency to prescribe medicine, for this is less time-consuming and is encouraged by the structure of the socialized medical system. People, therefore, visit the doctor for many problems that would have been taken care of within the family before the war. Cosmopolitan doctors, unable to help these patients adequately, complain about them but feel uncomfortable if they totally reject them.

The attitudes of patients to medication are also influenced by traditional beliefs. Like the doctors, the patients think holistically about their bodies—they expect to receive medicine to restore balance to the entire body. Many people prefer injections for just this reason—they feel that the whole body will be rapidly affected and that the most vulnerable part of Japanese anatomy, the stomach, can be bypassed. When people complain about overprescription it is not the number of kinds of medicine that is objected to, it is the *strength* of the doses that concerns most people. Synthetic medicine is still regarded somewhat like herbal medicine and, therefore, like a food: a mixture of several kinds of medicine will restore the balance if taken regularly, but excesses should be avoided. The fact that medicine prescribed for one member of the family is sometimes shared among family members (five families admitted to this practice, and other respondents avoided the question) indicates that the strength and specificity of synthetic medicine is not truly appreciated.

The practice of never rejecting patients may also stem from traditional beliefs. Since there is no concept of perfect health, an East Asian doctor never turns a patient away without treatment. The reluctance of modern doctors to send patients away with no medicine, and the expectation of all patients that they will receive something, arise perhaps from traditional practice.

This attitude is reinforced by yet another belief derived from East Asian medicine. It has been emphasized throughout this book that in general the Japanese are sensitive to the interrelationship of the environment and of social and psychological states and health. Traditionally, it was accepted that change and restoration of balance were most easily induced by first bringing about a physical change in the patient, which would then lead to restoration of balance in other realms. Even in cosmopolitan medicine both doctors and patients still seem to act on this premise. The doctor's role is to induce physiological change with his treatment, and if he does not supply some form of therapy, he and the patient both feel dissatisfied. Since there is still a strong feeling that the environment and social circumstances cannot be much changed, and because daily life is often seen as highly stressful, people *expect* to be off balance and unable to rectify it. The only remedy is to try to restore some order at the physiological level by resorting to medication. Before examination time, before the advent of New Year when everyone is busy, or before a stint of extra hard work at the office, people rush to the drugstore for a supply of tonics, vitamins, pep pills, and so on in anticipation that the demands of society will be so great that the body will need a boost to get back in balance. At times it seems that the excessive ingestion of medicine acts as "proof" of just how hard one has been working and sacrificing oneself for society.

The complaints of both doctors and patients, therefore, seem to have justification. Some doctors, of course, are largely bent on making a profit, and some patients are exploiting the health insurance system and the doctors' time. But most people are simply trying to satisfy their basic needs and beliefs about medical care in a socialized medical system, which was largely redesigned under American influence at a very troubled period in Japanese history. The "points system" is without doubt a major problem in that doctors will profit financially by seeing more patients each day (a pitfall that was avoided in the British National Health Service, for example). Other faults in the health insurance system are there because doctors and bureaucrats have fought to maintain certain traditional rights (such as the right of doctors to sell medicine), which are better applied to the East Asian medical system than to cosmopolitan medicine. Long-established cultural values are in conflict with present-day social structure and organizations. It appears that General Crawford F. Sams' point is well taken.

The Management of Acute and Chronic Diseases

Until recently in Japan, and particularly since the advent of socialized medicine, most people have assumed that traditional medicine was on a fast decline. Exceptions are the small percentage of the population who have a tradition-oriented lifestyle, who have never been fully accepting of trends in modernization, and who have always consistently made use of traditional medicine, and also those few families who try to avoid the use of all types of medical practitioners. Of my sample of fifty families only four fall into these categories. The other families all have a family, cosmopolitan style of doctor whom they consider to be their principal medical practitioner. However, as patterns of gift-giving and stated attitudes of informants indicate, the majority do not expect a particularly close relationship with their doctor, nor do they expect him to deal with social and psychological problems in their lives. On the contrary, they want the doctor to take an objective approach in which his role is to cure disease, using rational and mechanistic techniques. It appears that in recent years the biomedical model, the dominant professional medical model, has become in Japan what Fabrega (1975) believes it has become in the West: the dominant folk model. The rapid and impressive development of medical technology has made the Japanese, like other members of wealthy, industrialized societies, susceptible to the belief that all diseases can eventually be overcome through a reductionistic approach. Moreover, since acute infections presented a major medical problem at the time when antibiotics were discovered, it is not surprising that antibiotics were viewed initially, just as in the West, as "the magic bullet" with the promise of total control over the microbial world.

There are, however, other factors, which have already been discussed, related specifically to Japanese culture, which tend to reinforce the acceptance of the biomedical model. Since being unable to perform one's role adequately means not only that one is letting down oneself but also that strong feelings of guilt are generated about letting down the group, whether it be the family or one's co-workers, there is an incentive to avoid illness and to pay attention to preventive medicine. In fact, because people often feel a pressure of time in their daily lives, the practice of preventive medicine, with the exception of old people and of mothers on behalf of their children, is usually rather haphazard. When undergoing a period of time that is regarded as stressful, or at the sign of minor physical symptoms, however, many people—and informants all claim this is particularly true of men—tend to turn quickly to preparations of tonic waters, solutions, or shots of vitamins or other forms of patent and prescribed medicine designed to act as a general boost to one's physical state. The work ethic that pervades Japanese society is sustained through dedication to one's role, which means at times applying "perseverance and endurance to the point of masochism" (Lebra 1976, p. 163). If necessary, mind applied correctly can overcome the frailty of the physical body, but in daily rather than religious life, there is no harm in helping one's body along with medication. This type of attitude reinforces reductionistic rather than holistic thinking and appears to have long historical roots, since a similar attitude can be seen in traditional medical thinking: that the social order is given and the individual should adjust to it. As we have seen, doctors and patients do not usually attempt to manipulate social dimensions, which are seen as partially causal in illness; they focus instead on building up the patients' physical states so that they can cope once again with the demands of daily life.

Finally, I believe that Shintō beliefs have played a role in facilitating a general acceptance of the biomedical model. Since certain diseases, including cancer, are associated with fear and potential ostracism (see Chapter 6), and since they threaten the chances of making good marriages for immediate family members, it is desirable to have available, and to fund research to synthesize medication which can obliterate some diseases rapidly. The negative social consequences of sustaining tuberculosis, schizophrenia, or certain types of cancer are so great that a reductionistic approach to healing is infinitely preferable wherever possible.

The biomedical model is therefore attractive to Japanese physicians and patients for a number of reasons, and the majority of the population today go to the family doctor with their respiratory problems and intestinal upsets, assuming that they can be rapidly restored to health and the usual pattern of their daily life. It is when the medical problem fails to respond rapidly to treatment, or when general malaise becomes a chronic condition, that patients, like people everywhere when therapy is not effective, begin to question the system and search around for alternative forms of help. Under these circumstances the patients and their family, socialized to be sensitive to psychosocial and environmental factors in disease causation, begin to consider and try to isolate more general causes for the persistence of ill health. It is in response to chronic or mild recurring illnesses that patients give answers such as those given by patients at the *kanpō* clinic, and the causes of illness are then expressed in terms of environmental and psychosocial factors despite familiarity with bacteriology and physiology.

Once a chronic condition arises, most Japanese people have some knowledge and usually some experience among family members of the traditional East Asian medical system. At this juncture a visit to a traditional clinic is readily suggested by the family, although contact with and often treatment by the family doctor is maintained. Therapy received at a traditional clinic can stimulate associations with early socialization and with the family unit. Family members are often required to perform therapeutic techniques on the patient at home, or at least to prepare oral medication or a special diet. Techniques involving oral and tactile stimulation are used predominantly and are close to the preferred methods used to demonstrate care and affection toward children. This kind of stimulation is also associated throughout the life cycle with restoration of a calm emotional state after hard work or a stressful time. In this type of situation the association of illness with nurturance, feelings of dependency, and solidarity of the family unit come to the fore. In Freud's terminology, there are "secondary gains" from assuming the sick role, and it can be viewed positively. Under these circumstances a relatively slow recovery is acceptable, therapy should be mild, and the illness is consciously used as a time for family communication and for individual emotional development. Under these circumstances sickness and health are not viewed as a dichotomy—both are natural and necessary because one learns and grows from both situations. The therapeutic process is one of adjustment to the present situation rather than an expectation that the problem can be wiped out.

Despite the positive value associated particularly with mild illnesses, there is, of course, ambivalence about not fulfilling one's role. In the case of young married women who cannot take on the dependency role so readily, or the case of entrepreneurial, independently employed people who will cease to make a living while they are sick, the ambivalence is most marked. These people, along with the elderly, are the portion of the population who show the most interest in traditional medicine, largely as a form of security but also, they state explicitly, as a place where they can relax and receive some nurturant care.

Attitudes of Cosmopolitan Doctors
toward East Asian Medicine

Of the nine family doctors who were interviewed, eight responded that they have an interest in East Asian medicine and that more research related to it should be funded. All of the doctors give their patients support if the patient explicitly asks permission to use East Asian medicine, but only three doctors initiate this type of advice. The doctors who actively advise about East Asian medicine are the pediatrician, who recommends *kanpō* for chronic internal problems and acupuncture for *kan no mushi;* the orthopedist, who recommends acupuncture for whiplash, lumbago, and all problems involving pain; and an internist who, like four of the other practitioners, uses East Asian medicine himself. He lives and works in a poor section of Kyoto and recommends acupuncture and massage for chronic problems of all kinds. Two of the doctors who personally use East Asian medicine do not actively recommend it for their patients. One doctor uses *kanpō* for a stomach problem and acupuncture for sprains and pulled ligaments. A second doctor has several allergies, uses *shiatsu* to relieve the pain of lumbago, and takes *kanpō* for all internal problems. The pediatrician, who recommends East Asian medicine to his patients, sends his child, who has asthma, to the *kanpō* clinic described in this book, and is delighted with the progress the child has made. The wife of a fourth doctor had received several treatments of acupuncture for neuralgia. Six of the family doctors know the *kanpō* doctors and praised them strongly.

During the interviews the doctors made the following comments about East Asian medicine:

> "Because it is such an old tradition there must be something to it, otherwise it would have died out by now."

> "All Japanese doctors *should* use East Asian medical thinking; one should never forget the whole body."

> "Cosmopolitan and East Asian medicine should be better integrated."

> "Herbal medicine is not purified and therefore there are few side effects. It is effective for chronic diseases."

> "I feel closer to *kanpō* doctors than to American doctors."

> "I can't have a good relationship with acupuncture and

251

moxibustion doctors; they are at a different educational level, but I let them treat me anyway."

"Moxa is bad, burning the skin is bad."

The ENT specialist is particularly interested in acupuncture anaesthesia, use of which is limited in Japan almost exclusively to the extraction of tonsils and adenoids. He said that in this type of operation, acupuncture anaesthesia reduces bleeding during and after the operation and eliminates nausea.

Doctors who are actively opposed to East Asian medicine are usually young men, often working in large hospitals. There are, of course, some family doctors opposed to it, but they did not appear in the small sample interviewed. The Japanese ability to tolerate many points of view is well demonstrated in the attitudes of the Kyoto family doctors toward East Asian medicine. From the sample interviewed it appears that if there should be an official push for higher status and better recognition of East Asian medicine, this apparently would not evoke a totally negative response from cosmopolitan medical circles.

16

Conclusions

The Revival of East Asian Medicine

The *kanpō boomu* (boom in East Asian medicine), as it is popularly known, is a well-recognized phenomenon in contemporary Japan and much commented on in the mass media. In order to summarize the reasons for the revival of traditional medicine we must consider changes at both the macro and micro levels of Japanese culture and social organization.

Rapid change in the epidemiology of disease from a pattern of predominantly acute illnesses in the years before World War II to a pattern in which chronic illnesses are most frequent is, I believe, the most important variable to be considered in the revival of East Asian medicine. Since cosmopolitan medicine has as yet no straightforward remedies—"decisive technology," in Lewis Thomas's terminology (1974, p. 39)—with which to combat most chronic problems and hence their name, it is natural that alternative forms of medical care are sought out. It was shown in the previous chapter that, at the micro level, it is the actual experience of a chronic problem which usually stimulates an active interest in traditional medicine and then only after visits to a cosmopolitan doctor are assessed as ineffective. The fact, therefore, that cosmopolitan medicine is not at present adapted to meet the needs of many of its patients, in that it does not produce rapid cures for cancer, asthma, lumbago, neuralgia, and so on, is central in the revival of the traditional system. Although mild illnesses can be viewed positively and are actually welcome at times, chronic, nagging pain that impairs one's ability to lead a full life is something to be rid of, if possible. While many patients find that

253

cosmopolitan medical therapy furnishes them with temporary relief, they also try an alternative medical system in their search for a complete cure when faced with a debilitating chronic condition.

Related to the increase of chronic illnesses is a rising concern about the side effects of frequent ingestion of synthetic medicine. This concern has been actively fostered by the mass media. Many informants characterized their society as one that "likes to drink medicine too much" (*kusuri o nomisugiru*), and it was shown in the previous chapters how the belief systems of East Asian medicine, Shintō, and Buddhism have all contributed to this attitude, which is now compounded by the structure of the health insurance system and the doctors' right to sell medicine. Many patients at traditional clinics think of synthetic medicine as a poison or a purge; though it can be used briefly to bring rapid results, persistent use will weaken or even kill. Traditionally, there was no sharp distinction made between food, medicine, and poisons; all these items were thought of as being on the same spectrum, ranging from food materials, which are highly compatible with the human body, to medicine, which is moderately compatible, to poison, which is incompatible. Certain medicines were always at the extreme end of their range of the spectrum and were known to be close to a poison in action. Synthetic medicine appears to be categorized in this way by many patients. It is therefore regarded with fear and caution. The result is that patients with chronic respiratory problems, intestinal problems, dermatitis, and gynecological problems, for example, resort readily to East Asian medicine, either in the clinical setting or in buying herbal medicine from a pharmacist. Concern among pregnant women is most marked, and almost exclusive use is made of *kanpō*, both before and immediately after the birth of a baby.

The mass media has played a vital role in establishing East Asian medicine as a thriving medical system with a place in the modern world. Several practitioners are nationally known figures because of frequent television appearances, and recently a national television channel ran a series of twenty-four programs devoted solely to the topic of East Asian medicine. The history and traditional philosophy was dealt with at length, and the topic was presented in a serious and sympathetic fashion. There is also a regular series on *shiatsu*, which stresses its application within the home, and there are numerous programs on traditional diet. A leading newspaper ran a long series of articles by a well-known *kanpō* doctor, which dealt with traditional concepts and case histories. Almost daily there are reports of "successful cures" brought about by East Asian and folk practitioners, which are offset by extensive coverage on pollution problems and cases of malpractice in cosmopolitan medicine. Despite this, dissatisfaction with cosmopolitan medicine as such does not seem to be a major contributing factor to the *kanpō boomu.* Personal experience of a chronic illness rather than a general indictment of cosmopolitan medicine is much more significant. This may well reflect a continued lack of interest on the part of many Japanese in the universalistic nature of certain issues. The average Japanese is interested in the problem of pollution, for example, not in its global aspects, but only insofar as it affects one of the groups to which he or she belongs. When I asked questions about local pollution, informants rarely would respond in general terms. For example, they frequently gave answers like the following: "There is no pollution in my part of town so I cannot answer how I feel about it." Answers such as this indicate the continued primacy of interest in one's immediate group over more abstract universal issues, despite an increased sensitivity to the general issue of pollution on the national level. The situation is apparently similar with medicine.

The revival of traditional medicine has also received encouragement from outside Japan. Visitors, many from the West, and often M.D.'s, go to clinics to discuss traditional medicine, and foreign students are now accepted at several traditional medical schools. Second, the closer ties that Japan has forged with China are reflected in an ongoing exchange of medical practitioners and of information on research. Visits of Japanese doctors to China occur both formally and informally. Last, despite language barriers, several practitioners of traditional medicine have established an international reputation for themselves, which in turn enhances their image at home.

Another important source of impetus for the revival of traditional medicine comes from the scientific world itself. Trends in research in physics and biology are similar to recent developments in the West, and there is, of course, a continual exchange of information between Japan and the West in these areas. Recent interest in ecological and holistic models discussed in the introduction to this book is also apparent in Japan but is not as yet widely reflected in medical education and research as such.

One final point, which I regard as a major contributing factor to the revival of traditional medicine, is related to contemporary Japanese society in general and to the prevailing ethos of the times. In his essay "Values and Social Change in Modern Japan," Bellah (1970, p. 114) discusses his belief that although there have been great overt changes, the basic pattern of traditional Japanese values still largely dominates Japanese society today. He demonstrates that, despite the occurrence of several periods in history when the old value system could have been totally overturned, notably with the impact of the Jōdo Shinshū sect of Buddhism and later of Christianity, after a period of great upheaval which had profound and lasting effects, the potential for total reformation was lost: "it was drowned out by the ground bass . . . of the Japanese tradition of this-wordly affirmativeness."

The postwar impact of American culture with its emphasis on individualism, technological progress, universal, scientifically based education, and an interest in the subconscious have all provided massive impetus in the last thirty years for the complete overthrow of old values. Superficially, the change has occurred, but many observers of Japanese culture believe that despite some changes in social structure and despite rapid technological progress, business, politics, economics, and the family continue to function to a large extent with the backing of traditional values. (Bennett and Iwao 1963; Rohlen 1974b; Vogel 1968). The burning issue among Japanese intellectuals today is not new: the problem of individualism and how to transcend slavish adherence to social groups without experiencing alienation.

It seems that Japan may have embarked once again on the process that is self-consciously labeled *Nihonka* ("Japanization"), or that, to use Bellah's phrase, the "ground bass" is reaffirming its continued existence. The flood of information, material goods, and symbolic culture that has poured into Japan since the war is now being processed and a phase of critical reappraisal is under way.

The renewed interest in aspects of traditional culture is not limited to medicine. The arts, Kabuki, *noh* dramas, traditional crafts, and music are all enjoying a large revival, and the martial arts are expanding. A new trend in Japanese historiography is to examine rural society and folklore for the first time in a more than cursory way (Gluck 1978). Despite these trends, there is a second school of thought among scholars of Japan who believe that traditional values are dying, that the concept of individualism is making its mark, that dependency needs are less well tolerated, and that freedom of mobility and a chance for anonymity have helped produce profound and radical change. In general, scholars who come to these conclusions have studied lower-middle-class and working-class families, while scholars who stress continuity of tradition have devoted their time to observing middle- and upper-middle-class lifestyles. We shall return to this point shortly.

Pluralism in Japanese Medicine

Although Japan, when compared with many other countries, manifests a relatively homogeneous population and culture, pluralism in the major systems of belief has always played a vital role in its history. As the balance tips from favoring one system to another, the tension thus generated has frequently acted as a focal point for change. Moreover, it has often been noted, particularly in relation to religious beliefs, that, compared with West-erners, Japanese are readily able to sustain apparently conflicting systems of belief with little sense of ambiguity. Thus, even today, most people in reply to census surveys state that they hold both Buddhist and Shintō beliefs. The same attitude seems to have prevailed regarding medicine in historical times and is now emerging once again. The self-image of pragmatism seems justified; as Plath puts it, there is "a talent for blending different systems in practice and not posturing about false dichotomies" (personal communica-tion). Many doctors and patients seem willing to combine traditional and cosmopolitan medical theories and practice, if that will bring the best results.

The questions arise whether this revival of traditional medicine as an independent system will last, or alternatively, whether cosmopolitan medical practitioners will be prompted to adjust and adapt so as to absorb the parts of traditional medicine which have the most appeal. Both types of practi-tioners are engaged in scientific research regarding the effect of the therapeu-tic techniques of traditional medicine. The use of drugs derived from plant material has, of course, become a well-established part of cosmopolitan medicine. Some recent research is influenced, however, by new trends in biology, and some attempts are being made to consider the action of unrefined herbal mixtures on the human body.

Herbal medicine, acupuncture, and moxibustion can potentially be sub-sumed into cosmopolitan medicine as additional therapeutic tools and used quite apart from the belief system within which they were first applied, but I believe that if this should happen there would still be a demand for a separate traditional medical system. In many traditional clinics a type of care is provided that is not usually apparent in cosmopolitan medical practice and that is highly congruent with the needs of some Japanese patients. First, receiving therapy is often a social event; there is ample chance for an exchange of conversation between patients, and this activity is regarded very positively by patients and is considered in itself to be therapeutic. In other clinics there is a chance for introspection, also highly valued as therapy. Second, diagnosis (where it is performed) and therapy allow for the fulfillment of dependency needs through the use of nonverbal, tactile techniques. If a traditional diagnosis is not made, and if therapy is applied with the aid of machines and not by hand, then this advantage is lost. Furthermore, traditional practitioners are able to treat patients who have nonspecific somatic problems, including the culture-bound syndromes of *shinkeishitsushō* and *kan no mushi*. Cosmopolitan medicine is not designed to deal with such problems, which occur very frequently in Japan. Traditional practitioners may not "cure" these complaints, but they can provide therapy that both patient and practitioner believe to be effective and not iatrogenic. Related to the last point is the widely accepted concept of psychosomatic diseases and the belief that such problems are best dealt with through the use of therapy that focuses on inducing changes in the body. Psychotherapy is still regarded with deep suspicion in modern Japan, and traditional medicine fulfills a need in this respect. Last, patients tend to think holistically about themselves, and for many problems they expect treatment that will act in a general way on their whole body. Most of cosmopolitan medical treatment is not designed to do this, but it is widely accepted that traditional therapy acts holistically.

If cosmopolitan medicine were to be consciously modified and adapted in Japan to fit more closely with the cultural beliefs summarized above, then certainly there would be less demand for East Asian medicine. However, there are few signs, if any, of this happening at present, hence the traditional system fulfills an important and adaptive role.

In some developing countries, notably in China, there has been an attempt to maximize the use of traditional medicine during the process of modernization. Economic necessity is a driving force behind this type of thinking in that traditional medicine can be widely implemented relatively cheaply. The position taken recently by the World Health Organization and several developing countries, such as China, is one in which integration of traditional practitioners into cosmopolitan medicine is encouraged under carefully controlled conditions. There is, nevertheless, a tendency to accept the "convergence" hypothesis frequently applied to the process of industrialization and modernization. That is, it is assumed that traditional medicine will be rendered useless or very peripheral once economic development reaches such a level that cosmopolitan medicine is established as the primary source of health care. Just as business and industry will be organized and run on the same principles everywhere, so will medicine. Recently questions have been raised about the application of the hypothesis to industrialization (Austin 1976, p. 231) and similarly about its application to medicine (see, for example, Kleinman 1978, p. 82). The convergence hypothesis fails to take into account the fact that all medical systems, including cosmopolitan medicine, undergo a constant process or reevaluation and adjustment in light of changing health problems with which the system is confronted. Thus, as Lieban states (1973, p. 1031): "Health and disease are measures of the effectiveness with which human groups combining biological and cultural resources adapt to their environments." Insofar as the environment is constantly undergoing transformations, both biological and man-made, there will be new medical conditions to contend with, hence any medical system will always be in the position of trying to cope with some diseases with which it is not adapted to deal. In Dubos's words (1959, p. 2), "Complete and lasting freedom from disease is but a dream."

Cosmopolitan medicine in the West and in Japan is undergoing adaptation to meet the challenge posed by diseases that are chronic at the present time. The form of these diseases will change in the future, but there will always be patients with incurable problems. The existence of a pluralistic medical system offering a variety of approaches to the alleviation of suffering is highly functional, therefore, in that it can absorb the segment of the population whose problems are labeled chronic or incurable. We know very little about how effective traditional medical systems are in curing disease, but even if the rate of "cure" is not very successful, the very existence of alternative medical systems is essential to the psychological well-being of potential patients, and alternatives will continue to exist *because* of patients' demands. This holds true even when the economic necessity that encourages official support of alternative systems no longer exists. In situations of rapid change, migration, and acculturation, the need for alternative systems will increase to meet the demands not only of chronic patients but also of minority groups of all kinds whose expectations and theories of health and illness do not conform to those used in the dominant medical system.

There are further implications to be drawn from the Japanese situation that are applicable to medical systems in general and to the concept of pluralism. Despite educational and licensing requirements to practice East Asian medicine in Japan, it is clear that there is a great variety in the actual application of the system. This variety constitutes a response on the part of practitioners to the needs of patients. For example, if the predictions of Frager and Rohlen (1976, p. 255) are accurate, there will be a continuing demand by certain segments of the population for medicine to be practiced in a traditional manner. Rohlen demonstrated in an earlier work (1974b) that the concept of *seishin* training is still very important in many company training programs. *Seishin*, roughly translated as "spirit," is a traditional concept that includes the idea of accepting spiritualism over materialism; it is associated with the capacity to endure suffering and with being single-minded and serious, and also with a belief that one's happiness depends on inner attitudes rather than external conditions. As Frager and Rohlen state, in *seishin* training, "To accept the external world as it is and to cope with it on its terms is commonly reiterated advice." The concept is clearly related to attitudes found in traditional medicine. Frager and Rohlen find that a preoccupation with *seishin* is particularly pronounced in managerial classes or people who aspire to managerial positions. They also believe that older people in general rediscover this concept as they pursue activities usually associated with middle and old age. Finally, they find aspects of the *seishin* concept in many modern movements, including the "new religions," and come to the conclusion that modernization will enhance the *seishin* attitude as a means of countering the effects of urbanization and mechanization. If these predictions are accurate, many patients, particularly those with jobs at the managerial level, should continue to feel very comfortable with East Asian medicine in its traditional form. These patients in particular will appreciate a quiet, private therapeutic encounter that allows a chance for introspection and self-examination. On the other hand, Cole (1976, p. 165), in an essay that deals with the labor force in Japan, predicts serious alienation in the future, less adherence to the work ethic, and less paternalism on the part of employers. This is likely to affect the attitudes of employers toward sickness in employees such that generous sick leave may no longer be acceptable. If this should happen, blue-collar workers will seek out medical care that produces speedy removal of symptoms. In this case a reductionistic approach in either cosmopolitan or traditional medicine would be most acceptable. Kiefer (1976, p. 279) comes to the conclusion, from his study of the culture of an urban high-rise apartment complex, that in such surroundings the extended family will die out, community cohesion will decline, and individual autonomy will increase. In this type of situation a medical system that stresses, as classical traditional medicine does, the importance of the community and the family in the healing process will no longer be acceptable. However, it is in this same environment that many young mothers have such a close relationship with their children that a special term has been coined to describe the problem: *ikuji noiroze* (child-rearing neurosis), or alternatively, *danchi noiroze* (high-rise apartment neurosis) to describe the isolation of the mother. These types of problems, derived from a specific lifestyle, can best be dealt with by counseling or through the use of traditional therapy. It is acknowledged that meeting other people can help to overcome the problem, and traditional therapy in a group setting could be very helpful, whereas resort to a general practitioner could lead to iatrogenesis or to deep frustration for both doctor and patient.

Recent studies on Japanese women (N.H.K. 1976; Pharr 1976, p. 301) show that the overwhelming majority still accept the premise that a woman's role should be one of domesticity. Child-rearing is considered a vital and time-consuming activity, and the close relationships described by Caudill (1976) seem destined to persist for some time to come. Hence, the techniques of traditional medicine that stress the use of tactile and oral stimulation, and the atmosphere that prevails during treatment, should remain acceptable to many Japanese.

If traditional medicine is to sustain its rise in popularity, a pluralistic approach to practice within the system is a positive asset, and a push for modernization and rationalization so that it resembles cosmopolitan medicine more closely would reduce its utility. Despite this, some adjustments must be made to all medical practice, however tradition-oriented, to meet modern Japanese values. Since formal education throughout Japan stresses scientific concepts, scientific terminology has to be used with patients when it is appropriate. Second, since the nuclear family in Japan is on the increase and practitioners cannot assume that the patient has family support, it might be appropriate for large clinics to employ social workers or to encourage the formation of self-help groups. At the political level, the achievement of university status for training colleges would improve the self-image of practitioners and enhance confidence, so that the incentive would be to modernize traditional medicine on its own terms rather than as a poor relative of cosmopolitan medicine. Last, negotiations should be undertaken to include a full range of traditional medical practice in the national health insurance system with reasonable reimbursement rates for the application of traditional techniques both diagnostic and therapeutic.

It may be that medical clinics that stress an individual approach to health care, as the classical texts recommend, can have a particular appeal in the future for people who are young today. If indeed a greater sense of individuality is attained and sustained into middle age in future generations of Japanese, then the kind of treatment offered in clinics that retain traditional values, in which the relationship of each individual person to their environment is stressed, may be actively sought out.

East Asian Medicine as a Model for Holism in the West

Since the concept of holism is culture-bound, there is limited utility in looking toward the medical system of another country or another historical time as a possible model. There are, however, some general concepts to which we can become sensitive through an analysis of East Asian medicine.

Classics such as the *Nei Ching* and the Hippocratic corpus are rich documents in that a holistic and humanistic approach is emphasized, something that is comparatively rare in modern medical texts of both the East and the West. Therefore, a study of medical classics, even in translation provided it is of a reasonable caliber, can act as a contrast and a foil for the approach that is normally applied in cosmopolitan medicine today; such a study can make us sensitive to our own cultural biases. As we have seen in this book, the theory and actual practice of East Asian medicine do not conform very closely, and most practitioners have not read the classical texts that are regarded by scholars (but not by many practitioners) as the best theoretical sources. It is important, therefore, to bear in mind that the classics are not accepted as dogma in modern Asia and that much of the imagery used in a text such as the *Nei Ching* is relevant to its own historical period and is open to numerous interpretations today.

Among the concepts stressed in the classics, the following seem particularly relevant for the present day. First, preventive medicine is held in higher regard than therapeutic medicine. In the West, changing attitudes toward diet, exercise, and pollution of the environment indicate interest among the general public in preventive medicine, but this interest is not yet very prominent in the medical profession, in medical education, or among agencies that fund research. Prestige in medicine is not common in the fields of public health and preventive medicine. It may be, however, that economic necessity will provide impetus for change in this direction.

Recent developments in science have heightened an interest in the second concept, that of considering man in a continual interchange of energy with the environment and the acceptance of a model of adaptation to the environment rather than conquest of it. Models of cybernetics and open systems theory are highly relevant in this respect, but if such concepts are to be applied in medicine, closer links must be forged between the medical world and other aspects of social organization. If a more holistic approach is accepted and environmental conditions are considered important, responsibility for health and healing should not rest so heavily with the medical profession. Individuals, employers, and governments should also be recognized as responsible participants in health care. But the assignment of shared responsibility without the burgeoning of bureaucracy and legislation would, of course, be an enormously difficult task.

Another concept, stressed particularly in East Asian medical texts, is the importance of social behavior in groups and its effect on health. New approaches in the West, particularly in family therapy, also make extensive use of this idea, but in societies where individuality is heavily stressed, it is a difficult concept for patients and many practitioners to accept. Even where the idea is acceptable in problems labeled psychological, it is not so readily considered valuable where the problem is labeled organic. As with preventive medicine, psychosomatic medicine tends to be relegated to a marginal position in the medical profession. Finally, the impression obtained from the classics is that one should take time to look after one's health, that it can be a pleasurable pursuit, but that it is something to be cultivated and not assumed as a right.

In the actual application of East Asian medicine in contemporary Japan there is not much to be learned from practice that is highly reductionistic. But in clinics that aim to do more than remove symptoms, I believe that, of the lessons to be learned, one is especially important: despite an extensive education in the scientific approach to medicine, practitioners are able to accept subjective judgments on both their own and their patients' parts without feeling that this is a threat to their medical practice or their personal integrity. The science of medicine is not usually reified so that the art of medicine is lost, and both a reductionistic and a holistic approach are considered important.

If some of these concepts could be incorporated more fully into medical practice in the West, the experience could be useful, although it would entail major changes in education, values, and the relationship of politics and economics to medicine. But if Weisskopf is correct when he states (1972, p. 351): "The nature of most human problems is such that universally valid answers do not exist, because there is more than one aspect to each of them," then we should be striving toward complementarity in medicine and toward the use of both a reductionistic and a holistic approach. Since it appears to be difficult for specialists to cognitively accept and act on both concepts at the same time, perhaps the approaches should be kept somewhat autonomous, with independent educational, licensing, and professional organizations. This could facilitate more choice on the part of patients and less of a monopoly for one approach or the other. Moreover, since the meaning and experience of illness is shaped by culture, it will be essential in any complex society to foster a pluralistic system within both approaches, so that a variety of therapeutic techniques and concepts of efficacy are acknowledged and drawn upon according to the situation in question. Such a medical system would have to use the patients and their conceptions of reality as the focal reference point for medical decision-making. It is a situation toward which Japan is tentatively moving with the commencement of the "reign of *Kanpō*."

We do not dislike
everything that shines,
but we prefer a pensive shadow
to a thin transparence.

Junichiro Tanizaki,
In Praise of Shadows,
1934

GLOSSARY
OF
JAPANESE AND CHINESE TERMS

Amma　按摩

Chung-kan　中感

Ekiakudoku　穢気悪毒

Gomi　五味

Gosei　五性

Goseiha　後世派

Gotō Gonzan　後藤艮山

Hari　鍼

Hsüeh　血

Huang-ti Nei Ching　黄帝内經

In-sei　陰性

Jisshō　実証

Kanpō　漢方

Ki　気

Kohōha　古方派

Kyoshō　虚証

Manase Dōsan　曲直瀬道三

Manbyō-ichidoku-setsu　万病一毒論

Minkanyaku　民間薬

Nagoya Geni　名古屋玄医

Okyū　お灸

Shang han lun (Shōkanron)　傷寒論

Shên-nung pên t'sao ching　神農本草經

Shiatsu　指圧

Shih-ch'i-ping　時氣病

Shishin　四診

Shōyaku　生薬

Tanba Yasuyori　丹波康頼

Tokki　得気

Wai-kan　外感

Yoshimasu Tōdō　吉益東洞

267

BIBLIOGRAPHY

Association of National Training Institutes. 1973. *An Introduction to Kanpō.* Osaka.

Austin, Lewis. 1976. "The Political Culture of Two Generations: Evolution and Divergence in Japanese and American Values." In Lewis Austin, ed., *Japan: The Paradox of Progress.* New Haven: Yale University Press. Pp. 231–254.

Bellah, Robert N. 1970. *Beyond Belief.* New York: Harper and Row.

Benedict, Ruth. 1946. *The Chrysanthemum and the Sword: Patterns of Japanese Culture.* Boston: Houghton Mifflin.

Bennett, John W., and Ishino Iwao. 1963. *Paternalism in the Japanese Economy.* Minneapolis: University of Minnesota Press.

Bernstein, Jeremy. 1978. "Profiles: Biology Watcher." *New Yorker,* January 2. Pp. 27–46.

Blacker, Carmen. 1975. *The Catalpa Bow: A Study of Shamanistic Practices in Japan.* London: George Allen and Unwin.

Bowers, J. Z. 1965. *Medical Education in Japan: From Chinese Medicine to Western Medicine.* New York: Harper and Row (Hoeber Medical Division).

Carlson, Rick J. 1975. *The End of Medicine.* New York: John Wiley and Sons (A Wiley Inter-Science Publication).

Casal, U. A. 1962. "Acupuncture, Cautery and Massage in Japan." *Journal of Asian Folklore Studies,* 21: 221–235.

Caudill, William. 1962. "Patterns of Emotion in Modern Japan." In R. J. Smith and R. K. Beardsley, eds., *Japanese Culture.* Chicago: Aldine. Pp. 115–131.

———. 1976. "Everyday Health and Illness in Japan and America." In Charles Leslie, ed., *Asian Medical Systems.* Berkeley and Los Angeles: University of California Press. Pp. 159–177.

Bibliography

Caudill, William, and David W. Plath. 1966. "Who Sleeps by Whom? Parent-Child Involvement in Urban Japanese Families." *Psychiatry*, 29: 344–366.

Cole, Robert E. 1976. "Changing Labor Force Characteristics and Their Impact on Japanese Relations." In Lewis Austin, ed., *Japan: The Paradox of Progress*. New Haven: Yale University Press. Pp. 165–214.

Croizier, Ralph. 1968. *Traditional Medicine in Modern China: Science, Nationalism and the Tensions of Cultural Change*. Cambridge: Harvard University Press.

DeVos, George A. 1973. *Socialization for Achievement: Essays on the Cultural Psychology of the Japanese*. Berkeley and Los Angeles: University of California Press.

DeVos, George A., and Hiroshi Wagatsuma. 1959. "Psychocultural Significance of Concern over Death and Illness among Rural Japanese." *International Journal of Social Psychiatry*, 5, no. 1, pp. 5–19.

Doi, Takeo. 1973. *The Anatomy of Dependence*. Tokyo: Kodansha International, Ltd.

Dore, R. P. 1967. *City Life in Japan: A Study of a Tokyo Ward*. Berkeley and Los Angeles: University of California Press.

Douglas, Mary. 1966. *Purity and Danger: An Analysis of Concepts of Pollution and Taboo*. London: Routledge, Kegan and Paul.

———. 1970. "The Healing Rite." *Man*, 5: 302–308.

Dubos, René. 1959. *Mirage of Health, Utopias, Progress and Biological Change*. New York: Harper and Row.

———. 1961. *The Dreams of Reason*. New York: Columbia University Press.

———. 1965. *Man Adapting*. New Haven: Yale University Press.

———. 1968. *Man, Medicine, and Environment*. New York: Praeger.

Dunn, Fred. L. 1976. "Traditional Asian Medicine and Cosmopolitan Medicine as Adaptive Systems." In Charles Leslie, ed., *Asian Medical Systems*. Berkeley and Los Angeles: University of California Press. Pp. 133–158.

Eisenberg, Leon. 1977. "The Search for Care." *Daedalus*, Doing Better and Feeling Worse: Health in the United States, 106: 235–246.

Engel, George L. 1977. "The Need for a New Medical Model: A Challenge for Biomedicine." *Science*, 196, no. 4286, pp. 129–136.

Engishiki: Proceedings of the Engi Era. 1970. (Books 1–5) Felicia Grassitt Bock, trans. Tokyo: Sophia University Press.

Fabrega, Horacio. 1975. "The Need for an Ethnomedical Science." *Science,* 189: 969–975.

Frager, Robert, and Thomas P. Rohlen. 1976. "The Future of a Tradition: Japanese Spirit in the 1980's." In Lewis Austin, ed., *Japan: The Paradox of Progress.* New Haven: Yale University Press. Pp. 255–278.

Frank, Jerome D. 1964. Foreword to Ari Kiev, ed., *Magic, Faith and Healing: Studies in Primitive Psychiatry.* New York: Free Press. Pp. vii–xii.

Freidson, Eliott. 1970. *Profession of Medicine.* New York: Dodd, Mead.

Fuchs, Victor R. 1974. *Who Shall Live: Health, Economics and Social Choice.* New York: Basic Books.

Fujikawa, Yū. 1974. *An Outline of Japanese Medical History.* Tokyo: Heibonsha. Vol. I (Japanese text).

Gluck, Carol. 1978. "The People in History: Recent Trends in Japanese Historiography." *Journal of Asian Studies,* 38, no. 1, pp. 25–50.

Granet, Marcel. 1930. *Chinese Civilization.* London: K. Paul, Trench, Trubner and Co.

Hashimoto, M. 1966. *Japanese Acupuncture.* New York: Liveright.

Hayashida, Cullen T. 1975. "The Koshinjo and Tanteisha. Institutionalized Ascription as a Response to Modernization and Stress in Japan." In Toyomasa Fusé, ed., *Modernization and Stress in Japan.* Leiden: E. J. Brill. Pp. 84–94.

Heisenberg, W. 1958. *Physics and Philosophy.* New York: Harper Torchbooks.

Hoyle, F. 1955. *Frontiers of Astronomy.* New York: Harper and Row.

Huard, Pierre, and M. Wong. 1968. *Chinese Medicine.* World University Library. New York: McGraw-Hill.

Illich, Ivan D. 1976. *Medical Nemesis.* New York: Pantheon.

Ishikawa Takuboku. 1956. "The Romaji Diary." In Donald Keene, ed., *Modern Japanese Literature.* New York: Grove Press. Pp. 211–231.

Janzen, John M. 1978. *The Quest for Therapy in Lower Zaire.* Berkeley and Los Angeles: University of California Press.

Japan, Ministry of Education. 1971. *Religions in Japan.* Tokyo: Religious Affairs Section, Research Bureau, Ministry of Education, Government of Japan. 4th edition.

Katō, Genchi. 1926. *A Study of Shintō.* Tokyo: Meiji Japan Society.

Kiefer, Christie W. 1976. "The *Danchi Zoku* and the Evolution of Metropolitan Mind." In Lewis Austin, ed., *Japan: The Paradox of Progress*. New Haven: Yale University Press. Pp. 279–300.

Kleinman, Arthur M. 1973a. "Medicine's Symbolic Reality: On a Central Problem in the Philosophy of Medicine." *Inquiry*, 16: 206–213.

———. 1973b. "Some Issues for a Comparative Study of Medical Healing." In *International Journal of Social Psychiatry*, 19, nos. 3–4, pp. 159–165.

———. 1976. "Depression, Somatization and the 'New Cross-Cultural Psychiatry.' " *Social Science and Medicine*, 10: 1–8.

———. 1978. "International Health Care Planning from an Ethnomedical Perspective: Critique and Recommendations for Change." *Medical Anthropology*, 2, no. 2, pp. 71–94.

———. 1979. *Patients and Healers in the Context of Culture: An Exploration of the Borderland between Anthropology, Medicine, and Psychiatry*. Berkeley and Los Angeles: University of California Press.

Kunstadter, Peter. 1975. "The Comparative Anthropological Study of Medical Systems in Society." In Arthur Kleinman et al., eds., *Medicine in Chinese Cultures: Comparative Studies of Health Care in Chinese and Other Societies*. Washington, D.C.: U.S. Department of Health, Education, and Welfare, Public Health Service, National Institutes of Health, DHEW Publ. No. (NIH) 75–653. Pp. 683–695.

Kyōgoku, Kazuaki, et al. 1973. "Studies on the Constituents of 'Shikon.' Comparison of Contents, Constituents and Antibacterial Effects of Fat Soluble Fraction between 'Nanshikon' and 'Kōsikon.' " *Shōyakugaku Zasshi*, 27, no. 1, pp. 31–36.

Kyoto City Publications. 1974. The Health Insurance System. Kyoto. P. 4.

Kyoto City Statistical Records. 1973. Kyoto: Kyoto City Publications. P. 209.

Lalonde, Marc. 1975. *A New Perspective on the Health of Canadians: A Working Document*. Ottawa: Information Canada.

Lambo, T. A. 1975. Foreword to E. E. Meyer and Peter Sainsbury, eds., *Promoting Health in the Human Environment*. Geneva: World Health Organization.

Lanham, Betty B. 1966. "The Psychological Orientation of the Mother-Child Relationship in Japan." *Monumenta Nipponica*, 21, nos. 3–4, pp. 322–333.

Lebra, Takie Sugiyama. 1976. *Japanese Patterns of Behavior*. Honolulu: The University Press of Hawaii.

LeShan, L. L. 1959. "Psychological States as Factors in the Development of Malignant Disease: A Critical Review." *Journal of the National Cancer Institute*, 22: 1–18.

———. 1966. "An Emotional Life-history Pattern Associated with Neoplastic Disease." *Annals of the New York Academy of Sciences*, 125: 780–793.

Leslie, Charles. 1975. "Pluralism and Integration in the Indian and Chinese Medical Systems." In Arthur Kleinman et al., eds., *Medicine in Chinese Cultures: Comparative Studies of Health Care in Chinese and Other Societies*. Washington, D.C.: U.S. Department of Health, Education, and Welfare, Public Health Service, National Institutes of Health, DHEW Publ. No. (NIH) 75–653. Pp. 401–417.

Lieban, Richard W. 1973. "Medical Anthropology." In *Handbook of Social and Cultural Anthropology*, J. Honigman, ed. Chicago: Rand McNally. Pp. 1031–1072.

Lock, Margaret M. 1978. "Scars of Experience: The Art of Moxibustion in Japanese Medicine and Society." *Culture, Medicine and Psychiatry*, 2:151–175.

McKeown, Thomas. 1965. *Medicine in Modern Society*. London: Allen and Unwin.

———. 1971. "A Historical Appraisal of the Medical Task." In Gordon McLachlan and Thomas McKeown, eds., *Medical History and Medical Care*. Oxford University Press for the Nuffield Provincial Hospitals Trust.

———. 1976. *The Role of Medicine: Dream, Mirage, or Nemesis?* London: Nuffield Provincial Hospitals Trust.

Manaka, Yoshio. 1972. *The Layman's Guide to Acupuncture*. New York: John Weatherhill.

Mann, Felix. 1973. *Acupuncture: The Ancient Chinese Art of Healing and How It Works Scientifically*. New York: Vintage Books.

Marsella, Anthony J., David Kinzie, and Paul Gordon. 1973. "Ethnic Variations in the Expression of Depression." *Journal of Cross-Cultural Psychology*, 4, no. 4, pp. 435–458.

Morsbach, Helmut. 1973. "Aspects of Non-verbal Communication in Japan." *Journal of Nervous and Mental Diseases*, 157, no. 4, pp. 262–277.

Nakagawa, Yonezo. 1973. "La Medicine en el Antogua Japon." In *Historia Universal de la Medicina* (separata del tomo I). Madrid: Salvat Editores, S.A.

Nakane, Chie. 1970. *Japanese Society*. Berkeley and Los Angeles: University of California Press.

Navarro, Vicente. 1976. *Medicine Under Capitalism*. New York: Prodist.

Needham, Joseph. 1962. *Science and Civilization in China* (vol. 2). Cambridge: Cambridge University Press.

NHK (Japanese Broadcasting Service). 1976. *Survey on Women's Attitudes*. Tokyo.

Nihongi: Chronicles of Japan from the Earliest Times to A.D. 697. 1956. 2 vols. W. G. Aston, trans. London: George Allen and Unwin Ltd.

Nikkei Medical. 1973. "A Profile of Data on Japanese Doctors." 2, no. 1, pp. 48–49. (Japanese text)

Nishiyama, Hideo. 1962. *Chinese Herbal Medicine and Folk Herbal Medicine*. Osaka: Sōgensha. (Japanese text)

Ono, Sokyo. 1962. *Shintō, the Kami Way*. Tokyo: Bridgeway Press.

Ōtsuka, Yasuo. 1976. "Chinese Traditional Medicine in Japan." In Charles Leslie, ed., *Asian Medical Systems*. Berkeley and Los Angeles: University of California Press.

Palos, Stephen. 1971. *The Chinese Art of Healing*. New York: Herder and Herder.

Pelletier, Kenneth R. 1977. *Mind as Healer, Mind as Slayer*. New York: Delta.

Pharr, Susan. 1976. "The Japanese Woman: Evolving Views of Life and Role." In Lewis Austin, ed., *Japan: The Paradox of Progress*. New Haven: Yale University Press. Pp. 301–327.

Pomeranz, B., et al. 1976. "Naloxone Blockade of Acupuncture Analgesia: Endorphin Implicated." *Life Sciences*, 19: 1757–1762.

Porkert, Manfred. 1974. *The Theoretical Foundations of Chinese Medicine*. MIT East Asian Science Series, vol. 3. Cambridge: MIT Press.

———. 1976. "The Intellectual and Social Impulses behind the Evolution of Traditional Chinese Medicine." In Charles Leslie, ed., *Asian Medical Systems: A Comparative Study*. Berkeley and Los Angeles: University of California Press.

Powles, John. 1973. "On the Limitations of Modern Medicine." *Science, Medicine and Man,* 1: 1–30.

Public Health White Paper. 1973. Tokyo: Ministry of Finance Publications. Pp. 21, 27.

Reynolds, David K. 1976. *Morita Therapy.* Berkeley and Los Angeles: University of California Press.

Rhodes, Philip. 1976. *The Value of Medicine.* London: George Allen and Unwin.

Risse, Guenter B., ed. 1973. *Modern China and Traditional Chinese Medicine.* Springfield, Illinois: Charles C. Thomas.

Rohlen, Thomas. 1974a. "Ki and Kokoro: Japanese Perspectives on the Nature of the Person." Paper presented at the Regional Seminar on Japanese Studies, Center for Japanese and Korean Studies, University of California, Berkeley.

———. 1974b. *For Harmony and Strength: Japanese White Collar Organization in Anthropological Perspective.* Berkeley and Los Angeles: University of California Press.

Rosen, George. 1958. *A History of Public Health.* New York: MD Publications.

Sakaguchi, Hiroshi. 1963. "Concerning an Infusion of Peony and Licorice." *Kanpō Research,* pp. 46–55. (Japanese text)

Scotch, Norman, and H. Geiger. 1962. "The Epidemiology of Rheumatoid Arthritis." *Journal of Chronic Diseases,* 15: 1037–1067.

Sidel, Victor W., and Ruth Sidel. 1973. *Serve the People: Observations on Medicine in the People's Republic of China.* New York: Josiah Macy, Jr., Foundation.

Silverman, Milton, and Philip R. Lee. 1974. *Pills, Profits, and Politics.* Berkeley and Los Angeles: University of California Press.

Simonton, O. C., and S. Simonton. 1975. "Belief Systems and Management of the Emotional Aspects of Malignancy." *Journal of Transpersonal Psychiatry,* 7, no. 1, pp. 29–47.

Sjolund, B., et al. 1976. "Electro-acupuncture and Endogenous Morphines." *Lancet,* 2: 1085.

Smith, Wesley D. 1973. "Galen on Coan versus Cnidians." *Bulletin of the History of Medicine,* 47, no. 6, pp. 569–585.

Bibliography

Soloman, G. F., and A. A. Amkraut. 1972. "Emotions, Stress and Immunity." *Frontiers of Radiation Therapy and Oncology*, 7: 84–96.

Steslicke, William. 1973. *Doctors in Politics*. East Asian Institute, Columbia University. New York: Praeger.

Takenaka, Masao. 1959. *The Development of Social, Educational and Medical Work in Japan since Meiji*. The Hague: Van Keulen.

Tambiah, S. J. 1977. "The Cosmological and Performative Significance of a Thai Cult of Healing through Meditation." *Culture, Medicine, Psychiatry*, 1, no. 1, pp. 97–132.

Tanizaki, Junichiro. 1957. *The Makioka Sisters*. Edward G. Seidensticker, trans. Tokyo: Charles E. Tuttle Co.

Theobald, Robert. 1972. *Habit and Habitat*. Englewood Cliffs, N.J.: Prentice-Hall.

Thomas, C. B., and K. R. Duszynski. "Closeness to Parents and the Family Constellation in a Prospective Study of Five Disease States: Suicide, Mental Illness, Malignant Tumor, Hypertension, and Coronary Heart Disease." *Hopkins' Medical Journal*, 134: 251–270.

Thomas, Lewis. 1974. *The Lives of a Cell: Notes of a Biology Watcher*. New York: Bantam Books.

Topley, Marjorie. 1975. "Chinese and Western Medicine in Hong-Kong: Some Social and Cultural Determinants of Variation, Interaction and Change." In Arthur Kleinman et al., eds., *Medicine in Chinese Cultures: Comparative Studies of Health Care in Chinese and Other Societies*. Washington, D.C.: U.S. Department of Health, Education, and Welfare, Public Health Service, National Institutes of Health, DHEW Publ. No. (NIH) 75–653. Pp. 241–271

Tseng, Wen-Shing. 1975a. "The Nature of Somatic Complaints Among Psychiatric Patients: The Chinese Case." *Comprehensive Psychiatry*, 16: 237–245.

———. 1975b. "Traditional and Modern Psychiatric Care in Taiwan." In Arthur Kleinman et al., eds., *Medicine in Chinese Cultures: Comparative Studies of Health Care in Chinese and Other Societies*. Washington, D.C.: U.S. Department of Health, Education, and Welfare, Public Health Service, National Institutes of Health, DHEW Publ. No. (NIH) 75–653. Pp. 177–194.

276

Turner, Victor W. 1967. *Forest of Symbols: Aspects of Ndembu Ritual*. Ithaca: Cornell University Press.

———. 1969. *The Ritual Process: Structure and Anti-Structure*. Chicago: Aldine.

Varley, H. Paul. 1973. *Japanese Culture*. New York: Praeger.

Veith, Ilza, trans. 1949. *The Yellow Emperor's Classic of Internal Medicine*. Berkeley and Los Angeles: University of California Press.

Virchow, Rudolph L. K. 1958. *Disease, Life and Man: Selected Essays*. L. J. Rather, trans. Stanford: Stanford University Press.

Vogel, Ezra. 1968. *Japan's New Middle Class: The Salary Man and His Family in a Tokyo Suburb*. Berkeley and Los Angeles: University of California Press.

Von Mering, Otto, and L. W. Earley. 1965. "Major Changes in the Western Medical Environment." *Archives of General Psychiatry,* 13: 195–201.

Wagatsuma, Hiroshi. 1970. "Study of Personality and Behavior in Japanese Society and Culture." In E. Norbeck and S. Parman, eds., *Study of Japan in the Behavioral Sciences*. Rice University Studies, 56 (4): 53–63.

Weiss, Paul. 1970. "The Living System: Determinism Stratified." In A. Koestler and J. R. Smythies, eds., *Beyond Reductionism: New Perspectives in the Life Sciences*. New York: The MacMillan Co.

Weisskopf, Victor F. 1972. *Physics in the Twentieth Century*. Cambridge: MIT Press.

Whiting, John W. M. 1961. "Socialization Process and Personality." In Francis L. K. Hsu, ed., *Psychological Anthropology: Approaches to Culture and Personality*. Homewood, Ill.: Dorsey Press. Pp. 355–380.

World Health Statistics Annual. 1971. New York: World Health Organization. P. 48.

Yoshida, Yoichi, and Katsumi Yoshida. 1976. "The High Rate of Appendectomy in Japan." *Medical Care,* 14, no. 11, pp. 950–957.

INDEX

Abdomen (*hara*), 98; care of, 87, 105; disease originating in, 87, 105; Japanese concern with, 86–88; style of massage for, 180. *See also* Stomach

Abdominal palpation: contemporary use of, 55, 114, 129, 160; development of, 39, 54–55; Japanese text specializing in, 59, 60

Abortion, 170

Achievement motivation, 224

Acupuncture (*hari*), 15, 28, 40, 52, 53, 113; acting on only certain parts of the body, 173, 187; adverse reactions from, 184; anaesthesia, 252; applied in North America, 11; applied by *kanpō* clinic doctors, 136–137; factors influencing the application of, 43, 129–130, 133; classical techniques used in contemporary application of, 160, 208; attitudes of herbal pharmacists toward, 148, 149, 151, 153; attitudes of masseurs and their patients toward, 181, 182, 184, 185, 187; chiropractic diagnosis used with, 166, 209; compared to moxibustion, 171, 173, 175, 176; defined, 15; in early Japanese ministry of health, 50; effect of cosmopolitan medical beliefs on, 63, 206, 208–216; efficacy of, 137, 209–210; electrical, 161, 208–209; government rules for study and

practice of, 18, 64–65; introduced into Japan, 27, 42; meridians and pressure points used in, 35, 36–37, 42, 43; and national health insurance coverage, 17, 168–169; needles used in, 42, 136–137, 161, 169–170, 208; recommended by cosmopolitan family doctors, 251; research on, 65; to relieve pain, 159, 165; status of, 200; taught in East Asian medical schools, 197; treatment for children, 169–170; treatment of glaucoma and cataracts, 209–210; treatment of psychological problems, 190; treatment of rheumatism, 119; treatment for lower-back pain, 118–119; tube for needles used in, 60–61, 136

Acupuncture clinics, 157–170; compared to *kanpō* clinics, 160–161, 163–165; costs of treatment, 160, 161, 162, 168–169; criteria for selection of, 161–162, 166; description and settings of, 158–159, 166, 167, 168; diagnosis at, 160–161, 166, 168, 206–216; equipment and machinery at, 158, 166, 167; health insurance at, 168–169; herbal medicine prescribed at, 161, 164; in homes, 166, 167, 168; language used in, 158, 161, 162, 164; specialization among, 169–170. *See also* Patients at acupuncture clinics

Index

Acupuncture practitioners, 157–170, 203–216; attitudes toward traditional concepts, 203–216 *passim;* blind, 60–61, 136; classical diagnosis in, 160, 208; cosmopolitan medical practices used by, 206–216; licensed, 18, 167, 166, 168; in neighborhoods, 166; relationships with other doctors and status of, 61, 63, 166, 168

Acute illness, 190, 253; and acceptance of cosmopolitan medicine in Japan, 248; patients understanding of, 164; and trust of cosmopolitan family doctors, 243, 244

Adder's tongue, 41

Addiction to tobacco, 163, 190

Advertising of East Asian medicine, 92, 94, 160, 165, 170, 189, 254–255

Age: attitudes toward East Asian medicine influenced by, 94, 99–100, 129, 141, 245–246, 250; of East Asian doctors, 212; and yin/yang doctrine, 129. *See also* Old people; Youth

Akujunkan, and East Asian therapy, 138

Alchemy, 47, 52

Alcohol, 115

Alkaloids, isolation of, 65

Allergic disposition, 83

Allergies, 147, 223

Almanacs, 97

Aloe, 75

Amaeru: defined, 77; role in illness and the need to be nurtured, 77, 78, 79, 210, 222; inability to, 222; opportunity among women for, 80. *See also* Dependency

American children, compared to Japanese children, 74

American culture, impact in Japan, 256

American doctors, compared to Japanese cosmopolitan doctors, 233, 234, 238

American influence in Japanese medicine, 235

American mothers, compared to Japanese mothers, 71–74, 90

Amkraut, A.A., 37

Amma, defined, 15. *See also* Massage

Amulets, 48; for therapy, 52

Anatomical accuracy, 34

Anatomy, taught in East Asian medical schools, 195, 197

Ancestors, 145; disease caused by unsatisfied, 29; prayers for good health addressed to, 103, 104

Ando, Mr., acupuncture practiced by, 168–169, 206–207, 211

Angelica, 41

Anthrophobia, 223

Antibiotics, 134, 152, 172; discovery of, 3; Japanese attitude toward, 248; prescribed by cosmopolitan doctors, 237, 238

Antibody production, 175, 182

Anxiety, 222

Aorta, 36n, 39

Apartments, high-rise, and neurosis, 261

Apprentice, 168; master-apprentice system, 200

Apprenticed medical school graduates, 64, 199–201

Apprenticed pharmacists, 144, 146, 149

Aristocracy: access to licensed doctors, 58; East Asian medicine studied and used by, 51

Arrowroot, 24

Artery, radial, 39

Arthritis, 6. *See also* Rheumatoid arthritis

Asahi News, 112, 240

Asayama, Dr. Eizō, xiii

Asceticism: Buddhist compared to Taoist, 48; in Taoism, 46, 47, 48

Aspirin, 238

Association of National Training Institutes, 198

Asthma, 6, 147, 163, 190, 223; treated by East Asian therapy, 113, 172, 173,

Index

Index

methods of, 38–40, 160, 198, 199; inductive approach, 131–132; by *kanpō* clinic doctors, 114, 129, 131–133, 139, 140, 192; in medical schools, 196; in medical textbooks, 198–199; pulse-taking, 39, 114, 132–133, 139, 151, 160, 204, 210

Diet, 86, 114, 172; advice by herbal pharmacists, 148, 149–150; advice by *kanpō* clinic doctors, 115, 128, 133, 215; attitudes of contemporary East Asian specialists toward, 204, 206; and explanation of *kan no mushi*, 95; to maintain good health, 104, 105, 106, 133; foods not to be eaten together, 97. *See also* Nutrition

Directional lore, observance of, 98, 102, 104, 106

"Dirt," 92; elimination of, 91; fear of, 89, 91. *See also* Pollution

Disease: associated with fear and potential ostracism, 25, 91, 249; culture-bound expression and experience of, 221–222, 223–224 (*see also* Culture-bound syndromes in Japan); distinguished from illnesses, 220; "hard-to-cure diseases," 17; an ordered life to prevent, 100; of the stomach, 86, 87. *See also* Chronic illness; Illness

Disease causation, 3, 6, 58; and abdominal care, 105; attitudes of contemporary East Asian specialists toward, 204, 206, 207; attitudes of patients at acupuncture clinics, 165; attitudes of *kanpō* clinic patients toward, 124–125; beliefs of *kanpō* doctors, 127, 131; Buddhist theory of, 48; in classical East Asian medicine, 29, 36, 37–38, 44, 48; in contemporary East Asian medical textbooks, 197–198; East Asian and

early Japanese theories of compared, 45; in early socialization, 76–77; from hard work, 78, 118–119, 207, 214; early Japanese beliefs about, 24–26, 52; evil spirits in, 24–25; from industrial pollution, 6–7, 16, 65, 240; ontological vs. physiological theories of, 3–4, 10; personality type related to, 6, 83, 103, 129, psychosomatic concept of, 118–119, 119–120, 124, 137–139, 220, 221–228 *passim*

Diurnal variations: in classical East Asian medical theory, 33, 35, 38, 40, 43, 44; attempt to use by *kanpō* clinic doctors, 129; pulse quality influenced by, 133

Divination, 47, 52; and criticism of classical medical beliefs, 130; in medical books, 58; practiced by families, 98, 102; not accepted by contemporary East Asian doctors, 203. *See also* Fortune-tellers

Diviners, 50

Doctors, early Chinese, 29, 34; diagnosis utilizing basic senses of, 40; first medical books compiled by, 47; mixture of medicines prescribed by, 41–42; reimbursement of, 44–45; refusal to treat severe diseases, 44; specialization by, 40

Doctors of cosmopolitan medicine, 17–18; acute medical problems treated by, 151, 164, 243, 244, 248; attitudes toward East Asian medicine, 251–252; attitudes toward the national health insurance program, 231, 232–233, 238; clinics and hospitals owned by, 17–18; comparison of Japanese and American, 233, 234, 238; complaints against, 233–234, 242, 245; house calls by, 233, 237, 241; income of, 232–233, 235, 237, 247; initial standards and fees of, 62; influence of

Hashimoto, M., 32

Hayase, Machiko, xiii

Hayashida, Cuilen T., 90

Headaches, 38, 98, 103, 151; and environmental conditions, 130

Healing, role of the family in, 218–221. *See also* Therapy, East Asian, efficacy of

Health: culture-bound concepts of, 1, 11, 12; defined by the World Health Organization, 84; ministry of in early Japan, 50–51; policy planning, 6–7; role of introspection in, 192; standards in Japan, 16

Health, attitudes toward, xii, 1–2; by business and industry, 81–82, 184, 225, 260, 261; in classical East Asian medicine, 43; concept of *ki* in, 85; conflict among families, 99–101, 104, 106, 118; among contemporary East Asian specialists, 204, 206; among contemporary *kanpō* doctors, 127–128, 139; among contemporary *kanpō* clinic patients, 124–125; East Asian medical beliefs reflected in, 84; illness and health not viewed as a dichotomy, 85, 139, 142, 193–194, 250; learned during socialization, 69, 71–107; and meaning of therapeutic efficacy, 193–194, 224–228; among patients at massage clinics, 184; perfect health not the goal of East Asian medicine, 43, 84, 128, 139, 142, 246. *See also* Responsibility for health and illness; Psychotherapy

Health insurance system in Japan, 16–17, 18, 247, 248; at acupuncture clinics, 168–169; advantages of according to cosmopolitan doctors, 238; application of medical beliefs influenced by, 206; blamed for misuse of medication, 239, 242; criticized by cosmopolitan doctors, 231, 232–233;

and coverage of East Asian medicine, 18, 66, 190, 262; effects of, 169, 206, 231, 239, 242; faults in, 247; and "hard-to-cure" diseases, 17; gift-giving patterns changed by, 242; at moxibustion clinics, 173; not provided at *kanpō* clinics, 120

Health insurance system in Japan, points system of, 17, 18; used by acupuncturists, 168–169; and advice on preventive medicine, 246; impact on cosmopolitan medical practice, 232–233, 237–238, 247; and time for patient care, 232–233

Health through Garlic, 20

Heart: determining the condition of, 39; constrictor, 36, 132; disease, 16, 129; Western concept of compared to the Japanese concept of the abdomen, 86

Heisenberg, W., "Uncertainty Principle" of, 7–8

Herbal medicine, 52, 112; adherence to classical theory in use of, 214–215; associated with food, 96, 135, 190, 246; attitudes of contemporary East Asian specialists toward, 182, 204, 206; chronic diseases treated by, 113, 123, 139, 165; vs. cosmopolitan medicine, 172, 239; defined, 15; doctors specializing in, 61; efficacy of, 190; family use of, 96–98, 102, 104, 220; government standards and restrictions on, 66, 144; and health insurance, 66; introduced in Japan, 51; for nephrosis, 116–117; popularity of, 148; preferred by customers at massage parlors, 187, 188; prepackaged, 148, 150, 151; preparation of at *kanpō* clinics, 116–117; prescribed at acupuncture clinics, 161, 164; as a preventive measure, 185; references in early chronicles to,

Index

Itō Jinsai, 53

Iwao, Ishino, 256

Izumo, cult centered on, 24

Janzen, John M., 2

Japan: cosmopolitan medicine adopted as the official medical system in, 63, 234; doctors required to study Western medicine, 62; early medical beliefs and practices in, 23–26, 45, 52; first hospitals in, 48; health standards in, 16; introduction of East Asian medicine to, 2, 15, 23, 27, 49, 52; medical facilities in Kyoto, 17–20; modernized medicine in, 235; public anxiety about medical care in, 239–240; reasons for study of East Asian medicine in, 13–14; training in, 211. *See also* Pluralistic medical system in Japan

Japanese East Asian medical society, 127

Japanese Medical Association, 231, 232

Japanese mothers, compared to American mothers, 71–74, 90

Japan Times, 239

Jisshō, and therapeutic massage, 180

Joint problems, 163, 173, 177, 185, 187, 190

Judo, 167, 182

Kaden: example of, 174; tradition among herbal pharmacies, 146

Kamidana (household Shintō shrine), 105; in acupuncture clinics, 167

Kan no mushi, 169, 175; acupuncture for, 169, 190, 251; causes of, 95–96, 223; as a culture-bound syndrome, 258; disposition of the mother in explanation of, 95–96; moxa treatment for, 175, 176; and neurosis in adults, 223; susceptibility of boys to, 176; symptoms of, 175

Kanpō: defined, 15, 27; "reign of," 66, 264

Kanpō boomu, and revival of East Asian medicine, 151, 152, 253, 255

Kanpō clinics, 111–143; children as patients, 116, 120; compared to cosmopolitan medical practice, 258; compared to acupuncture clinics, 160–161, 163; costs of treatment at, 113, 115, 118, 119, 120, 123; criticism of, 123, 126; defined, 15; described, 112–113, 122; health insurance programs not provided at, 120; introspection encouraged at, 192; modern features of, 112, 113, 122; patients' needs fulfilled in, 258; social and psychological aspects of disease treatment in, 137–139, 193. *See also* Doctors of East Asian medicine, in *kanpō* clinics; Patients at *kanpō* clinics

Karma, 83, 139; disease caused by, 48; and Japanese attitudes toward therapeutic efficacy, 225

Karō (overwork), 207, 214

Katō, Genchi, 25

Ki, concept of, 84–85, 87, 197; attitudes among contemporary East Asian specialists toward, 204, 206, 207; believed by *kanpō* clinic doctors, 131; and disease causation, 85, 148; explanations of, 131; flow of, 86; and holistic treatment, 217; management of, 76, 85; research on, 204

Kidneys, 95, 130, 141–142, 198

Kiefer, Christie W., 225

Kinoshita, Dr., 174–176, 207, 210, 212, 213

Kinoshita, Yasuhito, xiii

Kinship terms, fictive, 80

Kinzie, David, 221

Kitasato Research Institute, 65

Kleinman, Arthur M., 2, 193, 220, 221,

Index

Index

CPSIA information can be obtained at www.ICGtesting.com

265384BV00001B/8/A